KU-603-383

GLAMORGAN, 1999

EXPLORATIONS IN SOCIOLOGY
British Sociological Association conference volume series

<table>
<tr><td>Sami Zubaida (editor)</td><td>1</td><td>Race and Racism</td></tr>
<tr><td>Richard Brown (editor)</td><td>2</td><td>Knowledge, Education and Cultural Exchange</td></tr>
<tr><td>Paul Rock and Mary McIntosh (editors)</td><td>3</td><td>Deviance and Social Control</td></tr>
<tr><td>Emmanuel de Kadt and Gavin Williams (editors)</td><td>4</td><td>Sociology and Development</td></tr>
<tr><td>Frank Parkin (editor)</td><td>5</td><td>The Social Analysis of Class Structure</td></tr>
<tr><td>Diana Leonard Barker and Sheila Allen (editors)</td><td>6</td><td>Sexual Divisions and Society</td></tr>
<tr><td>Diana Leonard Barker and Sheila Allen (editors)</td><td>7</td><td>Dependence and Exploitation in Work and Marriage</td></tr>
<tr><td>Richard Scase (editor)</td><td>8</td><td>Industrial Society</td></tr>
<tr><td>Robert Dingwall, Christian Heath, Margaret Reid and Margaret Stacey (editors)</td><td>9</td><td>Health Care and Health Knowledge</td></tr>
<tr><td>Robert Dingwall, Christian Heath, Margaret Reid and Margaret Stacey (editor)</td><td>10</td><td>Health and the Division of Labour</td></tr>
<tr><td>Gary Littlejohn, Barry Smart, John Wakeford and Nira Yuval-Davis (editors)</td><td>11</td><td>Power and the State</td></tr>
<tr><td>Michèle Barrett, Philip Corrigan, Annette Kuhn and Janet Wolff (editors)</td><td>12</td><td>Ideology and Cultural Production</td></tr>
<tr><td>Bob Fryer, Allan Hunt, Doreen MacBarnet and Bert Moorhouse (editors)</td><td>13</td><td>Law, State and Society</td></tr>
<tr><td>Philip Abrams, Rosemary Deem, Janet Finch and Paul Rock (editors)</td><td>14</td><td>Practice and Progress</td></tr>
<tr><td>Graham Day, Lesley Caldwell, Karen Jones, David Robbins and Hilary Rose (editors)</td><td>15</td><td>Diversity and Decomposition in the Labour Market</td></tr>
<tr><td>David Robbins, Lesley Caldwell, Graham Day, Karen Jones and Hilary Rose (editors)</td><td>16</td><td>Rethinking Social Inequality</td></tr>
<tr><td>Eva Gamarnikow, David Morgan, June Purvis and Daphne Taylorson (editors)</td><td>17</td><td>The Public and the Private</td></tr>
<tr><td>Eva Gamarnikow, David Morgan, June Purvis and Daphne Taylorson (editors)</td><td>18</td><td>Gender, Class and Work</td></tr>
<tr><td>* Gareth Rees, Janet Bujra, Paul Littlewood, Howard Newby and Teresa L. Rees (editors)</td><td>19</td><td>Political Action and Social Identity</td></tr>
<tr><td>Howard Newby, Janet Bujra, Paul Littlewood, Gareth Rees and Teresa L. Rees (editors)</td><td>20</td><td>Restructuring Capital</td></tr>
<tr><td>* Sheila Allen, Kate Purcell, Alan Waton and Stephen Wood (editors)</td><td>21</td><td>The Experience of Unemployment</td></tr>
<tr><td>* Kate Purcell, Stephen Wood, Alan Waton and Sheila Allen (editors)</td><td>22</td><td>The Changing Experience of Employment</td></tr>
<tr><td>* Jalna Hanmer and Mary Maynard (editors)</td><td>23</td><td>Women, Violence and Social Control</td></tr>
<tr><td>* Colin Creighton and Martin Shaw (editors)</td><td>24</td><td>Sociology of War and Peace</td></tr>
</table>

Thinking Identities

Ethnicity, Racism and Culture

Edited by

Avtar Brah
Senior Lecturer in Sociology
Birkbeck College
University of London

Mary J. Hickman
Reader in European Studies
and Director of the Irish Studies Centre
University of North London

and

Máirtín Mac an Ghaill
Professor of Sociology of Education
Sheffield University

First published in Great Britain 1999 by
MACMILLAN PRESS LTD
Houndmills, Basingstoke, Hampshire RG21 6XS and London
Companies and representatives throughout the world

A catalogue record for this book is available from the British Library.

ISBN 0–333–71773–2 hardcover
ISBN 0–333–71774–0 paperback

 First published in the United States of America 1999 by
ST. MARTIN'S PRESS, INC.,
Scholarly and Reference Division,
175 Fifth Avenue, New York, N.Y. 10010

ISBN 0–312–22317–X

Library of Congress Cataloging-in-Publication Data
Thinking identities : ethnicity, racism and culture / edited by Avtar
Brah, Mary J. Hickman and Máirtín Mac an Ghaill.
p.   cm. — (Explorations in sociology)
Includes bibliographical references and index.
ISBN 0–312–22317–X (cloth)
1. Race relations—Congresses.   2. Group identity—Congresses.
3. Ethnicity—Great Britain—Congresses.   4. Great Britain—Race
relations—Congresses.   5. Great Britain—Ethnic relations–
–Congresses.   I. Brah, A.   II. Hickman, Mary J.   III. Mac an
Ghaill, Mairtin.   IV. Series.
HT1505.T46   1999
305.8'00941—dc21   99–11251
                                                                                CIP

© British Sociological Association 1999

All rights reserved. No reproduction, copy or transmission of this publication may be made
without written permission.

No paragraph of this publication may be reproduced, copied or transmitted save with
written permission or in accordance with the provisions of the Copyright, Designs and
Patents Act 1988, or under the terms of any licence permitting limited copying issued by
the Copyright Licensing Agency, 90 Tottenham Court Road, London W1P 9HE.

Any person who does any unauthorised act in relation to this publication may be liable to
criminal prosecution and civil claims for damages.

The authors have asserted their rights to be identified as the authors of this work in
accordance with the Copyright, Designs and Patents Act 1988.

This book is printed on paper suitable for recycling and made from fully managed and
sustained forest sources.

10   9   8   7   6   5   4   3   2   1
08   07   06   05   04   03   02   01   00   99

Printed and bound in Great Britain by Antony Rowe Ltd, Chippenham, Wiltshire

Contents

Preface

This book is one of three volumes published by Macmillan which have derived from papers originally presented to the 1996 BSA annual Conference held at the University of Reading. The theme was 'Worlds of the Future: Ethnicity, Nationalism and Globalisation'. In organising the conference we had aimed to sharpen the political focus of the annual forum which the BSA conference represents and to widen the attendance so that it might include groups who do not always attend such events.

On both counts we estimate that we were successful. The first aim was realised in part by a series of excellent plenaries and panels. Doreen Massey gave the opening plenary 'Imagining Globalisation: Power-Geometries of Time-Space'. The other plenary speakers were Chandra Talpade Mohanty who spoke on 'Globalisation, Globe-Trotting, and other Stories of Democracy: Decolonisation, and the Challenges for Anti-racist, Comparative Feminist Practice' and Robert Miles on 'Analysing the Political Economy of Immigration Control'. The first panel involved three speakers on the relationship between Ireland, Northern Ireland and Britain. The speakers were Ailbhe Smythe, Robin Wilson and Liam O'Dowd. The other panel was entitled 'Is There Social Justice in Social Theory for Black Women', chaired Heidi Safia-Mirza. The conference closed with the Presidential Address which was given by Stuart Hall and was titled 'Identity and Difference in Global Times'.

The second aim was achieved in that many academics, both established and younger, drawn from a variety of ethnic minority and diasporic communities attended. The overall attendance was down, however, compared with the two previous conferences on 'The City' and 'Sexualities'. This we think partly reflects the continuing relative marginalisation by mainstream sociology of the issues being addressed in the conference. We hope this and the other volumes convey something of the flavour of the conference debates and will contribute to developing understandings in this field.

AVTAR BRAH
MARY J. HICKMAN
MÁIRTÍN MAC AN GHAILL

Notes on the Contributors

David Adamson has been Director of the Regional Research programme at the University of Glamorgan, where he is currently Head of the School of Humanities and Social Sciences. He is author of *Class, Ideology and the Nation: A Theory of Welsh Nationalism* and has been researching poverty and social exclusion in South Wales valley communities.

Avtar Brah is Senior Lecturer in Sociology, Birkbeck College, University of London. She is the author of *Cartographies of Diaspora: Contesting Identities* (1996), and co-editor (with Mary J. Hickman and Máirtín Mac an Ghaill) of *Global Futures: Migration, Environment and Globalization* (1999).

Graham Day is Senior Lecturer in Sociology and current Head of the School of Sociology and Social Policy at the University of Wales, Bangor. He is a founding editor of the journal *Contemporary Wales*, and he has published widely on aspects of economic and social change in Wales, with a particular interest in national, regional and local identities. Recent publications include articles in *The National Assembly Agenda* (Institute of Welsh Affairs, 1998), *Journal of Rural Studies* and *The Economic and Social Review*; and *Where Do We Go From Here? A Review of Community Participation* (Wales Council for Voluntary Action).

Mary J. Hickman is Reader in European Studies and Director of the Irish Studies Centre at the University of North London. Her main research interests are in the areas of Irish migration and diaspora studies, in particular the Irish in Britain and the USA. She also writes about multi-ethnic Britain and issues concerning the British state, the Union, Northern Ireland and British–Irish relations. Her publications include *Religion, Class and Identity: The State, the Catholic Church and the Education of the Irish in Britain* (1995), (with Bronwen Walter) *Discrimination and the Irish Community in Britain* (1997), and (with Bronwen Walter) *The Irish in Contemporary Britain* (forthcoming).

Máirtín Mac an Ghaill is Professor in the Faculty of Social Sciences at the University of Sheffield. His teaching and research interests include issues of contemporary social divisions and cultural differences in England. He has a specific interest in the question of the position of the Irish in Britain. He is author of *The Making of Men: Masculinities and Sexualities* (1994) and *Contemporary Racisms and Ethnicities: Social and Cultural Transformations* (1999).

Anoop Nayak is employed as a research associate in race and ethnicity at the Department of Education, University of Newcastle upon Tyne, UK. He is currently working as part of a research team on the institutional experience of ethnic minority student teachers and their life-history transition into work. He is also completing a PhD on whiteness that involves an ethnographic exploration of popular racism and the cultural identities of British youth. He has written and researched in the areas of race, ethnicity and whiteness, masculinities and schooling, ethnography, and youth subculture.

Sarah Neal is a Senior Lecturer at Middlesex University. Her research interests are dominated by the issues of race, racism, gender, femininity, representation and equality policy processes. Her recent publications include *The Making of Equal Opportunities Policies in Universities* (1998) and 'Embodying Black Madness, Embodying White Femininity: Populist Representations and Public Policy Responses – the Case of Christopher Clunis and Jayne Zito' (1998).

Rosemary Sales is Principal Lecturer in the School of Social Science at Middlesex University. Her research interests include gender and sectarianism in Northern Ireland, and gender, migration and social policy in Europe. Her recent publications include *Women Divided: Gender, Religion and Politics in Northern Ireland* (1997) and *Women, Work and Inequality* (edited with J. Gregory and A. Hegewisch, 1999).

Joyce I. Sherlock is Principal Lecturer in the School of Physical Education, Sport and Leisure, at De Montfort University. Currently she is analysing accounts of everyday training regimes, eating habits and role of the triathlon club in the lives of young female athletes. Her recent publications include articles in *Gender and Dance: A Special Issue of Women's Studies International Forum* (which she also edited), as well as articles in *Sociology of Sport*.

Max Silverman is Senior Lecturer in the Department of French at the University of Leeds. He has worked on areas of racism, nationalism, immigration and citizenship in modern France and also on wider questions of culture and society in contemporary France. He has published *Deconstructing the Nation: Immigration, Racism and Citizenship in Modern France* (1992), and his most recent publications include *Facing Postmodernity: Contemporary French Thought on Culture and Society* (1991).

Ruth Swirsky is Principal Lecturer in Sociology and Woman's Studies at the University of Westminster. Her research and writing focus on Jewish women's history and on prostitution issues.

Ravi K. Thiara is a Research Associate at the Centre for Research in Ethnic Relations, and she also works as an independent research consultant and lecturer. Her current research interests include the South Asian diaspora, gendered mobilisation, youth and citizenship, and violence against women. She is currently writing a book on Indians in South Africa, and her publications include *Transnational Ethnicities: Indians in South Africa, 1860–1998* (forthcoming) and *Redefining Spaces: The Needs of Black Women and Children in Refuge Support Services and Black Workers within Women's Aid*.

Joost van Loon lectures in social and cultural theory at the Nottingham Trent University and is affiliated with the Theory Culture and Society Centre. He has published extensively on cultural theory, media technologies and risk. He is co-editor of the journal *Space & Culture*, and has edited (with Barbara Adam and Ulrich Beck) *Repositioning Risk: Critical Issues for Social Theory* (forthcoming).

Andrew Thompson lectures in sociology at the University of Glamorgan. His current research activity is in media and national identity, nationalism and European integration, and the social impact of global communication technology.

Nira Yuval-Davis is a Professor and Post graduate Course Director in Gender and Ethnic Studies at the University of Greenwich, London. She is also the Vice-President of the International Sociological Association Research Committee on Race and Ethnicity. She has written extensively on nationalism, racism, citizenship, and gender relations in Britain, Israel and other settler societies. She recently carried out an ESRC research project (with Max Silverman) on racialised discourses on Arabs and Jews in Britain and France. She is a Founder Member of the International Research Network on Women in Militarised Conflict Zones, funded by the Canadian Research Council and the Ford Foundation. Her publications include *Racialized Boundaries* (co-authored with F. Anthias, 1992); *Unsettling Settler Societies: Articulations of Gender, Race, Ethnicity and Class* (edited with D. Stasiulis, 1995); *Gender and Nation* (1997); and *Women, Citizenship and Difference* (edited with P. Werbner, 1999).

1 Thinking Identities: Ethnicity, Racism and Culture

AVTAR BRAH, MARY J. HICKMAN and MÁIRTÍN MAC an GHAILL

This volume brings together research covering a diverse range of collectivities which are rarely analysed together: Welsh, Irish, Jewish, Arab, White, African, Indian, etc. The aim of the volume is to interrogate and critique orthodox theorisation of the processes which underpin the production of these identities. The background to the work is the changing political conditions of the 1990s: challenges to the configuration of the United Kingdom, a new Europe, nation-building in Africa, conflicts in Eastern and Central Europe and the territories of the former Soviet Union.

The fragmentation of social relations attributed to globalising processes is reflected in the increasing range of competing sociological attempts to respond to perceived major transformations. Key themes have emerged which are often condensed into such terms as Post-Fordism, the Risk Society, disorganised capitalism, or the over-arching concepts of postmodernism and poststructuralism. Hence much sociological debate has sought to evaluate the extent and direction of social and cultural change. This volume is concerned with the question of identity at a time of rapid social and cultural change and explores this from a number of different angles in the arena of the sociology of racism and ethnicity. The term 'identity' offers conceptual and political space to rethink issues of racialised social relations and ethnicity.

At the present time the concept of culture has become a central theme in a wide range of debates concerning social change within social and human sciences. In what is referred to as the 'cultural turn' there has been a shift away from the study of structure as the privileged feature of social relations accompanied by an increased critical interest in language and how it is used to produce meaning in social life. It is within this context of current theoretical advances, particularly

1

in poststructuralist and postcolonialist theory, that recent texts have argued for the need to return culture to the centre of the debate on how we are to understand contemporary changing meanings of 'race', racism and ethnicity. Said (1993) highlights the heterogeneous nature of these processes of cultural production by arguing for the need to perceive the politics of culture within 'overlapping territories' and 'intertwined histories'. Other writers have suggested the emergence of new identities marked by diaspora, late twentieth-century forms of globalisation and syncrenism (pluralistic forms of cultural belonging) (Bhabha, 1990; Brah, 1996; Brah *et al.*, 1999; Gilroy, 1993; Spivak, 1988).

One of the weaknesses of earlier anti-racist work in this area has been inadequate conceptions of racialised or ethnicised identity formations. More recently, theorists drawing on poststructuralism, psychoanalysis and semiology have provided new ways of thinking about subjective identities (Wetherell and Potter, 1992). They have critiqued dominant theoretical and 'common-sense' explanations of racialised differences, with their taken-for-granted definitions of majority (white) and minority (black) ethnic group identities, which are implicitly assumed to be ahistorical, unitary, universal and unchanging categories. For Hall (1992) talking of the emergence of new ethnicities and the decentring of the black subject, the idea of 'having' an identity is problematic because social situations produce varied subjective positions that may be occupied. As Bhabha (1986, pp. xvi–xvii) argues, 'The question of identification is never the affirmation of a pre-given identity, never a self-fulfilled prophecy – it is always the production of an "image" of identity and the transformation of the subject in assuming that image ... identity is never an *a priori*, nor a finished product; it is only ever the problematic process of access to an "image" of totality.' In contrast to many materialist accounts, poststructuralist theorists have emphasised that the actuality of these ethnic and sexual categories and divisions is more contradictory, fragmented, shifting and ambivalent than that suggested by the dominant public definitions of these categories.

'Old times' were once 'new times'. Locating earlier materialist representations of racism, ethnicity and social change within their sociohistorical context enables us to see how they resonated with wider social concerns and anxieties of their period. From a 1990s 'postcolonial' perspective, it is easy to dismiss these accounts by concentrating on their limitations, such as their essentialism, functionalism and overdeterminism. This is not our intention. Rather, we are exploring these earlier accounts in terms of their 'situatedness' at a specific moment, when notions of multiple racisms, new ethnicities and new definitions of processes of identity formation are helping to provide fresh sociological frameworks. If the latter position is addressing the key concerns of culture, identity, subjectivity and difference, a main strength of the former position has been to place on the social map such issues as the social reproduction of racist ideology, state regulation of racism, institutionalised racial discrimination and cultural exclusion. At the present time it is important to hold on to the theoretical and political achievements of this work. Doing so serves as a useful reminder of the historical amnesia that characterises many contemporary contributions in the field. There is a strong tendency in work on 'new times' to downplay or erase such issues as that of state power, social class divisions, institutional structures and hegemonic cultural capital. In such texts there is a suggestion that discourses and practices of representation have displaced the conceptual necessity of such terms as ideology and social reproduction. There is often little awareness that racism and ethnicity are the objects of both discursive *and* ideological labour (Cohen, 1988).

At a time of the conceptual ascendancy of the 'cultural', there is a need to return the 'social' to critical theory, but not as a bi-polar binary as some previous accounts have done. Instead, the categories of 'social' and 'cultural' as mutually constitutive elements should be brought into a productive dialogue. That is, to argue the need to renew the social and cultural analysis of racialised social relations and ethnic identity formations mapping out some of the more intricate and intimate positions as they articulate the shifting boundaries of class, gender, sexuality, ethnicity and generation (Cohen, 1997; Harvey, 1989). In other words, we are not suggesting the return to a sociological reductionism, that either views ethnic minority groups as unitary social categories, or a structuralist account that reifies racism as a monolithic state practice operating against ethnic minority groups. There is a need to re-engage with earlier academic and political representations of black and other ethnic minority groups, alongside critical explorations of whiteness, Englishness and the crisis in dominant forms of Anglo-ethnicity. This is particularly salient at a time when there is a lack of consensus in sociology concerning how we conceptualise our concern with commonalities of experience and specific experiences of the world in the context of rapid social and cultural transformations at global and local levels (Lash and Urry, 1994; Mason, 1995).

One of the surprising aspects of the earlier literature on the sociology of 'race' and ethnicity has been the under-theorisation of subjectivity. In contrast to a materialist position, with its primary focus on relations between social collectivities as if both the 'relation' and 'collectivity' were always pre-given, a poststructuralist position involves a deconstruction of the very process whereby the collectivity is constituted and positioned in relation to other groups. An implication of this is to argue that subjectivity is dynamically constituted. At a social level this perspective suggests that having a singular, coherent and rational subjectivity is inadequate because the interplay between different institutional regimes of power continually reproduces a variety of subjectivities. It is argued that, rather than social collectivities authoring self-identity through their intrinsic authentic claims, social collectivities are dependent upon the establishment of other social groups relationally to themselves. One way to conceptualise responses to the complex interplay of changing processes of racialisation and wider socioeconomic change is to view them as a set of narratives of self-production that are dispersed through a multiplicity of power relations. Hence, individuals are not the passive recipients or objects of structural processes. They are not such *'tabulae rasae*, to be injected or even constructed with the ideology of the day' but are constructively engaged in the securing of identities (Rowbotham, 1989: 18). The limitations of theorising subjectivities only in relation to state and institutional racist practices is that the question of agency may appear as a simple one-dimensional product of either the institutional practices or ethnic minority groups' cultural contexts. This is of particular explanatory significance in relation to the reductionist over-arching explanation evident in some anti-racist accounts in which the signifier of colour leads to a narrative of social closure of predetermined outcomes. By theoretically shifting from a focus on product to process, both minority and majority ethnic groups can be seen to be actively involved in the making and remaking of cultural identities. An aspect of conceptualising ethnic identity formations is to be spatially and temporally sensitive to the complex politics of their location, culturally contextualising them within local institutional sites.

This latter point in particular informed our selection of the essays in this collection. It highlights the shift away from a black–white dualistic model which has been the dominant paradigm for debating these related concerns for the past quarter of a century in Britain. This collection therefore enables the consideration together of: the underplaying of anti-Semitism and anti-Arab racism in dominant race relations and anti-racist models; the relationship of Irish, Welsh, Scottish, English and other social categories to 'Britishness'; the loss and dislocation of identity but also the potential for reformulating identities afforded transnational communities; an exploration of the interrelationship between different social divisions with particular reference to gender, class and sexuality; the critical examination of differences within racialised social collectivities; an exploration of ethnic majorities, including questions of whiteness; the contingent contestations which underpin Britishness and the 'sub-national' identities which constitute the hierarchical relationship which is the United Kingdom.

MANAGING 'DIFFERENCE' WITHIN THE NATION

It has become a truism of present-day social commentaries to declare that this is the age of the 'new politics of difference'. The implication of teleological trajectory which underpins many such accounts (despite the ostensible challenge to such projections) is reflected in the 'newness' ascribed to many aspects of culture and society deemed 'postmodern'. For example, many of the analyses studying the impact of and responses to the migration of people from the Indian subcontinent and the Caribbean to Britain in the 1950–70s have emphasised 'newness': new racism, new political discourses, new fears of an 'enemy within' (see, for example, Barker, 1981; Solomos *et al.*, 1982).

These claims to newness are hard to substantiate if the historical roots both of racist practices and of the politics of difference in Britain are examined in any detail. For example, 'new' racism is concerned with inclusion and exclusion – on the one hand specifying who may legitimately belong to the national community while simultaneously advancing reasons for the segregation or banishment of those whose 'origin, sentiment or citizenship' assigns them elsewhere (Gilroy, 1987: 45). Much of the sociology of 'race relations' rapidly embraced this 'new' conception of the basis of racism based on an assumption that a discourse of cultural differentialism formed a new basis for processes of inclusion and exclusion.

If the problematic of racism had been a more inclusive field of study, then this critical acceptance of the 'newness' of cultural racism might not have occurred. To take two historically and contemporaneously significant instances, both anti-Semitism and anti-Irish racism, as well as constructions of other colonised peoples 'out there', reveal that there is nothing new about cultural differentiation as a basis for racist discourse in this country. In Britain, the study of racism within the dominant paradigm, that of the 'race relations' problematic, has been constructed in exclusive and exclusionary ways. As a consequence, the frameworks and concepts with which processes of inclusion and exclusion are studied have had their own closures. This has the effect of concealing the multi-dimensional character of processes of exclusion and inclusion in Britain. It generated a view that colour was the predominant signifier of 'race'.

For example, it is instructive to examine the situation in Scotland, often overlooked in British 'race relations' debates. It is generally assumed that sectarianism, an acknowledged feature of Scottish society, is a completely distinct phenomenon to racism because it is deemed to be about 'religion'. The contemporary significance of the fact that discussion about Catholics in Scotland is taken as being about people of Irish Catholic descent is left unexplored. It is regarded as a subject fit only for historical investigation. That the term 'Catholic' in Scotland continues, in many contexts, to articulate both religious and ethnic/national origins, and remains a key component of racialisation processes and of possible discrimination, is generally ignored in discussions about racism in Britain (Hickman and Walter, 1997). The widespread acceptance in Britain of the premise that 'race' is primarily denoted by skin colour allows this occlusion.

The first chapter in this collection examines racism and national culture in Britain and France by comparing the racialised constructions of Jews and Arabs in both countries. It offers a critique of the black–white paradigm in Britain and highlights the centrality of the religious and the political for the theorisation of racism in France. Silverman and Yuval-Davis contrast, therefore, the 'race-relations' paradigm of Britain from which Jews have been excluded and Arabs marginalised, with the assimilationist republican tradition in France, in which Jews have been central, and the anti-colonial tradition which focused on Arabs. They use comparative analysis to question what is generally meant by racism, and explore the basis of different racisms.

The French national project of political rights and civic equality is both the antithesis of the 'racial model' and the root cause of a profound racism based on assimilationist social engineering and the rejection of difference. The problematic nature of attempting to reduce the other to the same or, alternatively, to fix the other as irredeemably different, is at the heart of this contradictory project. In official discourses the only way of categorising those residing in French territory is through nationality: you are either a French national (and therefore citizen) or a foreigner. Consequently, France accords full rights only to free and equal citizens before the law, and not to communities. This abstract model, founded on an individualistic egalitarianism and the uniformity of the public sphere, confines religious, ethnic or other differences to the private sphere and makes it impossible to conceive of the formal institutionalisation of communities. A powerful sense of national/cultural belonging has therefore been the major means of racialisation in France.

In contrast, these authors argue that racialised discourses in Britain developed around notions of 'race' and 'colour' and were closely connected with its historical experience as an empire. With the decline of the British empire, racialised discourses which were used to dominate abroad came to be used to establish boundaries within. After the Second World War, the defeat of the Nazi, the upward class mobility of Jews and their fear of invisibility had removed them from the 'centre stage' of racialised discourses. By the beginning of the 1970s, although 'the Jew' never lost the attention of Extreme Right organisations, Jews had virtually disappeared from the 'mainstream' British sociological literature dealing with racism, and this remained the case for two decades.

Silverman and Yuval-Davis think that there is now a convergence between Britain and France concerning theories of racism. They argue that the growing acceptance in both countries that the old biological basis of racism has today largely given way to cultural forms of racism is the most significant aspect of this convergence. It is associated in both countries with constructions of Islam as a major focus of otherness and the relationship between racism and concepts of the nation. In France it was the construction of the 'problem of immigration' in the 1970s that constituted the major contemporary paradigm for the theorisation of racism. It was at this point that 'immigration became politicised and racialised through the discourse of cultural difference and therefore (unassimilability) of North Africans in France'. The breakdown of the logic of 'assimilation' and the rise of cultural difference has left anti-racist movements in France oscillating between old concepts of (individualist) integration and (communtarian) difference: the former risks reproducing the official discourses and the latter risks reproducing the cultural differentialism of the New Right. The Front National is both anti-Maghrebian and anti-Semitic, while the fight against both these exclusions is central to most anti-racist organisations.

Silverman and Yuval-Davis point to the emergence in both countries of what they call a 'postmodern' frame for the analysis of racism. In Britain the postmodern frame has produced the problematisation of the black–white model and the acknowledgement by some theorists of the limitations of the colonial paradigm as a sufficient explanation for racism, and this in turn has led to the reconsideration of anti-Semitism as a major form of racism. In Britain there has been much debate about the category of 'race' and whether or not it should be used in academic analysis to refer to racialised social groups. Although 'race' is still used frequently it has been sidelined in favour of the concept of racialisation. Another significant factor contributing to convergence in theorisations of racism has been the harmonisation of national policies within the European Union, especially with regard to legislation on immigration and political asylum, and the construction of 'Fortress Europe'. In Britain, for example, legally the important distinction has ceased to be between an NCWP person and others, and is now between 'legal citizens' and 'illegal immigrants'.

The new 'politics of difference' therefore opens up the space for a variety of identifications and discriminations. In both countries this cultural/political project mobilises around the adoption of identity, rather than its predetermined and fixed nature. Silverman and Yuval-Davis ask whether this is leading to a new hegemonic paradigm. In this context the second chapter, by Thompson, Day and Adamson, is useful for its emphasis on national identity as a site of contestation; that is, national identity conceived as consisting of a number of *competing* conceptions, rather than one all-encompassing conception. If there is the outline of a new hegemonic paradigm emerging then one facet is the acceptance of the notion of plural identifications, the openness of the terrain of potential mobilisations for any individual or group.

Thompson *et al.* argue that the 'local' is an important terrain and has a critical role in the contestations which produce national identities. They set out to show the ways in which ongoing struggles to define locale, place and 'belonging' can contribute to the production of differing forms of national identity and their adoption. That is, how do individuals 'make sense' of issues of national identity in their relations with and interaction with other individuals in their immediate locale? Very localised cultural threats are pertinent in the constant processes of othering under way at this level. However, pursuing a point we made earlier, it would be difficult to argue that the contestations they analyse are new.

Thompson *et al.* critique the tendency of the modernists (e.g. Gellner) and the ethnicists (e.g. Smith) to explain national identity with recourse to the ideology of nationalism. Nationalism as an ideology is concerned with the production of the nation as a public, as a 'people', and is thus oriented towards concealing differences rather than recognising them. Their chapter, therefore, maintains the necessity of discriminating between nationalism and national identity. This is because theories of nationalism begin from the assumption that issues such as language, religion, territory or 'culture' are relevant to the individual, and that each individual expresses a similar attitude towards them rather than examining how these issues are made relevant by individuals through processes of negotiation with others within particular sociospatial contexts.

The authors view nationalism as 'free-floating' and capable of being articulated by any class or class alliance, albeit in different forms. Nation and related concepts such as community and language thus provide an open ideological terrain on which individual subjects can position themselves in relation to their lived experience. National identity is pervasive and not limited to the political sphere in the way that nationalism tends to be; individuals who have no nationalist political beliefs nevertheless will almost always have some sense of national identity. Therefore it is necessary to take cognisance of the national, local, communal and individual processes of identity acquisition and formation, as a sense of national identity will be produced from a complex interrelationship of all these levels. Thompson *et al.*'s argument is that concepts of community which are operationalised provide one of the principal criteria for inclusion and exclusion in processes of social closure by offering naturalised boundaries through which insiders and outsiders may be defined.

Taking Wales as an example they demonstrate that there is not a unified uncontested national ideology, and individuals and groups differ markedly in the particular version of community which they espouse, and that this has significant implications for their understanding of identity. The authors quote evidence from a recent survey of residents of South Wales Valleys communities which shows that within a clear sense of Welsh national identity there are sets of 'nested' identities located in life in the Valleys and the specific community to which the individual belongs. They argue that a reformation of identity is taking place; and directly link the dramatic processes of economic and social restructuring in Wales to the fact that none of the traditional markers of a distinctive Welsh identity has survived unscathed: religious nonconformity, political liberalism, Welsh language.

In a study of Bangor in northwest Wales they utilise a more qualitative approach in order to elicit the contextual specificities within which people employ notions of Welshness and nationality. The main 'communities' in Bangor are: Welsh-speaking students, non-Welsh-speaking students and the Bangor locals. Myriad sets of inclusions and exclusions maintain the 'differences' between the three groups and reveal the extent to which these local boundaries are inscribed with notions of national identity and social class. The divide between the locals and both groups of students is articulated in sociospatial terms as a division between 'Upper' Bangor (the students) and 'Lower' Bangor (the locals), and relations between the locals and both groups of students are distant. The differences between Welsh-speaking students and the non-Welsh-speaking students, reinforced by relatively distinct social circles, are encapsulated respectively as between the 'Welsh' and the 'English'.

This differentiation between 'Welshness' and 'Englishness' also inscribes relations between the Bangor locals and people from neighbouring towns and villages. Bangor has a lower proportion of Welsh speakers than other surrounding towns; consequently the 'Welshness' of people from Bangor is contested and the town is referred to as 'English Bangor'. In Bangor itself Welshness is expressed by the locals in the fervour with which the victories of the Welsh rugby or football teams are hailed. For many people in Bangor, therefore, although they are not opposed to the Welsh language, it does not represent an important feature of their sense of Welshness. The identification of Welshness with the language is represented by the locals in Bangor as a characteristic of the Welsh-speaking middle class; in the town this group is represented by the Welsh-speaking students in 'Upper' Bangor.

The locals legitimate their lack of identification with the language, a traditional marker of Welshness, with reference to the class differences which they believe underpin the division between Welsh-speakers and non-Welsh-speakers. Their own focus was on social issues such as housing and jobs for Wales. While the middle-class Welsh-speaking students prize an ability to deploy the Welsh language and culture as evidence of Welshness, the locals see being born in Wales and being proud to be Welsh as the crucial criteria of being Welsh. Thus in one small part of northwest Wales separate and competing conceptions of Wales coexist and highlight the differing 'lived experiences' of the different groups.

Thompson *et al.* show how even small-scale migration can make people aware of 'difference', for example, a visit to a pub in a different part of Bangor or a visit to a nearby town. They conclude by arguing that much of the construction of ideas of national identity takes place at local level, as people engage in drawing boundaries – real and symbolic – around their particular communities. These everyday conceptions of identity are far removed from the 'purified' and often stereotyped versions which eventually come to form part of more explicitly nationalist ideologies.

The local does, however, tell us about the production of the nation as a public, about the project of producing the 'people'; and it is the articulation of the latter with the local dimension which is of particular interest. This is borne out in Nayak's article (Chapter 4 of this book), in which he considers the significance of territorial racism. His chapter focuses on the cultural identities of young white males and the processes they deploy to enact particular forms of whiteness. Relatively little is known about the ethnicity of white youth and the way racism features in their lives, and the chapter is a contribution towards this in its exploration of whiteness, sexuality and national identity.

The young skinhead men interviewed for the research in Birmingham treasure a monolithic whiteness and refute any notions of their identities as fragmented through migratory experiences or multicultural influences. Being a black British citizen by birth was not enough, in their view, to claim the identity 'English'. For them an authentic sense of Englishness is confirmed only through a discourse of whiteness. They re-imagine white identities as stable and complete, as a continuum that has transcended epochs, as compared with their presentation of black identities as fluid and incomplete. This is an attempt to continually promote a polarised, unifying racial symmetry against the fractures and fragmentation of contemporary life. This accentuates notions of whiteness as superior, pure and uncomplicated, and involves a denial that they too inhabit a diasporic space (Brah, 1996). The investments in 'whiteness' are pivotal to identifying the techniques whereby young men locate their identities through particular narratives of the nation.

Nayak suggests that white masculinities are given the appearance of substance through synchronised routines. By drawing attention to the performative dimensions of whiteness he aims to expose the processes utilised to choreograph a coherent white identity. The choreographed exposition suggests whiteness is a repetitive, highly stylised ritual of display, and the lineage of whiteness as a constant that connects up young White men with the discourse of a 'stable past' helps to augment their situated performances. When deconstructed those performances reveal their two obsessions: 'being authentic' and 'being British'.

Boots were key signifiers of skinhead identity in the late 1960s and early 1970s, whereas for the young men in Nayak's chapter their haircuts are their main source of identity, a trademark of class, whiteness and masculinity. The close cut they usually adopted could articulate multiple fantasies of existence as soldier, ex-convict or someone who had to be institutionalised. The skinhead look is a choreographic pose adopted to display a performance of whiteness as quintessentially English and racist; for example, in tattoos of British bulldogs, Union Jacks or swastikas. Nayak describes both how these young men colonise the local landscape, marking out 'no-go' areas for other young people, and how their local identities are central to understanding the forms of whiteness they occupy within their locality.

Cohen (1997) has shown that the skinhead uniform can be abstracted from any specific reference or content in local social history and projected as a generic transnational image of white labour. Nationalisms of the neighbourhood, the football team, even the family can serve as supports for unofficial forms of immigration control directed against those whose faces do not fit the habitus of white male territorialism. In examining the choreographed whiteness of these boys Nayak is revealing how categories of race, nation or ethnicity are mobilised to reinvent or replace the culture of white labourism.

RE-PRESENTING WHITENESS

The chapter by Nayak illustrates one of the ways in which the conceptual and political space in rethinking the field of enquiry of race and ethnicity is being opened up; that is, through a focus upon the emergent issue of whiteness. This approach represents a departure from earlier work on race and ethnicity that foregrounded the experiences of black 'ethnic minorities'. The focus upon whiteness and white identities highlights the deracialisation of the ethnic majority, which in turn challenges the earlier frameworks that have constructed black ethnic minorities as a social problem (Bonnett, 1996). As film theorist Richard Dyer (1993) has shown, whereas black always 'speaks' colour, whiteness remains the unexamined norm, exhibiting an 'everything' and 'nothing' quality. For Brah (1992: 133–4) 'there is an urgent need to explore how and why the meaning of these words changes from plain descriptions to hierarchically organised categories under given economic, political and social circumstances'. This is part of a more general trend in culturally based theories whereby the ascendant social category in established binaries (for example, men, heterosexuals and whites) are becoming the new objects of critical appraisal.

The representation of 'racial' difference has a long history as one of the most contested arenas in the social and human sciences. A dominant understanding of representation is found in reflection theory, which suggests representations simply reflect a pre-existing reality that exists independently of its representation in discourses. A second understanding argues that the way things are represented has a constitutive role in actively constructing the object, giving 'questions of culture and ideology, and the scenarios of representation – subjectivity, identity, politics – a formative, not merely an expressive, place in the constitution of social and political life' (Hall, 1992: 254). Sarah Neal's and Joost van Loon's chapters work with the latter meaning. Contemporary cultural theory has been very successful in establishing the strategic significance of media amplification in the representation of 'racial' difference. Within the context of Britain this has been most graphically illustrated with reference to the coverage of the Rushdie Affair. However, contemporary cultural theory has tended to underplay the production and circulation of cultural representations of 'race', ethnicity and racism, failing to locate them historically within specific institutional contexts within which they are lived out. This is part of a bigger conceptual problem concerning culturally based theories of racism that tend to abstract practices from institutional contexts. There is a real danger, as we have already stressed, in this projected 'new times' of overstating the discontinuities with the past.

This is the background against which the next two chapters, by Neal and van Loon, are written. Neal's case-study analysis of the events surrounding Hugh Grant, Divine Brown and Liz Hurley, in June 1995, traces the populist configurations of 'race' and gender in media representations. The chapter is especially concerned with the social construction of white and black femininity and the relation of these to racist and nationalist ideologies. The chapter uses the Hugh Grant, Liz Hurley and Divine Brown incident of June 1995 to argue that racialised themes constantly surround and underpin the notions of femininity, gender and sexuality. Neal argues that the incident, very much played out in the public gaze, successfully counterpoised

Liz Hurley, a white (middle-class) model and actress with Divine Brown, a black (working-class) sex worker. Hugh Grant's payment for sex with a black woman pushed to the fore the antithetical constructions of white and black femininity. While Liz Hurley was (re)presented as a wronged and tragic woman, more significantly she came to symbolise purity and a specific Englishness. Conversely, Divine Brown, whose very name and occupation pushed her to an opposite location, evoked historical racist stereotypes centring on the notion of sexually permissive black women. These stereotypes were buttressed by the widespread questioning of why Hugh Grant had behaved as he had and the offered 'theory' that he wanted to experience the 'excitement' of sex with a black woman. Numerous media references to the (cheap) price of sixty dollars which Grant had paid Divine Brown reinforced this theme. Sarah Neal maintains that the incident, although appearing almost trivial and comical at an immediate level, demonstrates the currency of gendered and racialised stereotypes within contemporary populist discourse, and provides the terrain in which it is possible to identify the ways in which white femininity is central to broader notions of race and the construction of (female) black otherness.

The chapter by van Loon documents the way in which violence and racism are collocations frequently encountered at the global mediascape. He argues that, whether in the form of information or entertainment, racialised violence sparks off an acute awareness of the limitations of modernity, as far as its humanist–emancipatory ethos is concerned. This chapter deals with two particular forms of racialised violence – police brutality and urban 'riots' – and particularly focuses upon the way current technologies of mass-mediation have allowed these two to be brought together beyond the immediacy of local events. As a way of grounding this theoretical analysis, Joost van Loon describes the coming together of two specific events: the beating of Rodney King and the 1992 Los Angeles 'riots'. He raises the question: 'How can we explain the acquittal of the four police officers given the visual "evidence" of the videotape?' Arguing against the suggestion that it was simply a case of a miscarriage of justice, the notion of *hybrid media* is invoked to argue that we must not exclude judgement from violence itself. Re-interpreting the videotaped beating of Rodney King, the acquittal of his assailants by a nearly all-white jury in court, and the subsequent response by people in South Central Los Angeles and elsewhere, he argues that violence is a *hybrid energy*. Hybrid energy is engendered by the connectivity of different media.

This allows him to posit that all judgements, indeed all representations, are always violent enactments. The critical threshold of violence is thus not the difference between it being present or absent, but whether it engenders a transgression of the symbolic power. Analysing whiteness may help to remove it from its normative location as transparent, neutral and disembodied. Indeed, the chapters by Neal, Nayak and Van Loon draw attention to the relationship between constructions of black bodies and the production of whiteness in different social arenas. Neal and Nayak, respectively, discuss how representations of the black body can sustain differing femininities and masculinities. Sarah Neal exposes how sexualised images of the black female body are an underlying trope for mapping the contours of white femininities within an alternative repertoire of ethnicity, that demarcates blackness from whiteness. Meanwhile, Nayak explores how varied representations of black bodies (African–Caribbean and Asian) can be used to secure styles of white working-class masculinity in suburban neighbourhoods. For van Loon, careful examination of the media portrayal of the beaten body of the black motorist, Rodney King, illustrates how white anxieties can be re-articulated. The study of the racialisation of whiteness is still at an early stage. These three chapters illustrate the conceptual productiveness in opening up fresh questions in the area concerning shifting racialised social relations and complex identity formations.

COMPLEX SOCIAL DIVISIONS AND CULTURAL INTERACTIONS

In their chapters, Sales and Thiara explore other forms of cultural invisibility that have tended to be absent from academic and political representations of racial and ethnic difference. Rosemary Sales' chapter begins by discussing the gendered construction of the Protestant community in Northern Ireland. The dominance of the sectarian divide in Northern Ireland has marginalised concern with other social divisions, including gender inequality. The structure of the Northern Ireland state has created a form of politics which centres around community loyalties, leaving little space for alternative agendas. The conflict has often been portrayed as a religious dispute with the terms 'Protestant' and 'Catholic' having been used as 'boundary markers' for two groups. However, these different political and national identities stem from the different historical experiences of colonialism, and from their relations to the state in Northern Ireland. While these divisions are not about religious difference, the identification of the two communities with religious affiliation has institutionalised the power of the churches as a focus for community loyalty. Both churches have played a prominent role in welfare services, cultural life and schooling and the wider politics of the community, and promoted a conservative social agenda.

Sectarian divisions in Northern Ireland have therefore been associated with patriarchal structures which have served to exclude women from political life. This exclusion has been particularly strong in the Protestant community, in which women have remained largely invisible in formal politics.

Feminists from both communities have had to confront not only the ideological dominance of church teaching, but the idea that arguing a position contrary to the prevailing politics of the community is disloyal. The ties of Protestantism to the ascendancy have made it especially difficult for Protestant women to challenge 'their' state and politicians. Feminists are often seen as 'rocking the boat', and are identified as 'republicans'. Women who reject the politics of Unionism have found it particularly difficult to claim a positive identity as Protestant women.

Recent social and economic restructuring has undermined the ascendancy and increased fragmentation in the Protestant community. While the response has often been defensive and inward-looking, new possibilities have opened up for women to participate in economic and political life. Sales' chapter examines community divisions within Northern Ireland, both in terms of processes of exclusion and inclusion through the differential power of the two communities; and the gendered construction of sectarianism. It explores Protestant identity and the dominant gender ideologies and practices promoted by religious and secular institutions. It concludes by examining the increasing activity of Protestant women in community and women's groups. These groups have built co-operation around work on 'women's issues' through avoiding the major political issues which divide the two communities. The chapter explores the possibilities and limitations of these strategies.

Ravi Thiara, in her chapter, outlines a fresh perspective on forms of racialisation within South African society. As she argues, race and ethnicity have been the major guiding principles of South African society for many decades, creating hierarchies among its racialised groups. Within South African historiography, while attention has been focused on African/White or Indian/White relations, few attempts have been made to analyse interaction between African and Indian peoples.

Through a focus on a specific incident of conflict between African and Indian people in South Africa, her chapter attempts to move away from the simplistic Black/White binarism inherent in South African historiography. By highlighting the nature of differential racialisation in a colonial context, it points to the historical and political complexity that textures ethnic relations and which, it is argued, are critical to any adequate explanation of subordinate group interaction.

Through the lens of the 1949 Durban 'riots', which took place during a period of great political change, an attempt is made to assess their legacy for relationships between African and Indian people at a popular level. It is argued that the Durban 'riots' as an event have left an enduring psychological legacy which is of continuing significance to Indians. This event has become an 'epic' rooted in people's collective memory, and it has an ongoing longevity through its reproduction over the years. The need to examine in detail the competing texts that surround an 'event/epic', and the ways in which this assumes an independent logic, is also highlighted. The construction of the past and the 'message of history' for present-day discourses of ethnicity and ethnic conflict are importantly underlined.

MIGRATION AND IDENTITY

The last two chapters examine aspects of identity for two transnational communities: Jewish and Irish. Diasporic experiences are always gendered. Swirsky, in her chapter, is concerned with the loss and dislocation of identity as experienced by Jewish women in Britain. This is set in a migratory context in which many women feel compelled to offer a narrative of progress; their tales of displacement are therefore often hidden, tucked away in the corners of their personal accounts. Swirsky intends to prise them into view.

Swirsky examines the elements of both commonality and difference in the narratives of Jewish women who participated in two waves of mass migration, from Eastern Europe from 1880 to 1914 and from Nazi Germany and annexed countries in the 1930s. She draws on interviews made as part of the Jewish Women in London Group's oral history project. These were mostly interviews with the daughters of East European immigrants, because of the lapse of time.

The two migrations were different in a number of ways. That from Eastern Europe at the turn of the century was essentially economic, while the later wave was a migration of refugees. The former was largely working-class; the latter was middle-class; those from Eastern Europe settled in concentrated working-class communities, while the refugees of Nazism tended to disperse geographically, though in time they formed numerous societies and institutions which continue to provide cultural continuity.

It is Swirsky's contention that the experience of migration brings into focus the intersection of biography and history. In developing our life stories we draw upon ongoing stories and narrative structures available to us within our community and culture. The individual life and self is refracted through the narration of autobiography, and that narration ultimately leads us back to ourselves, to our identities. Exploring multiple autobiographies can also amount to a 'collective testimony'. Swirsky notes that many migrant women have difficulty in articulating and revealing the trauma and loss of migration, when they were migrating *to* something, a better life or safety, which almost requires the construction of a narrative of hope, of moving forward. From a series of women's commentaries she highlights the scars of uprooting, transportation, replanting, acclimatisation and development that women in both these periods of migration experienced. What is revealed is the psycho-geography of place: the dislocations not only of place but of self, the reconstructions of self within bodies occupying foreign spaces, the loss of lives that might have been within the world called 'home', the anger or guilt that often lies behind nostalgia. All who are migrants and their descendants live their lives with the shadow of a parallel life, the life that might have been lived.

Swirsky argues that there is an important difference between the two migrations in terms of loss. Economic migrants leave a home which continues to exist, with kith and kin and community continuing to have a concrete presence which acts as a reference point. Indeed today, in an era of accessible international travel and telecommunications, 'home' can be more easily visited or contacted to provide reassurance and help dispel the longing, assuage the emotional loss and mitigate the sense of dislocation. Political migrants may consist of those who are part of a political struggle and have a vision of a different society to which they might return, and those for whom exile seems irrevocable. Swirsky posits that political migrants who cannot go back have to turn their faces more resolutely forward. For refugees from Nazism there was a very specific sense in which departure was irrevocable because 'home' had been tainted, if not destroyed. The experience of migration and exile, of dislocation and loss, has therefore an almost universal quality, but it is also shaped by the historical specificity of the migration. The women who Swirsky writes about demonstrate that a singular, coherent and rational subjectivity as a successfully re-settled migrant masks a variety of subjectivities. Be they economic migrants or political refugees these women's subjectivities are dynamic and multiple.

In the final chapter Sherlock examines a different aspect of diasporic identity. Her analysis of *Riverdance* is a case study of how diaspora cultures work to maintain community, selectively preserving and recovering traditions, 'customising' and 'versioning' them in hybrid and often antagonistic situations (Clifford, 1994). The chapter is also a contribution to the cultural analysis of dance, and considers who creates dances, where they are located in society and whose interests they serve. The premise is that dance, as any cultural product in contemporary societies, may be subject to the global dominance of modernity; that is, the 'institutions and ideals of Western culture, configured alongside the capitalist nature of society'. Thus dance, far from being 'natural', is institutionalised not only in national contexts but at the global level.

Sherlock is especially interested in two aspects: how dance styles are changed by participants in relation to a search for identity; and how music and dance styles derived from one cultural location can be meaningful to another cultural group through evocations of life experiences structurally similar in capitalist social relations. *Riverdance* is set between cultures: the culture of Irish folk traditions abstracted from nineteenth-century nationalism: Irish, Spanish, Slavic, African–American popular cultural manifestations reinterpreted in the logic of stage and screen. In *Riverdance* traditional styles are modernised, and a levelling international style is produced. This is levelling up to unbelievable technical prowess, to incredible professional showmanship, to a signifying of Irishness, and perhaps other subordinate cultural groups, becoming modernised, disciplined and corporate and able to partake fully in industrialised labour.

Sherlock argues that the appeal of the show lies in: recognition of the skill of the footwork (the level of disciplined co-operation required undermines stereotypes of the lazy, boozy, inefficient, disorganised, spontaneous, fun-loving Irish); the precision, power and virtuosity create a feeling of belonging, legitimating a sense of no longer needing to succumb to the subordinate social location often implied by Irishness; its references to archetypal myths which are taken as common to all humanity (this comes over in the names of the dances); and in its evocation of particular myths about Ireland, especially the nationalist metaphor of nurturing Irish womanhood, in which the passion for an idea of homeland is kept alive.

Even in its traditional reinforcement of biological distinctions and male dominance, however, there is a modernist twist. The peasant woman of nationalist romance has been replaced by a 'couturier's waif'. Unlike the voluptuous Irish country lass, the women in *Riverdance* have the adolescent look of the fashion-conscious urban consumer, dieting and flat-chested rather than maternal and nurturing. In Ireland ideas of modern manhood and womanhood are under debate, but *Riverdance* ignores this reality, as it does the conflict in Northern Ireland. Thus at the point at which globalisation makes sexism redundant in principle, in practice it strengthens its hold and delineation.

The reality which *Riverdance* does negotiate, and allow to transform the way in which nostalgic memories and passions are evoked, is the hybridity of modern life for Irish–Americans or African–Americans – the urban struggle. The show is a reminder that struggle may be a necessary condition for gaining and maintaining credible identities in modern life, in its themes of humanity overcoming tragedies such as famine and slavery. *Riverdance* is therefore an example of how Irish–American diasporic consciousness has been formed from the collision and dialogue of cultures and histories in the 'new world' and a selective engagement with 'another place'.

REFERENCES

Bhabha, H. (1986) 'The Managed Identity – Foreword: Remembering Fanon', in F. Fanon (ed.), *Black Skin, White Masks* (London: Pluto Press).
Bhabha, H. (1990) *Nation and Narration* (London: Routledge).
Barker, M. (1981) *The New Racism: Conservatives and the Ideology of the Tribe* (London: Junction Books).
Bonnett. A. (1996) '"White Studies": the Problems and Projects of a New Research Agenda', *Theory, Culture and Society*, 13, pp. 145–55.
Brah, A. (1992) 'Difference, Diversity and Differentiation', in J. Donald and A. Rattansi (eds), *'Race', Culture and Difference* (London: Sage).
Brah, A. (1996) *Cartographies of Diaspora: Contesting Identities* (London: Routledge).

Brah, A., Hickman, M. J. and Mac an Ghaill, M. (1999) (eds), *Global Futures: Migration, Environment and Globalization* (London: Macmillan).

Clifford, J. (1994) 'Diasporas', *Cultural Anthropology*, 9: 3, pp. 302–38.

Cohen, P. (1988) 'Perversions of Inheritance: Studies in the Making of Multi-racist Britain', in P. Cohen and H. Bains (eds), *Multi-Racist Britain* (London: Macmillan).

Cohen, P. (1997) 'Labouring under Whiteness', in R. Frankenberg (ed.), *Displacing Whiteness* (London: Duke University Press).

Dyer, R. (1993) 'White', in *The Matter of Images: Essays on Representation* (London: Routledge).

Gilroy, P. (1987) *There Ain't No Black in the Union Jack* (London: Hutchinson).

Gilroy, P. (1993) *The Black Atlantic: Modernity and Double Consciousness* (London: Verso).

Hall, S. (1992) 'New Ethnicities', in J. Donald and A. Rattansi (eds), *'Race', Culture and Difference* (London: Sage/Open University Press).

Harvey, D. (1989) *The Condition of Postmodernity: An Enquiry into the Origins of Cultural Change* (Oxford: Basil Blackwell).

Hickman, M. J. and Walter, B. (1997) *Discrimination and the Irish Community in Britain* (London: Commission for Racial Equality).

Lash, S. and Urry, J. (1994) *Economies of Signs and Space* (London: Sage).

Mason, D. (1995) *Some Problems with the Concepts of Race and Racism* (Leicester: University of Leicester Press).

Miles, R. (1982) *Racism and Labour Migration* (London: Routledge and Kegan Paul).

Rowbotham, S. (1989) *The Past is Before Us: Feminism in Action Since the 1960s* (Harmondsworth: Penguin).

Said, E. W. (1993) *Culture and Imperialism* (London: Vintage).

Solomos, J., Findley, B., Jones, S. and Gilroy, P. (1982) 'The Organic Crisis of British Capitalism and Race: the Experience of the Seventies', in Centre for Contemporary Cultural Studies, *The Empire Strikes Back: Race and Racism in 1970s Britain* (London: Hutchinson).

Spivak, G. (1988) *In Other Worlds: Essays in Cultural Politics* (New York: Routledge).

Wetherell, M. and Potter, J. (1992) *Mapping the Language of Racism: Discourse and the Legitimation of Exploitation* (London: Harvester Wheatsheaf).

Part I

Managing Difference within the Nation

2 Jews, Arabs and the Theorisation of Racism in Britain and France

MAX SILVERMAN and NIRA YUVAL-DAVIS

INTRODUCTION

Until recently theories of racism in Britain have largely been constructed within a black/white and anti-colonial paradigm. However, over the last few years this has changed considerably. Today, new paradigms have emerged which have widened the discussion of racism to include, among others, Jews and Arabs. In France, on the other hand, the black/white paradigm has played a more marginal (if growing) role, whereas Jews and Arabs have for long been central to theorisations of racism.

The purpose of this chapter is to sum up and compare the major paradigms in which racism has been theorised in Britain and France, especially by sociologists, during the post-Second World War period, and the ways construction of Jews and Arabs and racisms against them have figured in these paradigms. It is our contention that the difference between the theorisation in the two countries is a result of both the construction of differences in their respective histories of racism, as well as the different processes of state, nation and colonial formation. We also argue that recently, as a result of a number of European and global processes, these differences have started to erode. This fact is reflected in the most recent theorisations in both countries.

The context in which this chapter has been written is our ESRC project on 'Racialised Discourses on Jews and Arabs in Britain and France'. Of necessity, the assertions in this paper are of a general nature and do not reflect all the work that has been done in the area. We do not include in this paper reference to works which concentrate exclusively on racism against Jews or (the much rarer cases) Arabs and, in general, limit ourselves to the sociological focus on these issues.

'RACE', 'COLOUR' AND RACISM IN BRITAIN

As in other European cultures, the British heritage of racism (that is, of constructing categories of 'others' with immutable boundaries in order to exclude, inferiorise and/or exploit them), has included Christian traditions of hatred towards Jews and Muslims. The rise of 'scientific racism' and Nazism in the early part of the twentieth century targeted Jews as the primary object of racism.

However, unlike most Western European countries, Britain was never under Nazi occupation (except for the Channel Islands). It therefore never became a central formative experience in its construction of the nation. Racialised discourses in Britain developed around notions of 'race' and 'colour' and were closely connected with its historical experience as an empire. As Miles (1987: 35) points out, the notion of 'race', as it emerged in the nineteenth century, served a dual object: to explain both the hierarchy of interdependence between the English and the colonial races, and the difference in productive relations in material wealth between England and much of the rest of the world at this time.

With the decline of the British empire, racialised discourses which were used to dominate other countries, came to be used to establish boundaries within. Paul Gilroy points to the patriality clause in the British immigration law of 1968 as a common articulation of British nationalism and racism, codifying 'cultural biology of "race" into statute law as part of a strategy for the exclusion of Black settlers' (Gilroy, 1987: 45).

British race relations legislation (especially the 1965, 1968 and 1976 Acts) were passed specifically in order to combat racism. However, there is a paradox inherent in the legislation: the Acts called for the elimination of various forms of racial discrimination while, at the same time, accepting the assumptions that the population is indeed composed of people of different races, and also that racism affects predominantly (if not exclusively) these races. The members of these races were identified in laws such as Section 11 of the 1966 Local Government Act as being members of the NCWP (New Commonwealth countries and Pakistan). Other forms of racisms, directed against other racialised minorities such as the gypsies, the Irish or the Chinese, were mostly excluded from this discourse, as too were Jews and Arabs.

It is not our intention here to enter into the critique of the 'race relations' paradigm, in both its multicultural and anti-racist variations,

which homogenises racialised minorities, reproduces racialised boundaries and does not – to use Ali Rattansi's words (1992: 32) – 'display
an awareness of contradictions, inconsistencies and ambivalences' (see
also Anthias and Yuval-Davis, 1992; Miles, 1993; Solomos and Back,
1996). Instead, we wish to highlight the fact that although some of the
associated theorisations, such as those of Banton (1967; 1977; 1988)
and Rex (1970; 1986), attempted to develop (in different ways)
general frameworks of analysis of racism, the minorities they were
concerned with in relation to the United Kingdom were the same ones
designated by the Race Relations Acts.

It is important to emphasise, however, that the particular theorisation of racism associated with this paradigm was not just that of post-
colonialism but also that of a particular class relations perspective. In
the introduction to the second edition of his book *Race Relations in
Sociological Theory* (1970, second edition 1983: xvi–xvii), John Rex
ponders whether or not the entry to Britain of middle-class Asian
refugees from East Africa after 1967 affects the validity of his 'race
relations' model. The African Asians clearly do not constitute an
underclass in Britain and yet have suffered from racism. Rex concedes
that his 'model of post-colonial society... has to be considerably
extended' to take account of these groups 'both at the metropolitan
centre and at the colonial periphery'. However, the existence in
Britain of other racialised minorities who are not post-colonial immigrants, and who do not share the class or colour positionings of Rex's
NCWP 'underclass', is not recognised by Rex in his model at all.[1]

Highlighting the link between racism and class relations (if not actually reducing the former to the latter) is also an important aspect of
the Marxist paradigm of analysis which was hegemonic during the
1970s and much of the 1980s in British sociology. In 1969, the British
Sociological Association dedicated its annual conference to the theme
of 'Race and Racialism' which can be considered as a symbolic
moment in the history of the study of racism in Britain. Sami Zubaida,
who edited the collection of conference papers (1970), argued in his
introduction against the hegemonic approaches which homogenise the
field of 'race relations' in Britain and the USA. He claimed that these
approaches were partly due to the concentration on 'social problems'
rather than on 'sociological problems', and partly due to the predominantly social, psychological and micro-sociological orientation of
research and discourse 'which results in obscuring the differences
between Negroes and Jews' (1970: 3). (Although Zubaida himself
comes from Iraq, the category of 'Arab' is not part of his discourse of

racism in this introduction.) Zubaida also mentions the importance of the historical legacy of colonialism in terms of shaping relationships between black or 'coloured' minorities and white majorities in Europe and the USA. From this point, 'the Jew' disappears from the introduction, from the book as a whole, and, virtually, from the hegemonic British sociological literature which deals with racism for the next twenty years (except when these relate to the social psychological study of fascists (cf. Billig, 1978) or in collections which deal with variants of 'ethnic cultures' in Britain (cf. Wallman, 1979).

The category of 'NCWP' was replaced in the 1980s by the category of 'Black' and then to 'Black' and 'Asians'. This shift highlighted two developments: the increased importance policy-makers attached to the second generation born in Britain, and the relative success of the promotion of the term 'Black' by the anti-racist movement inspired by the American Black Power movement. Unlike in the USA, however, where the category 'Black' was to a large extent homogeneous and signified the descendants of the African slaves, blackness as a political category was expanded in Britain to include the supposed 'organic unity' of the Asian 'coolie' and the Afro-Caribbean 'slave' (Sivanandan, 1982: 16), who share both the colonial and racist experiences. Essential to this perspective of anti-colonialist anti-racist black empowerment was the Fanonite perspective of 'The Wretched of the Earth' (1967) which was imported to Britain via the American Black Power movement.

In *Racialised Boundaries* (1992: 146–7), Anthias and Yuval-Davis quote at length a CRE fact sheet of 1985 in which country of origin becomes equivalent to immigrants' skin colour, and the countries of the world are divided into either white or black, the latter grouping made up of those countries which used to be included in the NCWP category. Unfortunately, it was not these absurdities which primarily brought about the move away by policy-makers from the use of the category 'Black' as an umbrella term to cover Britain's post-colonial immigrants, it was rather the effects of differences and power struggles among different groupings within the 'Black' category, especially between the 'Asians' and the 'Afro-Caribbeans' mainly about access to the state and state funds (Anthias and Yuval-Davis, 1992; Modood, 1988).

Whether united under the title of 'Blacks' or divided into 'Blacks' and 'Asians', and given the growing fascination with 'mixed race' people, the boundaries of these groupings did not embrace all the racialised minorities in Britain, omitting groupings such as the Irish, the gypsies and Chinese. Not even all those designated as part of the former NCWP category itself were necessarily included in these categories. For example, the Maltese and Cypriots, who officially belonged to the Commonwealth, were not automatically included in Britain's Black population. As Michael Banton pointed out (1988: 2), 'the British were never sure whether they should consider dark-skinned Mediterranean people as white or coloured'.

Although Arabs have been racialised into the 'Black' category (Lawless, 1995) and Jews into white (Brodkin Saks, 1994), neither of these racialised minorities ever really fitted the 'British Race Relations' paradigm. Before discussing the racialisation of Jews, Arabs and Muslims in Britain we shall briefly discuss the general framework in France within which questions of 'race', racism and anti-racism have formulated.

UNIVERSALISM AND THE REPUBLICAN TRADITION IN FRANCE

The conceptual apparatus of 'race' developed in Britain (and especially its accompanying black/white perspective) cannot simply be transposed onto diverse nations with different histories. In France, the 'race' perspective is seen as a peculiarly 'Anglo-Saxon' phenomenon (in which Britain and the USA are frequently collapsed into a single model). According to French commentators of all political persuasions, this model – founded on the institutional recognition of the category of 'race' for the definition and classification of social groups, and the recognition of the rights of communities rather than simply individuals – leads to the legitimisation of pseudo-scientific theories ('race') in defining social relations, the separation of people according to (spurious) 'racial' categories, the reification and essentialisation of these categories in terms of 'fixing' identity, the fragmentation of social and national unity and cohesion into a plurality of diverse communities (each with their own interests which are frequently antagonistic to those of other communities), and the consequent creation of ethnic ghettos, even 'soft forms of apartheid' (Rocard, 1989).

Hence, in formal terms, the French 'model' simply does not recognise 'race' as a valid conceptual or institutional category. Officially, the only way of categorising those residing on French territory is through nationality: you are either a French national (and therefore citizen) or a foreigner. Consequently, France accords full rights only to free and equal citizens before the law and not to communities. The French system is therefore one of individual *assimilation* (or *integration*) within the nation-state rather than the advancement of the rights of minorities.

From a British perspective, the French system appears antediluvian in its naïve faith in a formal equality with no developed institutional apparatus to advance the interests of minorities and to safeguard against the *de facto* reality of discrimination and racism.[2] Equal opportunities and positive action are considered by many as the least one can do to correct social inequalities. Yet it is necessary to situate the French system within the wider context of national and state formation in order to understand the difference in approach. Fundamental in this respect is the Enlightenment and universalist republican tradition underpinning the formation of the nation, and its accompanying ideological and institutional apparatus (Silverman, 1992). This abstract model, founded on an individualist egalitarianism and the uniformity of the public sphere, confines religious, ethnic or other differences to the private sphere and makes it impossible to conceive of the formal institutionalisation of communities ('racial' or otherwise). In the nineteenth century the 'racial' model became associated with Germany within a binary perspective which opposed French individual choice and equality with a German determinism of the *volk*. From this (republican) point of view, racial theories (and racist action) could conveniently be shown to have their origins in Germany and therefore be alien to the French system.[3]

Clearly, this schematic account of the formal definition of the French 'model' obscures a far more problematic reality. The Negritude movement of the 1930s and 1940s was an assault on the 'colour-neutral', ethnocentric and frequently racist nature of French universalism. Theorists such as Franz Fanon and Albert Memmi took these ideas further when viewed in the colonial context, and similarly highlighted the hypocrisy of formal declarations of equality and the 'Rights of Man'. The institutionalisation of the distinction between nationals and natives ('indigènes'), or citizens and subjects (Balibar, 1984) in colonised territories was clearly based on ethnic and discriminatory criteria, whilst the whole concept of the Enlightenment 'civilising mission' was founded on the assumed inferiority, backwardness and parochialism of those who had not yet 'evolved' to the 'higher' realm (hence the origin of the term 'évolué' for those who did finally attain this status).

More recently, research on the history of immigration in France has shown how immigration policy has frequently been infused with a discourse on desirable and undesirable immigrants according to racialised criteria (see, for example, Noiriel, 1988; Weil, 1991).

Research on the construction of the French nation-state has also demonstrated what Gérard Noiriel (1991) has termed 'the tyranny of the national' in establishing institutional/ideological frontiers between the national community and others. A powerful sense of national/-cultural belonging has been the major means of racialisation (and hence the construction of processes of inclusion and exclusion) in France (see especially, Balibar, in Balibar and Wallerstein, 1988; Citron, 1987; Galissot, 1985). Reappraisals of French national history have therefore revealed how republican universalism has effaced traces of racialised and other differentialist categorisations from within the French 'model' and displaced them onto other countries.

Nevertheless, the republican myth has had a powerful pull on conceptual and theoretical models. In the same way that there exists an ideological link between legislation for the Race Relations Act and the rise of the 'race relations problematic' as a distinct field of study in the British social sciences, so we can see the parallel link in France between policies of assimilation (or 'integration') within the context of the universalist republican nation-state and the major conceptual models for theorising racism. This is true both with regard to the place of antisemitism in theories of racism and the national/foreigner paradigm accompanying recent immigration. The next sections consider the different ways in which Jews, Arabs and Muslims were constructed as racialised groups in Britain and France.

THE RACIALISATION OF JEWS, ARABS AND MUSLIMS IN BRITAIN

Jews first reached Britain during Roman times and settled in large numbers in England after the Norman occupation. In Medieval times they constituted what Abraham Leon (1970) called 'a people-caste' and fulfilled specific socio-economic roles within feudal estate society. They enjoyed a certain autonomy as a community and the patronage of the feudal lords but their position also made them vulnerable. They were exposed to pressures and antagonism in periods of social and economic crisis, both from above (especially when they were owed large amounts of money by the lords) and from below (where they represented to the masses both the extractor of monies and the religious 'other' – the demonic 'anti-Christ').

Things came to a head during the crusades, both as a result of general social destabilisation and religious mobilisation and because of the heavy economic burdens imposed by the crusades. After a period of persecutions and pogroms and with the weakening of the economic resources of the British Jewish community, they were expelled from Britain in 1290 by a royal decree of Edward I – the first of a series of Jewish expulsions which took place in Western European countries, with the general rise of mercantile capitalism and national bouregoisies.

The first group of Jews to arrive in England again was composed of those expelled from Spain at the end of the fifteenth century. However, Jews only started to arrive in larger numbers in England after the establishment of the Commonwealth. During the seventeenth and eighteenth centuries both Sephardi Jews (originating in Spain and Portugal) and Ashkenazi Jews (originating Germany) settled in Britain. Despite several debates in the British Parliament regarding the legal status of the Jews in Britain, no agreement was ever reached on the subject, so that Jewish legal and political rights were largely achieved as a consequence of the rights given to Catholics and other non-established churches during the eighteenth and nineteenth centuries. The biggest influx of Jews to Britain took place towards the end of the nineteenth century and the beginning of the twentieth century, when Jews escaped persecutions and pogroms in Eastern Europe.

Jewish refugees continued to arrive in Britain before and after the Second World War, but their numbers were highly reduced by the developing machinery of immigration controls in Britain. The first law of this kind – the Aliens Act of 1905 – was prompted as a direct response to the Jewish immigration from Eastern Europe (Cohen, 1988). During the first half of the twentieth century, Jews were a major focus of anti-immigration agitation which, with the rise of fascism, combined with 'scientific racism' against them. However, after the Second World War, the defeat of the Nazis, the upward class mobility of Jews and their fear of visibility removed the Jews from the 'centre stage' of racialised discourses. This was reinforced with the mass arrival of NCWP immigrants to Britain in the 1950s and 1960s who then became the centre of racialised discourses about the 'coloured'. The Jews, however, never lost the attention of the marginal extreme right organisations (Silverman & Yuval-Davis, 1997).

Although Jews can be found in virtually every part of Britain and in every class group – from poverty-stricken east-enders to members of the lower aristocracy – there are still certain demographic trends which characterise British Jewry. They are mostly concentrated in Britain's large cities, especially in certain parts of Greater London; the percentage of those who have achieved high levels of education is slightly higher than among other sections of the population; and a higher proportion are either self-employed or professionals. Although traditionally the Jews were associated with the Labour movement, there have been several ministers of Jewish origin in recent Conservative governments, and the Jewish community as a whole was hailed by Margaret Thatcher and others as an example of an integrated/assimilated community. In actuality the situation has become much more polarised. As Brook (1989: 36) points out, 'religious authoritarianism is on the increase while the rate of assimilation into the non-Jewish community continues unabated'.

The relatively high economic and political power in Britain (relative, that is, to other racialised minorities), the hegemonic alliance between the organised Jewish community and Israel, and the continued reluctance of most Jews to be 'unnecessarily' visible so as not to become an easy target for discrimination and attacks, have been used by anti-Jewish racists as 'proof' of the Jewish conspiracy to 'take over the world' (Wistrich, 1990). At the same time, these general features have also been used by Anglo-Saxon sociologists of racism to reject the inclusion of antisemitism as a mode of racism. Oliver Cox (1970: 393), the first Black Marxist sociologist of racism in the USA, defined antisemitism as 'social intolerance' and reserved the term 'racism' for rationalisation of exploitation. Michael Banton, who quotes Cox, uses different reasons for rejecting the argument that antisemitism is a form of racism: 'Since Jews can be discriminated against on a number of grounds other than those of race, there is no merit in regarding antisemitism as a form of racism' (1992: 21). The other grounds mentioned by Banton are religious and political, that is, precisely those features which (as we shall see) are at the heart of the theorisation of racism in France, and which have also become important in Britain in the theorisation of racism against Arabs and Muslims.

Historically, the category of 'the Arab' and 'the Moor' slipped in and out of the 'Black' category. Othello, for instance, was a Moor, but his popular construction has been that of a Black man. Arab traders from Lebanon and seaman from Yemen, together with Somali seamen from Africa, constituted the first modern muslim immigration to Britain in the nineteenth century. Amongst the Black population in

Cardiff and South Shields – which were historically formed by the set-tlement of Mediterranean and African seamen – Arabs did not emerge as a separate racialised grouping but were 'invisible' (Halliday, 1992: 131). In 1919, after Arab boarding houses and cafés were attacked by crowds in South Shields, their official status was defined as that of 'coloured aliens' (Lawless, 1995: 3). The discourse on Arabs, however, has a different history to the discourse on other 'coloured' populations in Britain. On the one hand, the Muslim empires (Arab and then Ottoman) were the traditional political enemies of Europe from the time of the crusades until the end of the First World War. On the other hand, there has been a strong romantic tradition (sym-bolised by Lawrence of Arabia) of affiliation with the Arabs in their struggles against the Ottomans. As a result, an Orientalist racialised discourse (Said, 1985[1978]; 1993) has constructed the Arabs as the exotic 'Others', a representation in which cruelty, sensuality, noble-ness and sexuality were intertwined.

The ambiguity towards 'the Arab' has not simply concerned colour, but also that of the Arabs' 'postcolonial status'. The British actually ruled over many Arab countries, but there was no significant British set-tlement in the Arab world, which was officially part of the Ottoman empire, until after the First World War. Nor did the independent Arab states (or the state of Israel which was established after the end of the British mandate in Palestine) join the Commonwealth. As a result, the number of Arab immigrants to Britain was much smaller than that of those from NCWP countries (Arab League, 1990). They were also divided not only according to their country of origin and religion but also according to their class – for example, upper class, rich families from the oil countries, on the one hand, and poor migrant workers from Morocco on the other hand (Halliday, 1992). Although the category 'Arab' was included in the pilot 'ethnic' question for the 1981 census, it disappeared without trace when the ethnic question was eventually included in the census in 1991. Specific racist stereotyping towards 'the Arab' has tended to appear in times of crisis and war in the Middle East which affected Britain, as at the time of the oil crisis in 1973 and the Gulf War in 1991. In addition to racist stereotypes against Arabs as excessively rich and violent, the Arabs gradually came to be constructed during the 1980s as 'Muslim fundamentalists'.

While the Arabs have been 'telescoped' into Muslims (*CARF*, 1991), they have remained invisible, as a general rule, in the body of sociological work which has focused on racism against 'the Muslim' in Britain. The racialised constructions of Middle Eastern

Muslims – especially the Iranian 'Muslim fundamentalists', the Saudi 'Oil Sheikhs' and the Palestinian 'terrorists' – combine in the popular imagination to become the focus of a conspiracy theory somewhat similar to the anti-Semitic construction of the world conspiracy of 'the Elders of Zion'. This stereotype portrays the Arabs as ruthless barbarians who send money and people to spread their fanatic/fundamentalist/terrorist gospel. However, these racialisations have virtually been excluded from sociological studies of racism in Britain which have continued to target the Muslim communities within the former NCWP, especially those from South Asia (Joly, 1995; Modood, 1992; Rex, 1994). However, a certain shift occurred with the 'Rushdie Affair' and the Gulf War, which brought to the fore 'the Muslim' as a central racialised Other, whose religion and culture (rather than her/his colour or ex-colonial origin) constitute the most significant signifiers of racialisation. Questions were raised as to the possibility of a peaceful transition in Britain to a 'multiracial society' (Asad, 1990).

ANTI-SEMITISM AND COLONIALISM IN FRANCE

Until fairly recently, antisemitism was the major paradigm for the understanding and analysis of racism in France. This is, in part, due to the powerful tradition of antisemitism itself in modern France – running from Edouard Drumont at the end of the nineteenth century, through Maurice Barrès, the Dreyfus Affair of the turn of the century, Charles Maurras and *Action Française*, the virulent antisemitism of the 1930s, Vichy and the experience of occupation and collaboration during the war, to Jean-Marie Le Pen's Front National, war crimes and the question of French complicity in the Holocaust today. But this tradition of antisemitism can itself be traced to its origins within the French model of the nation. The Jews, emancipated in 1793 and then represented *vis-à-vis* the state through the 'consistoire israélite' under Napoleon I, became symptomatic of the power of the revolutionary ideal to free individuals from their parochial particularist backgrounds and bring them into the realm of light as free and equal citizens. They therefore came to be associated, like no other group, with the revolutionary republican and Enlightenment project of assimilation. The rise of the so-called 'Jewish question' at the end of the nineteenth century was symbolic of the struggle at that time between supporters of the republican project and anti-republicans, between advocates of the so-called political/civic model of the nation described above and those of the opposing ethnic model, founded on essentialist and deterministic notions of blood, earth and race. Pierre Birnbaum (1992) has termed this modern form of antisemitism a *political* antisemitism, in which both the new 'state' Jews, and the republican ideal which had allowed them to acquire high-ranking positions, have been attacked.

Between the two world wars, anti-republicans of all descriptions exploited the link between Jews and the Republic to highlight the decadence of political institutions in France since the Revolution. According to Birnbaum, nations with 'weaker' states, such as the USA and Britain, which placed less emphasis on systematically purging ethnic and religious attachments from the public sphere than France, developed more pluralist and hence less antisemitic political democracies. The interest of Birnbaum's theory lies in the link he makes between antisemitism and the model of the nation-state. This highlights the centrality of the nation (and its ambivalence) in theories of racism in France. On the one hand, the French national project of political rights and civic equality, assimilation and uniformity ('la République une et indivisible') is, as mentioned above, seen as the antithesis of the 'racial' model, and provides the foundations for a profoundly anti-racist vision of France. In this perspective, racism comes from outside the body politic and needs to be expelled like a foreign virus. On the other hand, this same model of the nation can be seen as the root cause of a profound racism based on assimilationist social engineering and the rejection of difference. The assimilationist tradition – making foreigners into Frenchmen – brought with it a profound ambivalence about sameness and difference, mimicry and 'authenticity' (cf. Bauman, 1991) which the Jews were to experience with painful consequences.

The problematic nature of attempting to reduce the other to the same (or, alternatively, to fix the other as irredeemably different) is at the heart of Jean-Paul Sartre's famous essay *Réflexions sur la question juive* (*Antisemite and Jew*), written in 1946. Sartre puts forward the theory that the Jew is the reflection of the antisemite's gaze, which fixes the other as a means of compensation for its own lack. This placed antisemitism within the complex construction of self and other, oppressor and victim – a theory informed by a mixture of Hegelianism and existentialist phenomenology.

It is at this point that we can see the convergence between theories of antisemitism and anti-colonialism, and between the racialisation of Jews and Arabs. Two of the major francophone theorists of colonialism were profoundly influenced by Sartre's theory. In *Black Skin, White Masks* (1952), Frantz Fanon openly acknowledged his debt to Sartre in his analysis of the effect of colonialism on the constructed pathology of the Black. Similarly, Albert Memmi (1957) used Sartre's model to construct his theory of difference and the relations between the coloniser and the colonised.

Sartre's fundamentally universalist perspective – in which difference could only ever be envisaged as imposed from without to restrain the freedom of others, rather than freely chosen by those others – was transformed by anti-colonial theorists into a positive affirmation of difference in a programme for liberation. From this time, in the French-speaking world, there was therefore not only a profound connection established between theories of antisemitism and anti-colonialism (whereas prior to the post-war period colonial racism had been virtually ignored by anti-racist and human rights organisations; cf. House 1997) but also a new tension in anti-racist discourse between the traditional discourse of universal human rights and the newer anti-colonial discourse of difference.[1]

However, it must be said that theories of difference frequently fell on barren ground in the context of French republican universalism. It is interesting to compare this with what happened in the USA, where some of the same theories were transformed in a very different way. The negritude movement of the 1930s and 1940s, for example, certainly presented a challenge to French universalism, but it was also profoundly marked by that tradition. In other words it was, like most cultural/political movements, a hybrid formation, born of the mixing of different traditions (cf. Gilroy, 1993 with regard to the wider formation of black intellectuals in the modern era). Yet within the USA, the movements' associations with 'French' cultural traditions tended to be effaced. This is very similar to the appropriation of Fanon's ideas in the USA. The profound influence on Fanon's analysis of French cultural traditions, the work on antisemitism which informed it, and especially Sartreian theory, tends to get largely written out when Fanon is invoked as a major spokesperson for Black Power in the 1960s. It is his anti-colonial credentials which are emphasised in this context, and Algeria is taken as an example of liberation to be copied by others. In the heat of the anticolonialist, anti-imperialist and anti-white differentialist moment, the complex and hybrid imbrication of 'traditions' tends to be sacrificed to more monolinear and essentialist visions of difference and history.

It is particularly interesting to consider the ambivalence of Fanon's remarks on 'Jews' and 'whiteness' in *Peau noire, masques blancs*, in which the 'Jew' can be both victim of oppression (and therefore in the same position as the black) and, in his 'whiteness', the mechanism of oppression (therefore entirely opposed to the black) (cf. Cheyette, 1995). Frequently, in Britain and the USA (and, perhaps, largely due to the construction of a dichotomy between black and white), Jews get subsumed within the category of the white oppressor. In France, on the other hand, the same conflation of 'Jew' and whiteness is not so common (cf. also the work of Sander Gilman (1991) on the 'blackness' of the Jew's body.)

THE RISE OF 'CULTURAL RACISM'

The rise of what has been termed 'cultural racism' is one of the factors leading to a convergence between Britain and France in recent years concerning theories of racism. It is associated in both countries with constructions of Islam as a major focus of otherness and the relationship between racism and concepts of the nation. Islam emerged as a central racialised discourse in Britain only in the late 1980s. However, cultural racism is far from being a new phenomenon, notwithstanding Tariq Modood's claims (1992). Historically, it has been a fundamental part of racialised discourses in Britain, even if the signifier for the racialised boundary has more frequently been skin colour.

Central to the crusade by A. Sivanandan and Jenny Bourne (Bourne, 1980) against the 'Cheerleaders and Ombudsmen' of the 'ethnic school' of British sociology in the 1970s was the fact that members of ethnic minorities in Britain were portrayed as being 'between two cultures' (Watson, 1977). As Solomos and Back explain (1996: 17) 'the rejection of "culture" (by anti-racist activists and scholars at that period) was tied up with the notion that the culturalist perspective of the 1970s did little more than blame the victims of racism' (see also Lawrence, 1982). The new centrality of the cultural dimension in the analysis of racism links racism to issues of nationalism, identity politics and the politics of cultural production.

In 1981 Martin Barker published his book *The New Racism*, in which he links the Powellite model of racism in Britain to a notion of difference founded not on constructions of 'race' but on essentially and unassimilably different national cultures which should not be mixed. Robert Miles, although criticising Barker for not differentiating between nationalism and racism, also shifts his analysis of British racism from being focused on class (1982) and links it with constructions of the British nation and empire (1993). Phil Cohen (1988) and Paul Gilroy (1987) articulated somewhat similar positions in this respect even earlier. Gilroy has also drawn attention to the centrality of culture in understanding the black community and relations between black and white youth, and insists that there is more to the black community than anti-racism. Anthias and Yuval-Davis (1992) have also shown that any signifier – whether biological, cultural, linguistic or religious – can be used to construct racialised boundaries.

The entry of 'the Muslim' into a significant position within the theorisation of racism in Britain (and the parallel attention to *cultural* forms of racism) has to be seen not only in the context of the political and demographic developments in Britain during the late 1980s and the 1990s. Another significant factor in the changing politics of 'race' in the UK has been the harmonisation of national policies within the European Union (especially with regard to legislation on immigration and political asylum), and the construction of what has been termed 'Fortress Europe'. Legally, the important distinction has ceased to be that between an NCWP person and others, but between 'legal citizens' and 'illegal immigrants' (although this policy has had wider repercussions on all 'visible minority' people in Britain). Another important consequence of this development has been the effect it has had on policy-makers, grassroots activists and sociologists in Britain, bringing them into closer contact with social and political realities and hegemonic discourses concerning minorities in other European countries. For the most part, social relations in these countries have not been conceptualised through the terminology of the white/black 'race relations' paradigm discussed above.

In France it is precisely the construction of the 'problem of immigration' in the 1970s that constitutes the major contemporary paradigm for the theorisation of racism. It was at this time that 'immigration' became politicised and racialised through the discourse of the cultural difference (and therefore inassimilability) of North Africans ('Maghrébins') in France (Silverman, 1992). The major signifiers of difference associated with this paradigm have, progressively, come to be cultural/ethnic ones, especially that of religion. During the 1920s and 1930s, on the other hand, when the religious 'visibility' of Maghrebian workers was seldom highlighted, there was instead a conflation of Maghrebian immigrants and 'Arabs' (even though large numbers were not Arabs but Berbers from the Kabylie region of Algeria). By the time of the Algerian war (1954–62), this conflation of the Maghreb, 'Muslim' and 'Arab' was a fundamental element in French orientalism. Pan-Arabism was also significant as a category of self-identification and political mobilisation. In France, even in the 1970s, movements like the Mouvement des Travailleurs Arabes (Arab Workers Movement) continued to mobilise politically around the category of 'Arab'. However, this changed completely with the more permanent establishment of families in the 1970s and the rise of the 'second generation' in the 1980s (a phenomenon resulting from the immigration flows from North Africa in the 1950s and 1960s). The decline of an Arabic identification accompanies the breakdown in the process of looking towards the 'mother country' as a means of identification, and the concentration, by a new generation, on forms of political and cultural identifications expressing their lives in France. In other words the decline of an Arabic identification accompanies the shift from the colonial/anti-colonial to the post-colonial era, one of whose major characteristics is precisely the use of cultural/ethnic/national terms (immigration, national identity, Islam and so on) as markers of racialised boundaries (the era, in Etienne Balibar's words, of a 'racism without races').

The breakdown in the logic of 'assimilation' and the rise of cultural difference has left anti-racist movements in France oscillating between old concepts of (individualist) integration (which risks reproducing the dominant official and political discourse) and (communitarian) difference (which risks reproducing the discourse of the cultural differentialist New Right and Jean-Marie Le Pen's Front National; cf. Benoist, 1986; Griotteray, 1984). Pierre-André Taguieff (1987, 1995) has highlighted the problems for anti-racism when, discursively, it finds itself constantly 'doubling' the conceptual logic of its racist adversaries. The headscarf affair of 1989 was perhaps the clearest example both of the way in which 'immigration' raises fundamental cultural, social and political questions concerning identity and belonging, and the problems posed for anti-racist movements as to forms of mobilisation in a post-colonial and pluralist era (Silverman, 1992).

The prevalence today of the paradigm associated with 'immigration' and nationalist discourses of Frenchness does not mean that anti-semitism has been displaced in France as a significant area of racist or anti-racist concern. The Front National is both anti-Maghrebian and antisemitic, while the fight against both these forms of exclusion is central to most anti-racist organisations. In general, recent developments have led to a broadening of the frameworks for theorising racism in both Britain and France. Our final section attempts to map out some of the other features of the contemporary paradigm.

THE 'POSTMODERN FRAME'

Under the rubric of 'the postmodern frame', Ali Rattansi (1994) discusses in detail some of the major approaches to racism and anti-racism today. We here adopt Rattansi's term as a means of outlining (in fairly schematic form) some of the factors which have contributed to a convergence in paradigms of racism and anti-racism in Britain and France.

Firstly, the modernity/postmodernity paradigm now constitutes a major framework for the theorising of today's racisms. If the age of modernity produced two major forms of racism – the first arising from the modern project of assimilation and uniformity through a state-led social engineering, the second arising from the theory of the biological hierarchy of races (ingesting or expelling the other) – then the postmodern age can be characterised by the clash of particularisms. In this perspective there is a shared analysis by theorists in both countries of the crisis of modernity in contemporary western democracies: the crisis of universalism, postindustrialism, postnationalism, globalisation of communications and culture, time–space compression, and so on (Hall *et al.*, 1992; Rattansi, 1994). In France the crisis is perceived by a number of theorists as a breakdown in the institutional structures of integration and solidarity (schools, trade unions, political parties and so on), leading to the creation of a new 'space' for the clash of ethnic/cultural particularisms (Lapeyronnie, 1993; Naïr, 1992; Touraine, 1992; Wieviorka, 1991). The postmodern scenario presents an awareness of the problems of universalism, on the one hand, and unfettered differentialism, on the other hand; or, in the words of Toni Morrison (1983: 62), 'blackening up or universalling out' (cf. Taguieff, 1987; Touraine, 1992; Wieviorka, 1993).

Secondly, the concept of multi-racisms (Cohen, 1988; Rattansi, 1994; Taguieff, 1995) opens up the possibility of a diversity of forms of discrimination aimed at a wide range of different groups. Those previously excluded from theories of racism now find a place in this wider definition. So, for example, in Britain the problematisation of the black/white model, and the acknowledgement by some theorists of the limitations of the colonial paradigm as a sufficient explanation of racism, has led to the reconsideration of antisemitism as a major form of racism (Gilroy, 1993: ch. 6; Miles, 1993).

Thirdly, the broadened perspective in both countries on what constitutes racism is underpinned by a wider perspective on constructions of difference. In Britain, especially, the theorisation of difference across a range of levels, of which 'race' is only one (including gender, sexuality, generation, class, and others), has opened up the possibility of situating racial stigmatisation and discrimination within the wider context of the multi-layered construction of social relations and their links with power (Anthias and Yuval-Davis, 1992). This has led to a more nuanced approach to the use of 'race' as a catch-all explanation of social behaviour. In France the crisis of universalism and the greater acceptance of theories of difference in the social sciences has, similarly, led to analysis of the articulation of differences (Balibar, in Balibar and Wallerstein, 1988). One of the most significant articulations treated by theorists is that between 'race' and nation (Anthias and Yuval-Davis, 1992; Balibar and Wallerstein, 1988; Galissot, 1985; Gilroy, 1987; Miles, 1987). A reappraisal of 'Englishness' and 'Frenchness' has illustrated the way in which a number of racialised discourses are central to, not simply on the extreme fringes of, the 'liberal' British tradition and the republican French tradition (Cheyette, 1993; Citron, 1987; Gilroy, 1987).

Fourthly, the growing acceptance in both countries that the old biological basis of racism has today largely given way to cultural forms of racism is perhaps the most significant aspect of this convergence (Balibar, in Balibar and Wallerstein, 1988; Barker, 1981; Gilroy, 1987; Taguieff, 1987). In France cultural racisms have perhaps always been more significant (hence the importance of anti-Semitism) but there is nevertheless a consensus on the view expressed by Taguieff that the concept of a hierarchy of biological races has given way to the relativism of cultural differences. In Britain, although 'race' is still used frequently, it has, for a number of theorists, been sidelined in favour of the concept of 'racialisation' (Miles, 1989; Anthias and Yuval-Davis, 1992). This is a broader definition of the essentialist construction of groups which accepts that this can be produced through the discourse of cultural absolutism as well as that of biological determinism. Taguieff (1987) and Bauman (1992) speak the same language when they talk of today's cultural differentialisms as the basis of racism, or (as mentioned in the previous section) when Balibar speaks of neo-racisms, or 'racism without races'.

Fifthly, the rise of 'cultural difference' is itself a symptom, in both countries, of the breakdown of a class-based and ideological politics – focused on the power of the state to regulate social relations – in favour of a more fragmentary identity politics. At the heart of this 'cultural turn' and the politics of identity is the use of the concept of ethnicity (Hall, 1990). In both countries this cultural/political project mobilises around the adoption of identity, rather than its predetermined and fixed nature. 'Ethnicity' has become a badge of self-affirmation and a sign for easy stigmatisation. Hence, the new politics of difference opens up the space for a variety (rather than simply a limited number) of identifications and discriminations.

Finally, the modernity/postmodernity paradigm is, for many, premised on a critique of the 'western' humanist concept of 'Man', itself founded on logocentric, ethnocentric and patriarchal assumptions. This perspective, theoretically underpinned by a large dose of French anti-humanist philosophy (Jacques Derrida, Michel Foucault, Jacques Lacan and others) but adopted by British and French theorists alike, views power and oppression in a far more diverse and fragmented way than previous theories (Marxism, for example). The break with a simplistic Hegelian master/slave model, and the awareness of the reductionism (and hence violence) of all binary oppositions (cf. Young, 1990), has led to the general concern with reappraising our treatment of the other in a new (non-binary) ethical framework, one based neither on ingestion nor expulsion of the other but a recognition of otherness within the self and the impossibility of a unitary and self-sufficient self (Bauman, 1993; Levinas, 1985). In this perspective racism is situated within the wider framework of 'fixing' the boundaries between self and other and general concepts of 'otherness'. This marks not only a point of national convergence (France/Britain) but also convergence across the disciplines (especially sociology, philosophy, psychoanalysis, critical theory, cultural studies and English studies).

CONCLUSION

The postmodern frame outlined above is not, of course, without its problems. Rattansi (1994: 24–6) criticises Bauman for his 'ethnocentrism' and exclusive focus on 'the Jew' as the modern symbol of ambivalence (hence ignoring the ambivalent construction of the Black inside and outside modernity developed by Gilroy in his *Black Atlantic*). He also criticises Foucault for being 'conspicuously silent about Europe's other Others, the "native" populations subjected to the brutal forces of slavery, colonial domination and racism' (p. 26).

We feel that these are important questions to which we might add more general queries about the possible Eurocentric nature of the modernity/postmodernity framework. However, our purpose in this chapter is not primarily to offer critiques of the specific paradigms for theorising racism, but rather to discuss tendencies. We need to consider further to what extent the convergence that we have outlined above is leading us towards one hegemonic paradigm (a new universalism?) and, if so, how the specificity of Jews and Arabs will be positioned within this conceptual framework.

NOTES

1. In a recent conversation between Nira Yuval-Davis and John Rex, the latter admitted that he had never studied racism against Jews or Arabs. His first article on the subject of anti-Muslim racism appeared only in 1994 (Rex, 1994).

2. This should not obscure the fact that the law against racism in France dates from 1972.

3. This argument was often voiced after the Second World War as a way of associating collaboration with German influence, thus preserving the idea of an unsullied and pure French republicanism. The Israeli historian Zeev Sternhell (1983) shattered this myth when he traced the roots of French fascism firmly within the traditions of the Right and the Left in France.

4. The major French 'anti-racist' movements of the early part of this century – the Ligue des droits de l'homme (LDH, founded in 1898) and the Ligue contre l'antisémitisme (LICA, founded in 1928) – were both human rights organisations which were born from the struggle against anti-Semitism in the context of the abstract egalitarian ideals of the universalist republican nation-state. The LDH came out of the Dreyfusard struggle at the end of the previous century, whilst the LICA was born from the fight against growing anti-Semitism between the wars. Both organisations therefore developed within the republican 'space of human rights and equality, liberty and fraternity', and both had a universalist, egalitarian and assimilationist programme at their very heart. This was also true for the Mouvement contre le racisme et pour l'amitié entre les peuples (MRAP), founded in 1949, and whose original name contained a reference to the struggle against anti-Semitism. As mentioned above, the anti-colonial struggles of the 1950s widened the focus of anti-racist movements in a number of ways, especially in terms of challenging their traditional assimilationist and egalitarian model of the Enlightenment version of human rights. As regards this new post-war tension between the discourses of universalism and particularism, it is

instructive to consider the reflections on 'race' promoted by UNESCO during this period. For the classic critique of the ethnocentric universalism and assimilationism of the West, and a plea for the acceptance of the relativism and coexistence of different cultures, see Lévi-Strauss (1952).

REFERENCES

Anthias, Floya and Yuval-Davis, Nira (1992) *Racialized Boundaries: Race, Nation, Gender, Colour and Class and the Anti-Racist Struggle* (London: Routledge).

Arab League (1990) *Arabs in Britain: Concerns and Prospects* (Riad: El-Rayyes Books).

Asad, Talal (1990) 'Ethnography, Literature and Politics: some Readings and Uses of Salman Rushdie's *The Satanic Verses*', *Cultural Anthropology*, 5(3), pp. 239–69.

Balibar, Étienne (1984) 'Sujets ou citoyens?', *Les Temps Modernes*, nos 452–3–4, pp. 1726–53.

Balibar, Étienne and Wallerstein, Immanuel (1988) *Race, Nation, Classe: les Identités Ambigües* (Paris: La Découverte).

Banton, Michael (1967) *Race Relations* (London: Tavistock).

Banton, Michael (1977) *The Idea of Race* (London: Tavistock).

Banton, Michael (1988) *Racial Consciousness* (London: Longman).

Banton, Michael (1992) 'The Relationship Between Racism and Antisemitism', *Patterns of Prejudice*, 26(1/2), pp. 17–27.

Barker, Martin (1981) *The New Racism* (Brighton: Junction).

Bauman, Zygmunt (1991) *Modernity and Ambivalence* (Cambridge: Polity).

Bauman, Zygmunt (1992) *Intimations of Postmodernity* (London: Routledge).

Bauman, Zygmunt (1993) *Postmodern Ethics* (Oxford: Blackwell).

Benoist, Alain de (1986) *Europe: Tiers Monde, Même Combat* (Paris: R. Laffont).

Bhabha, Homi (1986) 'Forwards: Remembering Fanon', in Frantz Fanon (ed.), *Black Skin, White Masks* (London: Pluto Press).

Billig, Michael (1978) *Fascists: A Social Psychological View of the National Front* (London: Harcourt Brace Jovanovich).

Birnbaum, Pierre (1992) *Antisemitism in France: A Political History from Léon Blum to the Present* (Oxford: Blackwell).

Bourne, Jenny (with A. Sivanandan) (1980) 'Cheerleaders and Ombudsmen: the Sociology of Race Relations in Britain', *Race and Class*, 21(4).

Brodkin Sacks, Karen (1994) 'How did Jews become White Folks?', in S. Gregory and R. Sanjek (eds), *Race* (New Brunswick, NJ: Rutgers University Press).

Brook, Steven (1989) *The Club – The Jews of Modern Britain* (London: Constable).

CARF (Campaign against Racism and Facism) (1991), no. 1.

Centre for Contemporary Cultural Studies (1982) *The Empire Strikes Back* (London: Hutchinson).

Cheyette, Bryan (1993) *Constructions of 'the Jew' in English Literature and Society: Racial Representations, 1875–1945* (Cambridge: Cambridge University Press).

Cheyette, Bryan (1995) 'Jews and Jewishness in the Writings of George Eliot and Frantz Fanon', *Patterns of Prejudice*, 29(4), pp. 3–17.

Citron, Suzanne (1987) *Le Mythe national: L'histoire de France en question* (Paris: Les Editions Ouvrières/EDI).

Cohen, Philip (1988) 'The Perversions of Inheritance: Studies in the Making of Multi-racist Britain', in Philip Cohen and Harwant S. Bains (eds), *Multi-Racist Britain* (London: Macmillan Education).

Cohen, Philip (1996) 'A Message from the Other Shore: Response to Tariq Modood', *Patterns of Prejudice*, 30 (1), pp. 15–21.

Cohen, Steven (1988) *From the Jews to the Tamils: Britain's Mistreatment of Refugees* (Manchester: South Manchester Law Centre).

Cox, Oliver (1970 [1948]) *Caste, Class and Race: A Study in Social Dynamics* (New York: Modern Reader Paperbacks).

Dubet, François (1989) *Immigrations: qu'en savon-nous?* (Paris: La Documentation française).

Fanon, Franz (1952) *Peau noire, masques blancs [Black Skin, White Masks]* (Paris: Seuil/Points).

Fanon, Frantz (1967) *The Wretched of the Earth* (Harmondsworth: Penguin).

Galissot, René (1985) *Misère de l'antiracisme* (Paris: Arcantère).

Gilman, Sander (1991) *The Jew's Body* (London: Routledge).

Gilroy, Paul (1987) *There Ain't no Black in the Union Jack* (London: Hutchinson).

Gilroy, Paul (1993) *The Black Atlantic: Modernity and Double Consciousness* (London: Verso).

Griotteray, Alain (1984) *Les Immigrés: Le Choc* (Paris: Plon).

Hall, Stuart (1990) 'Cultural Identity and Diaspora', in Jonathan Rutherford (ed.), *Identity: Community, Culture, Difference* (London: Lawrence & Wishart).

Hall, Stuart, Held, David and McGrew, Tony (eds) (1992) *Modernity and its Futures* (Cambridge: Open University Press, Polity).

Halliday, Fred (1992) *Arabs in Exile: Yemeni Migrants in Urban Britain* (London: I. B. Tauris).

House, Jim (1997) 'Antiracist Discourse in France', unpublished PhD thesis, University of Leeds.

Joly, Daniele (1995) *Britannia's Crescent: Making a Place for Muslims in Britain Today* (Aldershot: Avebury).

Lapeyronnie, Didier (1993) *L'Individu et les minorités: La France et la Grande-Bretagne face à leurs immigrés* (Paris: Presses Universitaires de France).

Lawless, Richard I. (1995) *From Ta'izz to Tyneside* (Exeter: University of Exeter Press).

Lawrence, Erol (1982) 'In the Abundance of Water the Fool is Thirsty: Sociology and Black "Pathology"', in Centre for Contemporary Cultural Studies, *The Empire Strikes Back* (London: Hutchinson).

Leon, Abraham (1970) *The Jewish Question* (New York: Pathfinder Press).

Lévinas, Emmanuel (1985) *Ethics and Infinity: Conversations with Philip Nemo*, trans. Richard A. Cohen (Pittsburgh, PA: Duquesne University Press).

Lévi-Strauss, Claude (1952) *Race et histoire* (Paris: Folio).

Lyotard, Jean-François (1988) *Heidegger et 'les juifs'* (Paris: Galilée).

Maffesoli, Michel (1992) *La Transfiguration du politique: La tribalisation du monde* (Paris: Editions Grasset et Fasquelles).

Memmi, Albert (1957) *Portrait du colonisé, précédé du Portrait du colonisateur*, preface by Jean-Paul Sartre (Paris: Payot).

Miles, Robert (1982) *Racism and Migrant Labour* (London: Routledge & Kegan Paul).

Miles, Robert (1987) 'Recent Marxist Theories of Nationalism and the Issue of Racism', *British Journal of Sociology*, 38(1), pp. 24–43.

Miles, Robert (1989) *Racism* (London: Routledge).

Miles, Robert (1993) *Racism after 'Race Relations'* (London: Routledge).

Modood, Tariq (1988) '"Black", Racial Equality and Asian Identity', *New Community*, 14(3), pp. 397–404.

Modood, Tariq (1992) *Not Easy Being British* (London: Runnymead Trust and Trentham Books).

Morrison, Toni (1983) *Tar Baby* (London: Triad Grafton Books).

Naïr, Sami (1992) *Le Regard des vainqueurs: Les enjeux français de l'immigration* (Paris: Grasset).

Noiriel, Gérard (1988) *Le Creuset Français: Histoire de l'Immigration XIXᵉ–XXᵉ Siècles* (Paris: Seuil).

Noiriel, Gérard (1989) 'Les jeunes "d'origine immigrée" n'existent pas', in Bernard Lorreyte (ed.), *Les Politiques d'intégration des jeunes issus de l'immigration* (Paris: L'Harmattan).

Noiriel, Gérard (1991) *La Tyrannie du national* (Paris: Calmann-Lévy).

Rattansi, Ali (1992) 'Changing the Subject? Racism, Culture and Education', in A. Rattansi and K. Reedar (eds), *Radicalism in Education* (London: Lawrence & Wishart).

Rattansi, Ali (1994), '"Western" Racisms, Ethnicities and Identities in a "Postmodern" Frame', in Ali Rattansi and Sallie Westwood (eds), *Racism, Modernity and Identity* (Cambridge: Polity).

Rex, John (1970, 1983) *Race Relations in Sociological Theory*, 2nd edn (London: Routledge and Kegan Paul).

Rex, John (1986) *Race and Ethnicity* (Milton Keynes: Open University Press).

Rex, John (1994) 'The Political Sociology of Multiculturalism and the Place of Muslims in West European Societies', *Social Compass*, 41(1), pp. 79–92.

Rocard, Michel (1989) *Le Monde*, 7 December.

Sahgal, Gita and Yuval-Davis, Nira (eds) (1992) *Refusing Holy Orders: Women and Fundamentalism in Britain* (London: Virago).

Said, Edward W. (1985 [1978]) *Orientalism* (Harmondsworth: Penguin).

Said, Edward W. (1993) *Culture and Imperialism* (London: Chatto & Windus).

Sartre, Jean-Paul (1954; first published 1946), *Réflexions sur la question juive* (Paris: Folio).

Silverman, Max (1992) *Deconstructing the Nation: Immigration, Racism and Citizenship in Modern France* (London: Routledge).

Silverman, Max (1998) 'Refiguring "the Jew" in France', in Bryan Cheyette and Laura Marcus (eds), *Modernity, Culture and 'the Jew'* (Cambridge: Polity).

Silverman, Max and Yuval-Davis, Nira (1997) *Research Report to the ESRC: Racialized Discourses on Jews and Arabs in Britain and France*.

Sivanandan, A. (1982) *A Different Hunger* (London: Pluto Press).
Solomos, John (1993) *Race and Racism in Britain,* 2nd edn (London: Macmillan).
Solomos, John and Back, Les (1996) *Racism and Society* (London: Macmillan).
Sternhell, Zeev (1983) *Ni Droite, ni gauche* (Paris: Seuil).
Taguieff, Pierre-André (1987) *La Force du préjugé: essai sur le racisme et ses doubles* (Paris: La Découverte).
Taguieff, Pierre-André (1995) *Les Fins de l'antiracisme* (Paris: Éditions Michalon).
Touraine, Alain (1992) *Critique de la modernité* (Paris: Flondayard).
Wallman, Sandra (ed.) (1979) *Ethnicity at Work* (London: Macmillan).
Watson, J. (1977) *Between Two Cultures* (Oxford: Blackwell).
Weil, Patrick (1991) *La France et ses étrangers* (Paris: Calmann-Lévy).
Wieviorka, Michel (1991) *L'Espace du racisme* (Paris: Seuil).
Wieviorka, Michel (1993) *La Démocratie à l'épreuve: nationalisme, populisme, ethnicité* (Paris: La Découverte).
Wistrich, Robert (ed.) (1990) *Anti-zionism and Antisemitism in the Contemporary World* (London: Macmillan).
Young, Robert (1990) *White Mythologies: Writing History and the West* (London: Routledge).
Yuval-Davis, Nira (1997) 'Ethnicity, Gender Relations and Multi-culturalism', in Pnina Werbner and Tariq Modood (eds), *The Dialectics of Cultural Hybridity* (London: Zed Books).
Zubaida, Sami (ed.) (1970) *Race and Racialism* (London: Tavistock).

3 Bringing the 'Local' Back in: the Production of Welsh Identities

ANDREW THOMPSON, GRAHAM DAY and DAVID ADAMSON

INTRODUCTION

The period since the mid-1980s has witnessed a growing interest in questions of national identity. In part this development has been inspired by a sense of urgency; by the necessity to understand, and respond to what has, perhaps somewhat misleadingly, been viewed as a surprisingly vigorous 'resurgence' of nationalism. Debates on the time–space consequences of globalisation processes have also raised crucial questions with respect to the future role of the 'nation', and the changing forms of 'national identity' (Featherstone, 1995); (Lash and Urry, 1994). Additionally, recent studies have pointed to the need to address the more 'banal' (Billig, 1995) processes implicated in the production of forms of 'national identity'. Furthermore, one of the most significant conceptual developments in sociology has been the re-prioritisation of the 'local', the implications of which have yet to be systematically explored with reference to national identity. While the notion of the 'local' has been a central feature of the debate on global-isation, it has also figured prominently, as might be expected, in exam-inations of 'community' and associated definitions of 'belonging', which we will argue have an intimate connection with ideas of national identity. Through the prioritisation of questions of 'space', 'place' and the 'local', particularly in terms of how they are socially constituted (and conversely, how social relations are spatially constituted), these studies have pointed to the contested nature of national identity.

In exploring the processes implicated in the production of national identities, this chapter draws on empirical research conducted by the authors into the subject of Welshness and the cultural politics of Welsh identity. As with the more general study of nationalism and national identity, the debate in Wales has received a renewed impetus in recent years, to become a leading topic in both academic and lay discourse. While this debate requires further elaboration with respect to the issue of 'national identity', a welcome feature of some recent additions to the literature has been the attempt to contextualise developments in Wales by drawing on broader conceptual arguments, and we suggest these moves to locate 'Wales' within a wider conceptual framework have generated the potential to avoid the pitfalls of earlier treatments of 'Wales', 'Welshness' and 'Welsh nationalism'.

NATIONAL IDENTITY: THE VIEW FROM BELOW

For those involved in the study of the 'nation' and nationalism the past ten years have seen significant developments, both in terms of the volume of studies dealing with these issues and with respect to the various modes of addressing them. While Symmons-Symonolewicz (1982: 215), writing in the early 1980s, could, with justification, argue that 'paradoxically in a rapidly developing field of studies in nationalism little attention has been paid to the central concept of the nation', the work which has emerged in the ensuing period may be viewed, partly, as an attempt to forge a more explicit critique of the 'nation'. Indeed, Anderson (1991: xii), introducing his revised edition of *Imagined Communities*, begins by commenting that the additions made to the literature since the early 1980s 'have, by their historical reach and theoretical power, made largely obsolete the traditional literature on the subject'.

However, the problem to which Symmons-Symonolewicz directed our attention – that earlier studies were principally analyses of nation*alism* – continues to constitute a problem, particularly with respect to the concept of national identity. Academic analyses have tended to treat national identity as a particular type of collective identity, the form and appeal of which can be grasped only in the context of the ideology of nationalism. Smith (1991: vii), for example, while arguing that 'we cannot begin to understand the power and appeal of nationalism as a political force without grounding our analysis in a wider perspective whose focus is national identity', goes on to add that it is 'nationalism [which] provides perhaps the most compelling identity myth in the modern world' (1991: viii). Similarly, Guibernau (1996: 65) maintains that 'the power of nationalism stems from its capacity to create a common identity among group members'. This emphasis on nationali*sm* as the primary focus for academic research serves to impose unnecessary limitations on the kinds of questions which may be asked with respect to differing ways of conceptualising national identity. There are, of course, various, and often sharply conflicting, accounts of nationalism, within which national identity receives differing inflections. This discussion elects to explore what Hutchinson (1994) has termed 'modernist' and 'ethnicist' accounts.

In the 'modernist' thesis it is nationalism which gives rise to the nation; as Gellner (1964: 168), explains: '[n]ationalism is not the awakening of nations to self-consciousness: it invents nations where they do not exist'. The underlying theme of the 'modernist' interpretation is that the rise of nationalism and the nation, in that order, must be explained in relation to the prerequisites for economic growth in industrial (or industrial capitalist) society. The nation, in this thesis, is explicitly connected to the state; it is the creation of a centralised, 'national' education system which instils a mass, common culture and it is the conferring of citizenship rights on all those perceived as possessing the correct cultural attributes which provides the foundation on which the modern nation is built. Given the congruity, in the 'modernist' thesis, between 'nation' and 'state' – 'one nation, one state' (Gellner, 1983: 134) – it follows that there can be only one (official) national identity.

The 'modernist' account, then, asserts that the process of industrialisation, with its demand for a unifying, common culture, 'flattens out' the forms of ethnic identity inherent in 'traditional' society (Gellner, 1994). Driven by the requirements of the division of labour in modern, industrial society, and fostered by the state through a variety of institutions, it is a shared culture, so Gellner (1983) maintains, that confers on each individual his/her identity. Underscoring the necessity of this form of identity in industrial society, he explains (1983: 111) that '[m]en really love their culture, because they now perceive the cultural atmosphere ... and they know they cannot really breathe or fulfil their identity outside of it'. Hobsbawm (1990) similarly stresses the role of the state in 'inventing' the national framework within which citizens conduct their daily affairs. During the late nineteenth and early twentieth centuries, he claims (Hobsbawm and Ranger, 1983: 264), 'the state increasingly defined the largest stage on which the crucial activities determining human lives as subjects and citizens were played out ... State, nation and society converged.'

The emphasis on an official, state-sponsored national culture, particularly in the work of Gellner, presupposes that individuals will recognise this national culture as *theirs* and that they will recognise others as sharing it. Gellner does not adequately address the dynamics of how the social relations of national identity are played out at a 'local' level, or how individuals 'make sense' of issues of national identity in their relations and interaction with other individuals. Breuilly (1993: 417), in a critique of Gellner's argument concerning the production of 'an homogenous "cultural zone" within which members of modern society act', contends that 'the point is that in this case the use of identity is related to specific problems in very specific settings'.

Perhaps the main criticism of the 'modernist' approach is that its 'top-down' analysis of the production of national identity, to draw on Hobsbawm's (1990: 11) critique of Gellner, 'makes it difficult to pay adequate attention to the view from below'. For other commentators, however, such as Smith (1986, 1995) and Llobera (1994), it is precisely the subjective identity of the individual which is central to their respective accounts of nationalism. In sharp relief to the 'modernist' thesis, the 'ethnicist' approach maintains that the persistence of rituals and traditions associated with ethnic identity are central to explaining the rise, and continuing salience, of nationalism and national identity.

Smith acknowledges that the 'core doctrine' of nationalist ideology emerged only in the late eighteenth century, and stresses that the modern nation differs from premodern ethnic communities, or *ethnie*, in a number of fundamental respects. Yet he explains that '[i]f nations are modern, at least as mass phenomena legitimated by nationalist ideology, they owe much of their present form and character to pre-existing ethnic ties which stemmed from earlier *ethnies* in the relevant area' (Smith, 1995: 57). In periods marked by dislocating social change, Smith argues (1995: 159), the appeal of national identity is that it responds to needs for 'cultural fulfilment, rootedness, security and fraternity'. National identity, then, is a fundamentally *collective* identity which acquires a popular resonance through public rituals.

Explicit in Smith's analysis is an attempt to explore how, through the cultural practices implicated in the reproduction of the 'nation', the 'personal' is linked to the 'public'. However, in his thesis – and here he shares common ground with Gellner – the prioritisation of the production of *a* national identity in the public sphere does not allow for the articulation of alternative, or competing, conceptions of national identity; indeed, Smith (1995: 156) appears to acknowledge as much when he writes that 'most members [of the nation] to this day continue to identify with the ideal version of the nation portrayed by nationalism'. Mass, public, commemorations, of the form described by Smith, undoubtedly represent an important method of reproducing the 'nation' at a collective level, of constituting the nation as a public. Yet, as Billig (1995: 45–46), noting the significance of 'great days of national celebration', comments: 'these are by no means the only social forms which sustain what is loosely called national identity. In between times, citizens of the state still remain citizens and the state does not wither away'. While Smith's analysis of national identity does not rely solely on these periodic events, his emphasis on the *collective* celebration of the nation appears to assume that the meaning of the 'nation' is the same for each individual. Put another way, there is little consideration of how the lived experience of the individual in 'local' social contexts inform his/her understanding of the 'nation' and 'national identity'.

The theoretical paths forged by 'modernists' and 'ethnicists' seek to explain national identity by recourse to the ideology of nationalism. This is a necessary project, in that it examines the way in which 'nation' and 'national ideology' are inscribed in institutional practices. Moreover, in their respective studies of nationalism, Gellner and Smith *do* attempt to explain how issues of national identity permeate the private world of the individual. Nevertheless, nationalism as an ideology is concerned with the structuring of the nation as a 'people', and as such, is oriented towards concealing differences rather than recognising them. Consequently, it becomes difficult to conceive how a theoretical account of national identity embedded in an understanding of nationalism can address the plurality of national identities which are the product of negotiations and interactions between individuals. Calhoun (1995) has commented on the need to establish a more critical account of nationalism along these lines, writing that '[i]t is necessary to overcome the naturalizing notions of ethnicity and nation ... and to approach the themes of peoples, publics, and nations with attention to a world of possibilities and inner tensions, not just one of static entities' (1995: 273). As Calhoun (1995: 253) correctly points out, nationalism may 'depend very much on individualism', but

> [i]t establishes the nation both as a category of similar individuals and as a sort of 'super-individual'. As a rhetoric of categorical identity, nationalism is precisely not focused on the various particularistic relationships among members of the nation.
>
> (1995: 253)

At the heart of the matter is the need to move beyond theories of national*ism* in accounting for national identity. Some commentators

(Billig, 1995; Schlesinger, 1987; Tomlinson, 1991) have already pointed to the attendant problems of attempting to explore national identity within the framework of theories of nationalism. Tomlinson (1991: 79), for example, notes that '[d]iscussions of national identity are mostly found in the literature of the politics of nationalism ... [y]et the specific psychological contents, the "phenomenology", as it were, of national identity is rarely probed in detail'. Other writers, such as Billig (1995) and Jenkins (1995), have argued the need to adopt a more 'flexible' conception of nationalism, which allows us to comprehend the (re)production of national identity through 'banal routines' (Billig, 1995: 44), or is 'concerned with nationalisms rather than nationalism' (Jenkins, 1995: 385). We would go further in maintaining the need to discriminate *between* nationalism and national identity. In addressing issues of language, religion, territory or 'culture' and their relationship to national identity, theories of nationalism tend to presume that these issues are both relevant for the individual and that each individual expresses a similar attitude towards them, rather than examining how these issues are made relevant by individuals through processes of negotiation with others. Moreover, distinguishing between nationalism and national identity allows us to explore ways in which national identity is produced 'locally', that is between the individuals involved and within a particular sociospatial context. In mapping this particular line of argument it is possible to show how questions of national identity, generally, and Welshness, specifically, enter into more 'routine' social relations. In examining processes through which national identity is inflected and utilised in social relations, we point to its contested nature, to the production of national identi*ies*.

THEORIES OF NATIONALISM AND NATIONAL IDENTITY IN WALES

Studies of the influence of ethnic and national considerations within the society and culture of Wales have reflected the tendencies identified above, by situating questions about identity within the politics of nationalism, viewed as one of the central ideologies shaping popular identity in Wales. They have concentrated mainly upon the formal political structures of the nationalist movement, and the organisations associated with its cultural wing (Balsom *et al.*, 1982; Madgwick *et al.*, 1973; Philip, 1975). A fundamental limitation of this approach has been to treat Welsh nationalism as a unified ideology, constructed historically from the key building blocks of Nonconformist religion, political Liberalism, and the Welsh language (Evans, 1974). The political movement itself did much to create such a view during the inter-war years, when it was dominated by a deeply conservative cultural nationalism rooted largely in the past and current development of rural Wales. This perception remained largely unchallenged until the internal organisation of nationalism itself began to change in the 1960s.

With new patterns of recruitment drawing, for the first time, significant membership from the industrial communities of South Wales, different perceptions of nationhood and Welshness started to emerge. The first serious attempt to describe this differentiation was developed by Rawkins (1979), who distinguished between sets of nationalists who had different attitudes to the Welsh economy, differing affiliations to the language and culture, and who adhered to different conceptions of Welshness. Those he referred to as 'modernists' were drawn from industrial Wales, and were more concerned with questions of economic development and social justice than were the 'fortress nationalist' and 'militant cultural nationalist' tendencies that he saw as being drawn from the same broad social classes in rural society, and who shared a primary concern with linguistic and cultural survival/revival. The distinction between the 'fortress' and 'militant cultural' nationalists was one of age and political strategy – the acceptance by the latter of non-violent direct action as a means of securing recognition of the Welsh language by the British state.

Through its recognition of the existence of differing, and to some extent conflicting conceptions of Welshness, Rawkins' analysis represented a considerable advance in the understanding of Welsh nationalism. It suggested that different versions of national identity could be associated with contrasting social and economic positions in Welsh society. Rawkins' 'modernists' were clearly drawn from the urban working class of South East Wales, and their sense of national identity was strongly influenced by the socialist tradition and working-class collectivism of that region; hence their vision of Wales was less centred upon language and cultural identifications; if anything, they held a class-based ideology which saw the Welsh as a dominated economic class and consequently treated the 'English' as a class category . Such an argument was given added credence by Michael Hechter's influential theorisation of Celtic nationalism as a response to 'internal colonialism' (Hechter, 1975), whereby cultural differences had come to form the basis for an economic and political division of labour. However, despite the ability of the theory to provide considerable sustenance for nationalist ideology, the excessive reliance placed on processes of social closure in Hechter's concept of the 'cultural division of labour' and the faulty empirical basis of his analysis offered little in the way of adequate explanation for the contemporary nationalisms of the 1960s and 1970s (Adamson, 1984; Day, 1979).

In contrast to the Weberian approach taken by Hechter, this period also saw a parallel attempt to apply Marxist analysis to the issue of Celtic nationalism. The historical difficulties of deriving a satisfactory theory of the national question from Marx's work were even more evident in the context of the small nation neo-nationalisms of the Celtic fringe. Nairn's contribution tied the development of these movements to the historical experiences of the peripheral bourgeoisie, set within the context of the uneven development of capitalism and processes of modernization (Nairn, 1977). Nairn remained firmly wedded to the Marxist tradition of treating nationalism as a bourgeois ideology. Yet experience in Wales suggested a less genetic connection between class and nationalism.

Developments in social theory during the late 1970s and early 1980s provided the opportunity to develop more sophisticated analyses of the complex interplay of social and economic forces that had brought Welsh nationalism into existence. Two of the contributors to this chapter (Adamson, 1984; Day, 1984) produced accounts which suggested that complex class relations, characterised by alliance and fracturing of the primary classes, were involved in the emergence of Welsh nationalism during the nineteenth century. Adamson used Althusserian and Gramscian concepts of ideology and hegemony to suggest that nationalism could be seen as a class-neutral ideology which was given its form and substance by the manner of its insertion into class struggle. Rather than seeing nationalism as inevitably bourgeois, as had Nairn, it can be viewed instead as 'free-floating' and capable of being articulated by any class or class alliance, albeit in different forms. Nation, and related concepts such as community and language, thus provide open ideological terrain on which individual subjects can position themselves in relation to their lived experience, and high levels of class, linguistic, religious and cultural variation can be overlooked by reference to those things that are (or appear to be) held in common. A similar conception of nationalism as constituting an *exceptionally* flexible ideological field was advanced by Day and Suggett (1985), who argued that ideas of nation and nationality should not be seen as fixed, but rather as an evolving matrix of shifting definitions and competing constructions. This implied, they suggested, that 'the retention and creation of a distinctive identity is a practical problem for many Welsh people, and that any realistic nationalist movement must seek to reconcile these diverse meanings' (1985: 92).

These contributions point to the existence of a plurality of meanings attached to Welshness, depending upon the class and social location of the individual subject. This introduces a clear link between the study of nationalism and a more specific analysis of national identity, while at the same time enabling the topic of identity to be dealt with separately from the examination of formal nationalist political movements. National identity can be seen as all-pervasive, and not limited to the political sphere in the way that nationalism tends to be; individuals who have no nationalist political beliefs nevertheless will almost always have some sense of national identity, and the particular form it takes will be the consequence of a complex relationship between national, local, communal and individual processes of identity acquisition and formation. In the remainder of this chapter we draw upon more recent discussions of national identity within Wales, and our own empirical research, to illustrate this point.

THE 'LOCAL' PRODUCTION OF WELSH IDENTITIES

The dramatic transformation brought about by processes of economic and social restructuring in Wales in recent years is by now well documented (Day, 1991; Rutherford, 1991). The disappearance of much of the traditional industrial base, the consequent class and gender recomposition of the Welsh population, and the substantial levels of migration that have resulted, have meant that few, if any, local Welsh communities have been left unchanged, while many have altered out of all recognition. These changes have brought issues of Welsh identity into greater prominence, and at all levels within Wales the nature and meaning of Welshness and its relationship to such alternative identifications as 'British' and 'European' have been debated with considerable intensity. None of the 'traditional' markers of a distinctive Welsh identity has survived unscathed. Religious nonconformity commands the allegiance of a relatively elderly minority population; political Liberalism and radicalism are vestiges of their former strength; and despite its recent revival, the Welsh language remains the possession of less than a fifth of the total population, with its use concentrated in particular geographical areas. More fundamentally, change has fragmented the earlier solidarities and commonality of experience that arose from the dominance within Wales of a limited number of basic industries – coal, steel, slate, and agriculture – and the communities which grew up around them. Wales is now a far more diverse place, and Welsh people are having to make sense of a greater variety of situations and experiences than in the past. It is a 'fragmented and fractured country' (Osmond, 1988), and identity is more problematic as a result. This is apparent from research conducted in different parts of Wales.

Survey data from a recent study of the South Wales Valleys indicate a complex connection between issues of community, locality and identity (Adamson and Jones, 1996). Within a clear sense of Welsh national identity there are sets of 'nested' identities located in Valleys' life, and in the specific communities to which individuals belong; 85 per cent of respondents defined themselves as Welsh, and only 9 per cent as British. Although only a fifth of the sample could speak Welsh, most of whom declared themselves to be learners, two-thirds stated they would like to be able to speak the language, suggesting a strong affiliation with Welsh even within Anglo-Welsh culture, a conclusion supported by evidence of growing demand for Welsh language education throughout South East Wales. Half regarded being Welsh as either 'extremely important' or 'very important', about the same proportion as strongly identified with a Valleys' identity. A powerful sense of community informed responses throughout the interviews, with 70 per cent seeing the sense of community as the primary distinguishing feature of Valleys' life; this had tangible effects, in terms of patterns of neighbourhood support, high levels of community density, and a low propensity for labour mobility. This distinctiveness, however, was seen as under threat, with 89 per cent viewing the Valleys as changing, and nearly 30 per cent of these referring to some aspect of declining community values as the major social change taking place.

Survey data, however, produce no more than an aggregate impression of local conceptions of identity. In order to understand more fully the dynamics which underpin the formation of such identity constructs it is necessary to take a more qualitative approach which pays greater attention to the particular contexts within which people employ their notions of Welshness and nationality.

Further evidence of an evolving 'Valley Welsh' identity is presented in a recent study of communities in a Gwent mining valley (Roberts,

1995). Employing the concept of 'social image', Roberts suggests that changes in class boundaries and consumption practices, and the emergence of new work and family processes, have all served to redefine the 'social imagery' of the area. Again the notion of 'community' is central in providing the mechanism for defining categories of insiders and outsiders, and ethnic criteria play a key role in this process. The study suggests that whereas, conventionally, analysis of cultural identity in the Welsh Valleys has emphasised the class and work aspects of mining communities, this has disguised the real transformations occurring as a consequence of economic changes which predate the collapse of mining but which have accelerated since. The outcome appears to be a diminishing influence for class identity and an increasing saliency of a reformed or redefined Welshness.

The result is that Valley people are questioning the meaning of 'local' and 'Valley' identity and are re-examining 'Welshness'. In short new identities are being *explored*: a sense of 'Welshness', that is neither of the Welsh-speaking area nor of British Wales.

(Roberts, 1995: 80)

Likewise, the recent Rural Lifestyles study has shown that there are a plurality of ways of living within rural Wales, associated with 'conflicting and renegotiated notions of Welshness' (Milbourne *et al.*, 1995). In the rural context these are articulated primarily in relation to the impact of the inward movement of newcomers, who are perceived as 'English' and whose presence is often interpreted as posing a threat to established patterns of behaviour and values. English incomers are viewed as 'importing specific constructs of rural lifestyle – many of which were in conflict with existing cultural norms and practices' (Milbourne *et al.*, 1995: 15). Similar issues are raised by Day and Murdoch in their examination of the impact of economic and social restructuring in a rural community in Mid Wales, where questions of who belonged, and who did not, were central to people's understanding of both their local and their wider social identities (Day and Murdoch, 1993).

The closeness of the association between ideas of community, and the sense of a national identity, is further highlighted in a study of nationalism in North West Wales (Borland *et al.*, 1992). Concerned to explain the 'simultaneous surge in support of both parliamentary and extra-parliamentary nationalism' (1992: 49) this has much to say of relevance to the wider issue of national identity. Concepts of 'community' are held to play a key role in the mobilization of support for political nationalism. Borland *et al.* see the concept of community as central 'because it lies at the heart of the fundamental question of national identity, namely "Who is of this place?"' (1992: 52). Community is an 'imagined' social construct which has concrete effects in social processes, in that it provides one of the principal criteria for inclusion and exclusion in processes of social closure, by offering naturalised boundaries through which insiders and outsiders may be defined. The paper seeks to demonstrate that, even within a limited geographical space such as North West Wales, there exist a 'number of social constructions of community' (1992: 54) and hence, of identity. This helps advance our understanding of the complexity of national identity and of the ways in which diverse senses of Welshness can coexist in groups with close geographical and sociocultural proximity. The authors conclude that it is possible to argue that community in North West Wales operates as a 'site of resistance' which binds individuals together (1992: 66); but at the same time it is also clear that individuals and groups may differ markedly in the particular version of community which they choose to espouse, and this is bound to have significant implications for their understanding of identity.

WELSHNESS AND LOCAL SOCIAL RELATIONS

So far our aim has been to point to the existence of national identity, in general, and Welshness, in particular, as sites of contestation and change, and to illustrate how 'Welshness' may be given a diverse array of inflections as a result of the impact of various 'local' factors. The examples reviewed show how the articulation of Welshness is a chronic process inextricably bound up with the ongoing struggles to define place and 'belonging'. As noted by both geographers (Harvey, 1993; Massey, 1994) and sociologists (Urry, 1995), places do not possess a single identity. Rather, places may have any number of different connotations for different social groups and individuals. At the same time, certain narratives of place may come to acquire greater public legitimacy than others. To talk of a 'Valleys identity', for example, is to imply notions of common experience forged over time, of how 'the Valleys' were created through the rise and fall of the coal industry and to invoke ideas of a Valleys 'culture'. Similarly, Gwynedd, in North West Wales, has come to acquire a particular identity and, like the South Wales Valleys, occupies a particular privileged position within discourses of Welshness. Gwynedd represents a significant proportion of what has been termed *Y Fro Gymraeg*, or the 'Welsh-speaking heartland', with over 60 per cent of its population speaking Welsh (Aitchison and Carter, 1991). In political terms it is a nationalist stronghold, with three out of its four parliamentary seats held by *Plaid Cymru* (the Welsh National Party). Language questions have become the subject of much debate in Gwynedd, linked as they are to issues of public sector employment, education, and in-migration as well as to the sphere of formal politics. Trosset (1993) maintains that in North Wales a particular form of Welshness has become 'ideologically dominant' in that it is 'sufficiently widespread that it affects everyone's thinking about society and their individual places in it ... and its dominance results from certain processes involving particular categories of people working through a variety of social institutions' (1993: 17). Other commentators have similarly noted how the ability to speak Welsh is central to the local sense of Welshness. Bowie (1993: 179) argues that the 'notion that by learning and, of course, by speaking Welsh one becomes a fuller member of the community is axiomatic in much of Gwynedd'.

There are centres of population within Gwynedd, however, such as the coastal area around Conwy and Llandudno, which contain significantly smaller numbers of Welsh-speakers. The university city of Bangor also has a lower proportion of Welsh-speakers than the surrounding area; although over half of the city's population speak the language (Aitchison and Carter, 1994); this contrasts markedly with neighbouring towns such as Caernarfon and Bethesda, both more than 80 per cent Welsh-speaking. The impact of the growth of the university and migration to Bangor from northwest England in the aftermath of the Second World War help explain this disparity.

Many local people in Bangor, although able to understand and speak Welsh, routinely use English as their preferred medium of communication. Residents of Bangor are fully aware that, partly for this reason, some of their neighbours regard them as not being 'proper-Welsh'. A local shop-owner in his late-50s remarked that 'if someone asks you, "Are you Welsh?", and you say "Yes, I'm from Bangor", they'll say "Oh, Bangor-Welsh, sort of half-and-half. You can't speak proper Welsh". Once they know you're from Bangor they'll speak English to you.' This view is confirmed by those who have moved in from nearby towns; one Welsh-speaking student observed that he had 'been made more aware of being Welsh now than I was before coming here from a totally Welsh place, basically absolutely Welsh. I've come here and it has increased my awareness. Even though it's Bangor it's basically England.' That Bangor has come to be identified as 'English' in sharp contrast to other 'Welsh' towns is also evident when Bangor locals, especially young adult males, visit the surrounding area. Speaking of the history of trouble between young men from Bangor and their counterparts in neighbouring towns, a local man in his late 20s explained:

> We never go out of Bangor without being involved in trouble. It's always Bangor, because it's predominantly English, everywhere around Bangor's Welsh, so if we went up to Bethesda, Caernarfon, anywhere in Anglesey it's always '*Saes* Bangor', 'English Bangor', and straight away there's conflict there. You can feel it as soon as you walk into the pubs. If me and my friends walk into a pub in Caernarfon, we're strangers moving into their pub. You can feel the animosity as soon as you walk through the door. It's the same if they come into Bangor.

While these particular incidents may represent a more general 'politics of turf', the characterisation of Bangor as 'English' remains a significant factor in framing relations between these neighbouring populations. Encounters between people from Bangor and other local centres serve as reminders of difference as well as being crucial for the reproduction of contrasting meanings of place. In examining the articulation of a local form of Bangor Welshness it is useful to note how, even for non-Welsh-speakers in Bangor, what is held to be 'Welsh' tends to be talked about in terms of an ability to speak Welsh and how places can similarly be described unproblematically as 'Welsh' ('everywhere around Bangor's Welsh'). Nevertheless, Bangor locals will strongly assert that not speaking Welsh does not make an individual any less Welsh. Explaining how he thought Bangor people felt about the symbolic importance of the Welsh language, an informant stressed that 'everybody in Bangor counts themselves as Welsh, and they're proud to be Welsh, but they're not fanatical about it, the language to them is irrelevant really'.

Such views concerning language do not necessarily imply strong objections to measures to ensure the future development of Welsh. Where objections do arise is in relation to perceptions of an emerging social divide between Welsh-speakers and non-Welsh-speakers, and in particular to the perceived 'elitism' which now surrounds the Welsh language. A local man, who had returned as a mature student to study at the university, contended that the 'classification in the Welsh language between those who go to college and the working-classes is beginning to present itself', adding that he was concerned 'that the language ... is becoming elitist'. For people in Bangor who do not speak Welsh or who, for the large part, elect to speak English, the existence of a dominant Welsh language-centred form of Welshness, particularly in Gwynedd, and the growing status of the language over the past 25 years, has raised doubts about the pedigree of their Welsh identity. A young woman, who maintained that she had suffered discrimination by virtue of being a Welsh-learner, stated that she did not understand 'why people say you have to speak the language to be of that certain identity ... it makes no difference if you speak the language, it's if you believe in Wales then you are Welsh'. Others expressed similar concern with what they viewed as a growing militancy among some Welsh-speakers about the importance of speaking Welsh, and actively sought to distance themselves from specific images of Welshness. A local lay preacher, for example, stated:

> You cannot define yourself as Welsh because 'Welshman' to one man is the ability to speak Welsh, whilst to another man it is to help your heritage and culture. If I was asked 'Am I Welsh?' I can claim to be Welsh by heritage and birth, having got family steeped in Wales ... .that way you can claim to be Welsh. But if you say to be Welsh is to go around bombing, destroying homes, tearing down signposts, writing slogans on walls then I'm not Welsh and if you mean to be Welsh is to ostracize the English or any incomers, then I don't want to know.

The actions of certain organisations, such as *Cymdeithas Yr Iaith Gymraeg* (the Welsh Language Society), have had a considerable influence in heightening public awareness of these language issues. As a result of campaigns by these organisations and the development of an emergent Welsh language popular culture, through the media and the commercial success of particular pop groups, the Welsh language has taken on a more positive inflection among Welsh-speakers and non Welsh speakers alike. Significant changes in the role of the Welsh language in business, media, and education have also served to strengthen its position and create growing opportunities for Welsh-speakers, although often in Cardiff, rather than Gwynedd (Giggs and Pattie, 1992). With respect to questions of national identity, these changes are reinforcing 'dominant' ideas of Welshness. The impact of 'routine' practices, such as in work, watching television or socialising with friends, are crucially important for the reproduction of national identities, whether these are experienced consciously or unconsciously, as 'forgotten reminders' (Billig, 1995). For non-Welsh-speakers, such as those local to Bangor, completing a form or application in English than rather Welsh, not speaking Welsh in work or even not liking to view Welsh-language television will be significant in reproducing the social and cultural divide between themselves and Welsh-speakers. While non-Welsh-speakers continue to exist outside the 'dominant' Welsh identity, changes in the status of the Welsh language will remain largely irrelevant or threatening for them.

CONCLUSION

In this chapter we have argued that studies of national identity need to direct greater attention towards analyses of the routine practices and local social relations which inform the production of its contending forms. This should not be read as simply being a call for more empirical work on questions of national identity, although this is, of course, an important task. Rather, we are suggesting that it is necessary to begin to recognise some of the attendant problems of talking about national identity in its singular sense, particularly its part in reifying the idea of the culturally homogeneous nation. In pursuing this approach three main concerns have underpinned our discussion. Firstly, an exploration of some of the definitional struggles which centre on issues of place, 'community' and 'nation'. Secondly, the need to examine the everyday processes through which we remember 'who we are' as well as how 'we' are different from 'them'. Finally, we have stressed the significance of unpacking the larger discourses of the nation by identifying the existence of competing versions of national identity, in general, and Welshness, in particular.

The pace of change in Wales, as elsewhere, during the past two decades has been such as to bring about significant dislocations of community and personal identities. In the process of remaking their identities people draw upon conceptions of nation and nationality, and make use of criteria of ethnic belonging, to distinguish between themselves and others. 'Community' is central to this process; but since there is no single version of community to which all can agree, definitions of nationality also tend to be varied, and often conflicting. We would suggest that much of the construction of ideas of national identity takes place at the local level, as people engage in drawing boundaries – real and symbolic – around their particular communities, and that these everyday conceptions of identity are far removed from the 'purified' and often stereotyped versions which eventually come to form part of more explicitly nationalist ideologies. Indeed, much of the tension within nationalist movements and organisations arises from the efforts they must make to integrate varying, and possibly incompatible, forms of national identity.

REFERENCES

Adamson, D. L. (1984) 'Social Class and Ethnicity in Nineteenth-century Rural Wales', *Sociologia Ruralis,* XXIV, 202–15.
Adamson, D. L. (1988) 'Community, Ideology and Political Discourse: the Concept of Community in Welsh Nationalist Politics', International Conference on Utopian Thought and Communal Experience, New Lanark.
Adamson, D. (1991) *Class Ideology and the Nation: A Theory of Welsh Nationalism* (Cardiff: University of Wales Press).
Adamson, D. and Jones, S. (1996) 'The South Wales Valleys: Continuity and Change', paper 1, Occasional Papers in the Regional Research Programme (University of Glamorgan, Pontypridd).
Aitchison, J. and Carter, H. (1994) *A Geography of the Welsh Language* (Cardiff: University of Wales Press).
Anderson, B. (1991) *Imagined Communities: Reflections on the Origins and Spread of Nationalism* (London: Verso).
Balsom, D., Madgwick, P. and Mechelen, D. V. (1982) 'The Political Consequences of Welsh Identity', *Studies in Public Policy,* Centre for the Study of Public Policy no. 27, University of Strathclyde.
Billig, M. (1995) *Banal Nationalism* (London: Sage).
Borland, J., Fevre, R. and Denney, D. (1992) 'Nationalism and Community in North West Wales', *The Sociological Review,* 40, pp. 49–72.
Bowie, F. (1993) 'Wales from Within: Conflicting Interpretations of Welsh Identity', in S. Macdonald (ed.), *Inside European Identities: Ethnography in Western Europe* (Oxford: Berg).
Breuilly, J. (1993) *Nationalism and the State* (Manchester: Manchester University Press).
Calhoun, C. (1995) *Critical Social Theory* (London: Blackwell).
Day, G. (1979) 'The Sociology of Wales: Issues and Prospects', *Sociological Review,* 27, pp. 447–74.
Day, G. (1984) 'Development and National Consciousness: the Welsh Case', in H. Vermeulen and J. Boissevain (eds), *Ethnic Challenge: The Politics of Ethnicity in Europe* (Gottingen: Edition Herodot).

Day, G. (1991) 'The Regeneration of Rural Wales', in G. Day and G. Rees (eds), *Regions, Nations and European Integration* (Cardiff: University of Wales Press).

Day, G. and Murdoch, J. (1993) 'Locality and Community: Coming to Terms with Place', *Sociological Review,* 41(1), pp. 82–111.

Day, G. and Suggett, R. (1985) 'Conceptions of Wales and Welshness: Aspects of Nationalism in Nineteenth-century Wales', in G. Rees, J. Bujra, P. Littlewood, H. Newby and T. L. Rees (eds), *Political Action and Social Identity* (London: Macmillan).

Evans, G. (1974) *Aros Mae (Land of My Fathers)* (Swansea: John Penry Press).

Featherstone, M. (1995*) Undoing Culture: Globalisation, Postmodernism and Identity* (London: Sage).

Gellner, E. (1964) *Thought and Change* (London: Weidenfeld & Nicolson).

Gellner, E. (1983) *Nations and Nationalism* (Oxford: Blackwell).

Gellner, E. (1994) *Encounters with Nationalism* (Oxford: Blackwell).

Giggs, J. and Pattie, C. (1992) 'Wales as a Plural Society', *Contemporary Wales,* vol. 5 (Cardiff: University of Wales Press).

Guibernau, M. (1996) *Nationalisms: The Nation-State and Nationalism in the Twentieth Century* (London: Polity).

Harvey D. (1993) 'From Space to Place and Back Again: Reflections on the Condition of Postmodernity', in J. Bird, B. Curtis, T. Putnam, G. Robertson and L. Tickner (eds), *Mapping the Futures: Local Cultures, Global Change* (London: Routledge).

Hechter, M. (1975) *Internal Colonialism: The Celtic Fringe in British National Development, 1536–1966* (London: Routledge & Kegan Paul).

Hobsbawm, E. J. (1990) *Nations and Nationalism since 1780* (Cambridge: Cambridge University Press).

Hobsbawm, E. J. and Ranger, T. (eds) (1983) *The Invention of Tradition* (Cambridge: Cambridge University Press).

Hutchinson, J. (1994) *Modern Nationalism* (London: Fontana).

Jenkins, R. (1995) 'Nations and Nationalisms: Towards More Open Models', *Nations and Nationalism,* 1(3), pp. 369–90.

Lash, S. and Urry, J. (1994) *Economies of Signs and Space* (London: Sage).

Llobera, J. (1994) *The God of Modernity: The Development of Nationalism in Western Europe* (Oxford: Berg).

Madgwick, P., Griffiths, N. and Walker, V. (1973) *The Politics of Rural Wales: A Study of Cardiganshire* (London: Hutchinson).

Massey, D. (1994) *Space, Place and Gender* (London: Polity).

Milbourne, P., Cloke, P. and Goodwin, M. (1995) 'Wales and England: Identity, Community, Cultural Change and English In-movement to Rural Wales', paper presented to the Conference on 'Ideas of Community' (Bristol: University of the West of England).

Nairn, T. (1977) *The Break-up of Britain: Crisis and Neo-Colonialism* (London: New Left Books).

Osmond, J. (1988) *The Divided Kingdom* (Llandysul: Gomer).

Philip, A. B. (1975) *The Welsh Question* (Cardiff: University of Wales Press).

Rawkins, P. M. (1979) 'An Approach to the Political Sociology of the Welsh Nationalist Movement', *Political Studies,* XXVII: pp. 440–57.

Roberts, B. (1995) 'Welsh Identity in a Former Mining Valley: Social Images and Imagined Communities', *Contemporary Wales*, 7, pp. 77–93.

Rutherford, T. (1991) 'Industrial Restructuring, Local Labour Markets and Social Change: the Transformation of South Wales', *Contemporary Wales*, 4, pp. 9–44.

Schlesinger, P. (1987) 'On National Identity: Some Conceptions and Misconceptions Criticized', *Social Science Information*, 26(2), pp. 219–64.

Smith, A. D. (1991) *The Ethnic Origins of Nations* (Oxford: Blackwell).

Smith, A. D. (1991) *National Identity* (Harmondsworth: Penguin).

Smith, A. D. (1995) *Nations and Nationalism in a Global Era* (London: Polity).

Symmons-Symonolewicz, K. (1982) 'The Concept of Nationhood: Toward a Theoretical Clarification', *Canadian Review of Studies in Nationalism*, 12(2), pp. 215–22.

Thompson, A. (1995) 'The Social Construction of Welsh Identities', unpublished PhD thesis, University of Wales.

Tomlinson, J. (1991) *Cultural Imperialism* (London: Pinter).

Trosset, C. (1993) *Welshness Performed: Welsh Concepts of Person and Society* (Tucson, AZ: University of Arizona Press).

Urry, J. (1995) *Consuming Places* (London: Routledge).

Part II
Re-presenting Whiteness

4 'Pale Warriors': Skinhead Culture and the Embodiment of White Masculinities

ANOOP NAYAK

INTRODUCTION

This chapter aims to expose the processes used to enact a white identity. In doing so it argues that whiteness is a choreographed identity, repetitively sustained in corporeal actions. The chapter analyses ethnographic data, based upon interviews with explicitly racist young men, to interpret their stylised investments in adopting a hostile posture of whiteness. It is argued that a key way in which these white identities are consolidated are through racist practices and an investment in a certain type of working-class masculinity. By exploring the performativity of whiteness, and drawing attention to the contradictions and uncertainties underpinning white masculinities, the work aims to make an intervention into debates about whiteness, racism and the cultural experiences of working-class young men.

'THE THORNS OF RACISM': WHITE MASCULINITIES AND SUBURBAN CONFLICT

Kempton Dene lies on the very outskirts of Birmingham amidst white picket fences and rose bushed gardens.[1] With a mere 2 per cent black populace, suburban areas such as 'the Dene' appear as stark enclaves of whiteness when placed alongside the broader, vibrant metropolis of a city which boasts that approximately a quarter of its million people are non-white residents.[2] Statistical evidence drawn from police records and the Birmingham Racial Attacks Monitoring Unit (BRAMU) indicates that the vast majority of racist attacks are

71

concentrated in the outer band of the city and that the perpetrators of racist violence are invariably groups of young white men in their teens and early 20s (14–25 years). Consequently, it is the cultural identities of these young men that I shall focus on, in order to interpret the enactment of whiteness within provincial localities. The empirical data suggest that the image of the suburban rose, as a quaint motif of Englishness, conceals thorns of white hostility which are rooted in a volatile 'rural racism'.

The research group consisted of seven working-class young men predominantly in their mid-teens, who all resided in the Kempton Dene estate situated on the south-east borderlands of Birmingham. Five of the young men identified themselves as White (Daniel, Robbie, Darren, Paul, Mark) while Calvin and Leonard were of mixed-heritage with white mothers and black fathers. Significantly, the young white men were all from large families who had lived on 'the Dene' for a number of years. These families had notorious reputations within the community and were feared by many residents. It was rumoured that most of the criminal activities which occurred on the estate were attributable to one of three families, from which the young men all belonged. The reputations of these families were further enhanced by images of the estate as racist and 'hard', by people who lived in neighbouring areas. This portrayal was often contested by older members of the community as being a misrepresentation, but was publicly celebrated by the research group:

> *Does it mean a lot to you to live around here?*
> Robbie: Yeah, I love it. Got a name, that's what I like.
> *What kind of name?*
> Darren: Born on the Dene and I'll live on the Dene all my life.
> Robbie: Ruff 'n' tuff. That's what we are. We stick together.

The regional identities of the group are, then, central to understanding the forms of whiteness they came to occupy within the suburban locality. The comment about 'sticking together' is both a statement about working-class community and white male bonding. At the time of the research the young white men were either unemployed, about to leave school, or, in the case of Daniel, had even been expelled for 'paki-bashing'. None of the respondents were in permanent employment and they had a fragmentary work experience at best, gained from temporary manual labour helping out their fathers when situations arose. Consequently, they spent long stretches of time out on the streets, but during evenings occupied a local youth club where interviews were conducted, involving myself and colleague Les Back.[3]

SUBCULTURE, ETHNOGRAPHY AND THE CCCS

Much sociological literature on youth is marked by a distinct lack of engagement with the ethnicity of white young people (Hewitt, 1986; Jones, 1988). As Avtar Brah remarks:

> it is important to stress that both black and white people experience their gender, class and sexuality through 'race'. Racialization of white subjectivity is often not manifestly apparent to white groups because 'white' is a signifier of dominance, but this renders the racialization process no less significant.
>
> (1993: 133–134)

Writers from the Birmingham Centre for Contemporary Cultural Studies (CCCS), who remain some of the most eloquent exponents of youth cultures to date, have tended to discuss skinhead style, for example, in terms of working-class resistance and generation differentiation. The class-generation dynamics that help fashion youth subculture remain pertinent where skinhead style may be read as 'a reaction against the contamination of the parent culture by middle-class values' (Cohen, 1972: 24). This approach has tended to emphasise the social class location of young men and, to a lesser degree, has tentatively considered the ways in which masculinities operate within these peer-group settings. For CCCS writers in the mid-1970s investments in skinhead style were thought to have little to do with securing whiteness; instead they were viewed as 'rituals of resistance'. Here, the retrospective harking-back to a bygone 'golden age' offers therapeutic comfort against harsh economic realities, where a 'magical recovery' of community is evoked:

> Our basic thesis about the Skinheads centres around the notion of community. We would argue that the Skinhead style represents an attempt to re-create through the 'mob' the traditional working class community, as a substitution for the real decline of the latter. The underlying social dynamic for style, in this light, is the relative worsening of the situation of the working class.
>
> (Clarke, 1976: 99)

These comments have powerful resonance for interpreting the actions of skinhead youth today, where a consistent erosion of the manufacturing base has led to a rapid decline of unskilled manual labour. The closure of large factories in the West Midlands has undoubtedly affected the employment situation of many working-class males and, in part, may explain the skinheads' obsession with colonising 'territory' (shops, streets, bus stops, the youth club) by way of response. For the early CCCS writers, heavily influenced by Marxist and neo-Marxist approaches (Gramsci, 1971) these practices were thought to be the reaction of working-class youth to fierce postwar consumerism and a sharply visible unequal distribution of wealth. Consequently, Clarke (1974: 249) claims skinheads had a 'subordinated view' of their situation where 'acceptance of racial scapegoating . . . displaced antagonisms from their real structural sources'. A feature of these perspectives was a tendency for researchers to subsume the complex lived experience of working-class lifestyles, within a sometimes rigid, Marxist theoretical framework. Thus, Pearson in his 'paki-bashing' study expands upon his fragmentary observations to provide an all-encompassing economic thesis:

> Only if we enter into the heart of working class life can we understand these beliefs and actions. 'Paki-bashing' is a primitive form of political and economic struggle. It is an inarticulate and finally impotent attempt to act directly on the conditions of the market – whether the exchange value which is contested concerns housing, labour power or girls.
>
> (1976a: 69)

This 'Ruling Ideas'[4] framework attempts to incorporate complex and diverse social phenomena (violence, sexual politics, racism) within a complete philosophy. In this analysis the 'impotent' 'skins' occupy a castrated/subordinate masculinity *vis-à-vis* their socioeconomic location, the anger for which is displaced in violent outbursts. Here, the 'skins' are shadow-boxers extraordinaire, flexing their muscles in choreographic displays, without ever altering their 'real' social class situation. But there is more to this than mere shadow- boxing, as the perspectives of 'paki-bashing' victims would no doubt inform.[5] In these earlier studies the elaboration of a social class politics was often at the expense of issues of masculinity and racism.

Rather than treating white racist activities as the pointless stretching of symbolic sinew, Pearson's paper suggests that such practices aid the mutual consolidation of masculinity, sexuality and white ethnicity in working-class culture. Indeed, the over-rational economic account does not capture the deeper motivations for exhibiting whiteness. It does not adequately explain, for example, why it is *young men* who are engaged in such hostile actions, or why not *all* working-class males synthesise a racist white identity. There remains an absence of individual agency in these accounts which allows Pearson to conclude his analysis with the concept of the 'mis-directed heroism of the "paki-basher"' (1976a: 86). This nostalgic portrayal of (male) working-class heroes depicts them as passive victims of the State, acting under a 'mis-directed' *false consciousness.* I would suggest that skinhead style can be said to be a ritual of resistance, but its reactionary effects are too easily explained away. The romanticism with violence that researchers have imputed to working-class youth cultures has served only to produce an imaginary 'noble savage', the often-patronised working-class hero. A further consequence of this sentimental stance has been a tendency to ignore differences within working-class formations of gender, sexuality, age, region, etc.

Furthermore, Les Back (1993: 217) has noted that: 'While an enormous amount of attention has been paid to the study of ethnic minority young people, little is known about the ethnicity of white youth and the way racism features in their lives'. This chapter hopes to go some way towards redressing this imbalance, by exploring the process whereby explicitly racist young men evoke whiteness within their suburban neighbourhood. The research will draw upon primary ethnographic data derived from the skinhead subculture who form the respondents in this study. This methodological approach is unusual, as the majority of skinhead studies comprise what Moore (1994: 15) has termed 'a sociology of appearances', frequently based on secondary data and media reporting. As Moore (1994) goes on to note, this is all the more surprising considering the numbers of insightful media critiques conducted at CCCS, and the production of some classic ethnographies (see especially Willis, 1977).[6]

A further complication with subcultural studies has been the tendency to assume these youth formations as distinct, mutually incompatible categories. Contemporary variations in skinhead style are present in racist, anti-racist, gay and black subcultures. Despite some of the limitations of older CCCS research on youth subculture, this chapter remains indebted to these insights, which undoubtedly form the backdrop to the research. Notably, the respondents in this analysis defined themselves against both an imaginary 'black' inner-city

(Birmingham) and the wealthier middle-class suburbs that bordered the estate. It was precisely because white working-class masculinities were felt to be 'in crisis' at these levels that they were so virulently asserted in the space of the local. This appears to have left working-class males without a secure identity, where investments in specific styles of whiteness become a substitute for the masculine-affirmative process of manual labour.

SKINHEAD MOVEMENTS – DANCE OF THE PALEFACE

The nostalgic portrayals of white working-class men are voiced in bodily descriptions of them as 'the backbone of the nation', 'the salt of the earth', 'the heart of the country', etc. Such earthy, corporeal metaphors not only articulate notions of class and gender, but are premised on static notions of a rooted white community. Rather than seeing whiteness as the unchanging, anatomical identity fetishised here, I want to suggest that white masculinities are given the appearance of substance in *embodied* action and synchronised routines. Through ethnographic interviews I will discuss how such a comportment draws on racist discourses to convey the illusory coherence of whiteness as an identity of supposed permanence and stability. By drawing attention to the performative dimensions of whiteness I aim to expose the very processes utilised to *choreograph* a coherent white identity.

Hebdige (1982) has compared the performativity of skinhead style with the motions of dance. Here, 'skins' move to a *dissonant* rhythm, out of synch with much of society:

> Just watch the way a skinhead moves. The posture is organised . . . The head twists out as if the skin is wearing an old-fashioned collar that's too tight for comfort. The cigarette, tip turned in towards the palm, is brought down from the mouth in an exaggerated arc and held behind the back. It's a gesture reminiscent of barrack rooms and Borstals, of furtive smoking on the parade. That's the dance of Skin . . . nervous and twitchy. . . . They're always on their toes, ready to respond to the slightest provocation, ready to defend the little they possess (a football end, a pub, a street, a reputation). The dance of Skin is, then, . . . the mime of awkward masculinity – the geometry of menace. . . . Two obsessions dominate the style: being *authentic* and being *British.*

> (Hebdige, 1982: 27–8)

The aim of this chapter is to deconstruct the working-class, white masculinities of a skinhead subculture by explaining the 'two obsessions' with 'being authentic' and 'being British'. The 'dance of Skin' which Hebdige refers to will be developed to consider the *choreography* of whiteness, a style fashioned in an attempt to embody a desired working-class, white masculinity. In skinhead subculture the enactment of whiteness can be seen as a highly regulatory posture that achieves further recognition through group simulation. The activity suggests that whiteness is a repetitive, highly stylised ritual of display. The metaphor of choreography touches on the performative aspects of whiteness, which enable skinhead style to be likened to a 'ghost dance of white ethnicity' (Mercer, 1994: 123). The ethnographic evidence in my research indicates that emulating the dance requires practice, timing, correct use of costume and careful body regulation. The apparent ease with which young men are able to mimic a phantasmal mode of whiteness conceals the intensive labour involved in presenting a coherent white masculinity. Even so, I will go on to identify times when the performance is revealed as an 'act', and moments at which young men are seen to be 'out of step' with the regulatory specificities of simulating whiteness. The chapter will then also reveal the contradictions embedded in skinhead style and action.

'Shadow Cuts': Skinhead Style and White Corporeality

Having a skinhead haircut, the way you dress, you've made a vow to each other. You can't mingle and get away with things. You're hardcore. You're living it out. You're dedicated. You're living a life as a racist, patriot, nationalist, every minute of the day. Not when it suits you. When you look at us, you know what we are straightaway.

(Quoted in Regan, 1993: 10)

Skinhead style developed from mod subcultures of the mid-1960s, and was further influenced by the dance-hall scene of Jamaican Rude Boys who espoused cropped hair, narrow ankle tapered trousers and smart jackets (see Ferguson, 1982; Hebdige, 1987; Knight, 1982). This literature suggests that the act of dressing as a 'skin' is highly ritualistic, symbolic and self-conscious; indeed, subtle inflections within skinhead style were recognisable to those within the cult (Ferguson, 1982; Moore, 1994). Skinheads would often alter their dress according to context and situation: if they were on the football terraces expecting 'aggro', at night-clubs hoping to attract members of the opposite sex, or simply hanging out on the street (Robins and Cohen, 1978).

The symbolic structure of skinhead style is evident in Richard Allen's eponymous cult fiction novel first published in 1970, simply entitled *Skinhead*.[7] Throughout Allen's narrative we learn of how the working-class EastEnd[8] hero Joe Hawkins 'immediately felt two feet taller' (1992: 38) when he wore his boots. Here, symbols of working-class life are adopted as treasured icons of skinhead style. Consider the ways 'bovver boots' are used to convey authenticity, masculinity and working-class power:

> The boots were the most important item. Without his boots, he was part of the common-herd – like his dad, a working man devoid of identity. Joe was proud of his boots. Most of his mates wore boots bought for a high price in High Street shops. But not Joe's. His were genuine army-disposal boots; thick-soled, studded, heavy to wear and heavy to feel if slammed against a rib.
>
> (Allen, 1992: 14)

In this passage the army-surplus boots of early skinhead style become a signature or thumb-print for the central protagonist, Joe Hawkins. The boots speak volumes about who Hawkins is, when we are told that without them he remains 'devoid of identity'. His boots are a metaphor for the stereotypical skinhead – 'genuine', 'thick', 'heavy' – and are also capable of delivering excruciating violence. The boots can be thought to symbolise the character of Joe Hawkins represented as a macho, working-class, 'genuine' skinhead. Richard Allen recently claimed, in a retrospective on his series, that 'Joe Hawkins and his ilk were, essentially, patriots fighting for a heritage . . . prepared to regain their rightful place in a homeland they had never relinquished' (1992: 5). The interviews conducted with contemporary skinheads suggest that these xenophobic emotions have not disappeared. As Jamie (15 years), a heavily built skinhead, explained, 'The English fight for their territory. . . . That's why we want them out of this country.'

However, where the boots were key signifiers of skinhead identity in the late 1960s and early 1970s, the young men interviewed in this study emphasised their haircuts as the main basis of identity. They each sported closely cropped hair styles which were subtle variations on skinhead styles.[9] Here the shaven-headed appearance was an essential means for embodying a particular, regional, working-class masculinity, as we shall see. Despite stylistic differences from older 'skins', the Kempton Dene males nevertheless identified themselves as 'genuine' skinheads.

Did you shave your head for a skinhead style?
Darren: Yeah, that's what everyone has down the Dene: a skinhead. Don't they?
Robbie: It's the trademark
Darren: I used a BIC [type of razor] and ...
What's it a trademark for?
Robbie: Don't mess with the Dene.
Darren: Don't mess with the skinheads!
Robbie: [*chanting*] Skiiiiiin-'eads! [*sic.*]

The image is one of aggression, a celebratory 'trademark' that is believed to be representative of the 'hard' regional culture of the community. The term 'trademark' indicates that the young men see the skinhead cut as an immediate guarantee of working-class masculinity. The shaven-headed appearance accentuates the 'geometry of menace' which Hebdige (1982) identified earlier, and is given resonance in the comments 'Don't mess with the skinheads!' The interconnection between skinhead style, whiteness and masculinity was given further emphasis when the young men we interviewed sprayed 'Don't fuck with Whites!' in white paint on a nearby wall of the youth club. The research group embodied forms of whiteness in the verbal and visual styles of dress code, body language and discourse. As such, the skinhead look is a body styling display that choreographs white working-class masculinity as powerful and threatening. An example of the choreographic machismo embodied in skinhead style is found in the 'skinzine' *Tighten Up*, where Toast (age 15) describes the management of his body:

I didn't walk to the sea front. I swaggered. I felt I could take on the whole world. And when I saw the first group of skins, my heart would fill with pride. I was part of an army and for a day the town would be ours.

(Quoted in Marshall, 1994: 99)

The 'geometry of menace' is then worked out simultaneously on the body and on the social landscape. The militaristic overtones and explicit bravado function to demonstrate how power is evoked through collective simulation in particular spaces. Choreographing white masculinity through skinhead style is about costume, bodily performance and collective spatial action.

For the young men in our research there were critical moments when the skinhead look had to be backed up with direct racist violence. It appeared that there was nothing more demeaning than having white masculinity called into question.

Mark (16 years): You get people, like one black kid saying things like, 'Oh I'm gonna batter 'im, he's a white blah, blah. Thinks he's hard 'cos he's got a skinhead', all this. And that's what everyone says. Then you come face to face with them, give them a smack. If they ask for it they get it back.

To be a skinhead in this reading means being genuinely 'hard', and capable of asserting violence when required, 'If they ask for it they get it back.' The relating of fight narratives was a popular pasttime for the group who could appraise one another's actions accordingly, for as Moore (1994: 142) explains: 'The good time is the act, the story the evidence, and authenticity the verdict brought down on this act.' However, this masculine identification with being 'genuine' also evoked a sense of being loyal to one's regional working-class roots. The overlaps between class and masculinity are commented on by Pearson (1976b: 206), who writes of how 'The skinheads' uniform (boots, braces, cropped hair) was almost a caricature of the working dress of the model working man, and in their hooliganism and their "aggro" the skinheads seemed to reaffirm the working-class values of manliness and toughness.'

But while it appeared to be complying with a manual work ethos, skinhead culture was in direct conflict to the 'drop-out' generation of hippie subculture. In the late 1960s skinheads eschewed what were felt to be the bourgeois, effeminate trappings of long-haired hippie culture to opt for a 'straight', no-nonsense proletarian crop.[10] The close cut was not only functional but could articulate multiple, masculine fantasies of existence, as Knight explains:

If you get in a fight, short hair is an advantage since your opponent cannot grasp it. It has another practical benefit in that it is easy to keep clean and to wash. It is also easy to manage when you are working. . . . Generally, short hair is associated in the public mind with convicts, prison camp inmates and the military. It was exactly this mean look which the skins wished to cultivate.

(1992: 13)

For the Kempton Dene males the cut also signified a 'mean look'; they were 'ruff 'n' tuff', not to be 'messed with'. Although the cut connects up with elements of working-class manual labour in the way Knight (1982) describes, as none of the young men interviewed was in employment it was the *fantasy* of the macho style that was particularly attractive. Cohen (1972: 25) has accurately described such 'machismo' as 'the unconscious dynamics of the work ethic translated into the out of work situation'. Here, the skinhead haircut is consciously emblematic of working-class identifications and a broader bourgeois social alienation. Perhaps the cut itself could be viewed as a cultural register for the 'hard times' of 1990s Britain, and thereby be said to conceal a certain naked vulnerability: the bald truth of a bleak future. For the interviewees the macho-class dimensions of the cut pertinently drew upon the *already* established image of the skinhead as male, working class and violently racist. Critically, the 'trademark' was a socially recognisable symbol of white power in the Kempton Dene context, where other youths regarded the young men as racist extremists by dint of their communal style. However, few elements of older skinhead style remained in the dress codes of the Kempton Dene males, though students in a local school referred to them as part of the 'bomber jacket brigade'.[11] A school student, Nicola (15 years) referred to the dress code and activities of the 'skins': 'Yeah, they're in the NF . . . and they write it all down the walls and on the roads and everything and they wear green jackets with the orange inside which is the NF coat'.[12]

According to the police and local residents the Kempton Dene 'skins' were influenced by Adam, an older youth in his 20s who was continually in and out of prison. He featured as a key actor in many of the violent narratives told by the 'skins', where 'doing time' bolstered masculine reputations in the locality of the working-class peer group. Mr Sidhou, a local Sikh shopkeeper who was himself a frequent recipient of the group's racism, explained how the severe 'ex-con' haircut of Adam was quickly reproduced among male youths. He notes how Adam 'had a shave of a different type', a particularly short skinhead style which the group sought to emulate: 'The others, four or five, shaved their hairs exactly to match his style.' Collective simulation of white masculinity is important. This goes some way to explaining desired investments in the area as 'hard', 'that's what everyone has down "the Dene", a skinhead'. The concept of skinheads as representative of the community was a consistent theme in the accounts of the Kempton Dene males.

Roger Hewitt's research on young people and racism found such outward encoding to be popular among 'skins', where 'the semiotics of class and politics were written into their involvement with skinhead style at many levels' (1986: 34). He notes how braces represented working-class identifications, and colour-coded socks or bootlaces could indicate an affiliation to either the British Movement or National Front. However, by the end of his research Hewitt found such marked dress styles to be in decline, a view echoed in Back's (1996) recent work, similarly based in South London. Another bodily display of whiteness by certain skinheads is found in the use of tattoos where British bulldogs, swastikas, union jacks and Blood and Honour motifs are not uncommon among far-Right extremists (Regan, 1993). Moore (1994) found that skinheads in the Western Australian suburb of Perth, due to their migrant situation, were more likely to assert ethnicity before class through adopting English styles (though he refers to Hebdige's claim that in England the reverse is more common). Similarly Cohen (1972: 24) has claimed that 'while the mods explored the upwardly mobile option, the skinheads explored the lumpen', to affirm their working-class heritage.

For the discussants in this research, racist graffito became a key spatial practice for exhibiting white ethnicity. School students indicated that this would accompany the wearing of 'White Power' badges and the use of neo-Nazi stickers, though none of these was evident during interviews.[13] However, the use of racist symbols was to play a key part in removing the young men from the youth club. They had been suspended from using the facilities after a 'paki-bashing' rampage which occurred during a night-time excursion involving other youth clubs from the inner city.[14] For a trial period they were accepted back into the club on the explicit terms that any similar type of behaviour would result in a permanent ban. During this time the young men scrawled various National Front insignia on club walls, posters and the pool table, which resulted in a final expulsion.

Two-tone Dialogues: The Contradictions of 'Skin'

> Even the skinhead 'uniform' was profoundly ambiguous in origin. The dialectical interplay of black and white 'languages' (dress, argot, focal concerns: style) was clearly expressed in the boots, sta-prest and severely cropped hair: an ensemble which had been composed on the cusp of the two worlds, embodying aesthetic themes common to both.
>
> (Hebdige, 1987: 57)

According to Dick Hebdige there have always been contradictions in skinhead style, and a long standing association with fetishising aspects of black culture. In Kempton Dene, the haircut became the main signifier of difference between skinheads and other youth groups. However, the stylistic elements of skinhead culture are often ambiguous and have been creatively reappropriated by organisations such as the Anti-Nazi League, and contemporary Queer subcultures.[15] Paradoxically, the fashion of the skinheads from 'the Dene' re-worked black cultural style, though they were a far cry from the 'braces-'n'-bovver-boots' appearance of previous periods. The interviewees frequently wore loose checked shirts, training shoes, baggy jeans and hooded anoraks; familiar accessories found in the wardrobes of many African/Caribbean males in Birmingham. The monocultural whiteness the young men chose to celebrate, disguised the hybrid exchanges that had occurred in their appropriation of dissonant styles. Consequently, the 'skins' were engaged in a 'post-imperial mode of mimicry' (Mercer, 1994: 123), adopting elements of black cultural style and synthesising this into a white working-class repertoire of style. Where former skinhead cultures looked to reggae, bluebeat and ska for inspiration, the young men in this study looked to the equally contradictory black influence of 'rave', ragga and hip-hop. The alteration in styles of dress and music by contemporary skinheads in outer-city Birmingham is possible, as these are "plastic" forms not directly produced by the subculture but selected and invested with sub-cultural value' (Cohen, 1972: 23). Thus, hardcore 'rave' music could be appropriated as a white working-class youth culture, while its black cultural roots were overlooked. This suggests that skinhead style has developed, while continuing to be in 'dialogue' *with* and *against* black culture.

Skinhead style as a manifestation of white pride is, at once, structured in contradiction. Hebdige (1987) metaphorically notes how skinheads bleached the black roots embedded in their stylistic identities. The haircuts of the Kempton Dene males ranged from the 'no. 1' (the severest grade on an electric shaver), through to 'crew cuts' and 'flat tops'. These cuts draw upon the black soulboy look of the mid-1960s, so as a motif of white authenticity remain highly suspect (Mercer, 1994). Effectively, the genuine 'trademark' that the Kempton 'skins' hope to achieve only produces a synthetic whiteness, as the style was fabricated through black/white interaction. Rather, the skinhead style remains, to all purposes, an inverted parody of blackness, what Kobena Mercer (1994: 123) has compared to 'a photographic negative'. Here, the shadowy image of a black 'Other' is the film through which whiteness is constituted. In other words, essentialising black-ness to trace and locate an authentic white being, only produces another ephemeral imitation, a copy of a copy. It seems that behind the dazzling dance of the paleface may lurk the smudged shadow outline of black history.

But skinhead subcultural style was also in 'dialogue' with another organic influence, primarily associated with white working-class males – football. British working-class culture mediated and refracted the Jamaican influence, and in so doing translated the style into a 'new' cultural form, the 'skinhead'. Here, aspects of 'yardie' protest culture (music, dress, resistance) could be readily appropriated by British, white working-class youth. The working-class culture of the 'host' community inflected Jamaican culture to produce a style that was always something more than just the pale reflection of blackness. Rather, the street styles formed a cultural collage of fusion and mix that resulted in new youth styles. Ultimately, skinhead style remains an ambiguously situated mode of whiteness, where a performance is worked out on the surface of the body and the local territory, to convey specificities of class, whiteness and gender.

REGULATING SEXUALITY: 'THE UNBEARABLE WHITENESS OF BEING'

Throughout interview the skinhead group simultaneously expressed horror and fascination with black sexuality, an ambivalence which Frantz Fanon (1968) captures in his renowned couplet, *'fear/desire'*. This process was evident in relation to a favourite programme at the time, the television screening of Hanif Kureshi's novel *The Buddha of Suburbia*. Set in 1970s Britain, the production explores issues of hippie spirituality, gay and interracial sexuality; the very themes the youth-club males detested. Although this series represented the very antithesis of the white suburban utopia the 'skins' were trying to evoke, it retained a curious collective appeal. The 'skins' claimed to be viewing the series to 'watch the shaggin'', yet in many ways the programme was a depiction of their darkest fears, an apocalyptic suburban nightmare.

Although the young men could insert themselves into a discourse of rampant heterosexuality in this instance to explain contradictory desires, the technique was not always effective. The most pertinent example of this occurred when the group were asked if they would date someone of a different colour. The young white men were adamant that they found black sexuality repulsive, yet this view was challenged by the mixed-heritage youth who remembered a previous conversation with one of the group members. This revelation opened up the ambiguities of whiteness and racism.

Would you go out with somebody who wasn't the same colour as you?
Robbie (white):   A nigger?
Mark (white):   Wouldn't even entertain one!
[. . .]
Calvin (mixed-heritage):   Daniel would.
Leonard (mixed-heritage):   [*raising voice*]   You told us! Janet Jackson, Tina Turner...
Daniel (white):   [*grudgingly*] Tina Turner yeah. Not Janet Jackson.
[*Swelling laughter and jeering as Daniel starts to go very red*]
ALL: Blushing!
Robbie (white):   Nigger-lover.

In this extract Calvin and Leonard seize upon the contradictory practice of Daniel's behaviour and 'shame' him in front of the group. The hatred of blackness he espouses is compounded with a covert attraction for black sexuality. Robbie quickly reprimands him as a 'Nigger-lover', a regulatory term used to 'police' whiteness and white sexual behaviour. These comments are a form of category maintenance work, a means of policing the sex - race identities of 'Self' and 'Other'. Daniel was perhaps the most virulently racist young male in the group and had even been expelled for 'paki-bashing', claiming, 'It's what I got thrown out for, battering pakis. I don't go school anymore.' His volatile racism made the desire for the black body appear all the more ambiguous. The ambivalence of a whiteness structured through *fear* and *desire* could, then, erupt to expose multiple contradictions.

Mark (white):   White boys should go out with white girls; black girls should go out with coons; pakis should go out with pakis.
Leonard (mixed-heritage):   An' half-castes should go out with both!
[. . .]
Leonard (mixed-heritage):   Who should half-castes stay with?
Daniel (white):   Fucking half-castes.
Leonard (mixed-heritage):   There's not many is there?
Robbie (white):   Exactly, because no white people would sleep with black people. 'Cos they don't like 'em . . . Point, point.
Leonard (mixed-heritage):   Fact, fact.

The choreographic performance of white masculinities is revealed in the careful routines young men must adhere to, where 'White boys should go out with white girls.' This crude sexual matching acts as a mantra for behaviour and attempts to secure a 'racial' symmetry across a rigid axis of colour/ethnicity. However, the passage is riddled with multiple contradictions. There is the underlying ambiguity that has already seen a white racist male forced into confessing a sexual attraction towards the black icon Tina Turner. Surprisingly, it is the group *themselves* who have orchestrated this situation and alienate Daniel for allowing his mask of whiteness to momentarily slip. Such was the sense of disruption that Daniel, who had been seated at the front, later removed himself to the back of the room. Here, the costs of fracturing the image of a coherent whiteness were acutely felt. The question of 'who should half-castes stay with' also poses a dilemma to monolithic conceptions of 'race' as inherently pure, distinct categories. This makes Robbie's comment appear all the more ridiculous, 'no white people would sleep with black people. 'Cos they don't like 'em'. A final contradiction is seen when Leonard, who has a black father and a white mother, accepts this point as 'fact', thereby sewing together the ragged fabric of white incoherence.

The struggle to perform a coherent white masculinity is seen when Daniel's desire for Tina Turner is denounced by the group. Here, white masculinities must be constantly asserted, celebrated or patched up when punctured with such verve. Daniel unsuccessfully attempted to retract his statement about Tina Turner as the conversation developed by claiming, 'she's too old ain't she?' However, the group were unwilling to allow him to retrieve a position of white authenticity and drove him to admit, 'I said she's nice looking'. As these words left his lips Robbie quipped, 'She's a nigger though', underlining the 'impossibility' of inter-racial attraction where a strict code of whiteness is in operation. Even in an avowedly racist group it appeared white identities can never rest, lie still and simply 'be'. Indeed, the taken-for-granted status of white identity as 'natural' is never quite achieved in the skinhead subculture, forever bound to rehearsals of whiteness. The intense labour involved in cultivating a coherent white skinhead identity suggest the project of whiteness is always underscored by the performance, the need to act, display, exhibit. Rather than conveying a 'natural' white masculinity, the choreographic process suggests whiteness is only given meaning through repetitive, fraught, hyperbolic exhibition.

These contradictions suggest that whiteness is itself an activity secured through repetitive dramatisation. Rather than being a stable identity, a point from which actions follow, whiteness is made intelligible through the various expressions and activities it claims are 'natural'. Whiteness can be seen to be constituted in and through action where white identities are made to appear creditable through choreographic styling. The performance, which aims to convey an essential whiteness, simultaneously reveals the process whereby these identities are exposed as parodic reiterations of an imagined form.

The sexual policing of whiteness remained a volatile issue for the Kempton Dene males, who frequently insisted that 'you should stay with your own kind'. Here is an example of the regulatory techniques deployed to govern whiteness.

Calvin (mixed-heritage):   If a white bloke sees a white girl with a black guy they might get jealous.

Robbie (white):   No they say, 'Oh look at that dirty bitch with a black man'.

Mark (white):   That's what I'd say if I saw a white girl with a black man, I'd call her a bitch.

What about a white bloke with a black girl?

Robbie (white):   Batter 'em.

Mark (white):   I'd still call her a bitch.

You'd call her a bitch and not him?

Mark (white):   I'd call 'em both wank.

Daniel (white):   Batter the coon, batter the wipe.

Leonard (mixed-heritage):   The wipe? The ass wipe.

In the passage there is a denial of jealousy for black masculinity which is displaced through violence and sexual abuse. Here, white women's bodies become the discursive terrain for asserting white masculinity (see Frankenberg, 1994; Ware, 1993). White women who are potential 'race' traitors are sexually vilified as 'dirty bitches'. Black women, precisely because of their blackness, are already marked as 'bitches' regardless of their sexual behaviour. Meanwhile, white men who transgress the 'racial' symmetry are also said to be risking potential violence. If the Tina Turner extract was an example of the internal 'policing' of whiteness by the 'skins', here we see how sex–race boundaries of other young men and women are regulated. The range of sanctions is informative of the differing social costs incurred when challenging whiteness through lived experience. However, women's bodies were not the only anatomical landscape for choreographing whiteness, as I shall show in the section below.

BODIES OF EVIDENCE: 'ACTING WHITE, GENDERING ETHNICITY'

> 'paki-bashing' can be read as a displacement manoeuvre whereby the fear and anxiety produced by limited identification with one black group was transformed into aggression and directed against another black community. . . . Every time the boot went in, a contradiction was concealed, glossed over, made to 'disappear'.
>
> (Hebdige, 1987: 58)

Whiteness was found to be embodied in physical action, demonstrative style and bodily display, yet claimed as 'natural' by the skinheads. It was evident that a key mechanism for enacting whiteness was to assert the cultural difference of racialised 'Others'. Here, the skinheads used stereotypical notions of blackness to highlight their own distinctiveness from these social groupings. This allowed them to claim their choreographic routines as 'natural' actions emanating from an essential whiteness, while simultaneously disparaging the enactment of black identities. In their minds these activities and social practices were regarded as the outcome of occupying a particular racialised identity. Following on from this, the young men insisted that people should 'act their own colour', which led to a discussion of the meaning of these statements, when I asked:

> *What do you mean 'act your own colour'?*
> *Mark*:   We act like we act, and get all the black people like walking, swinging their fucking arms like fucking apes.
> *Darren*:   We wear jeans. Niggers wear cuts in their jeans. Pakis wear pyjamas.
> *Daniel*:   And fucking towels.

In this extract, whiteness is consolidated through fixed, identifiable categories of ethnic difference. It is through notions of blackness that whiteness is made intelligible. The comments about 'acting your own colour' suggest an inherent way of 'being' white which involves an intrinsically different body schema than those adopted by black or Asian youths. Accordingly, black people are identified as animals indulging in hyperbolic choreographies, 'swinging their fucking arms like apes'. Meanwhile, white identities are naturalised in the phrase 'We act like we act', which disguises the regulatory styling required to sustain these identities and allows whiteness to be presented as the 'norm'. This neutrality is represented through the mundane, western symbol of 'jeans', an effect which film theorist Richard Dyer found to portray whiteness as 'emptiness, absence, denial' (1993: 141). The denial of white performativity is particularly remarkable in this group when we consider the accomplished choreography of skinhead style. The normalising of whiteness is a point picked up by various British anti-racist writers who have noted that, while black identities have been too readily interrogated, the identity 'white' remains undisclosed, masked and beyond discussion (Bonnett, 1996a; Gillborn, 1996; Jeater, 1992).

In order to understand the processes used to choreograph white masculinity, we need to recognise that notions of 'race' simultaneously 'articulate' dynamics of gender and sexuality. The comment that 'niggers wear cuts in their jeans' locates African/Caribbean identities as urban, streetwise ethnicities that are potentially threatening and dangerous, indeed, ape-like. The racist articulation of blackness creates a *hyper-masculine* image of African/Caribbeans. The desire embedded within fantasies of black machismo are displaced, by depicting blacks as primitive, savage beasts. The ambiguities of these processes have encouraged Stuart Hall to write of how 'fear and desire double for one another and play across the structures of otherness, complicating its politics' (1993: 256). The coded street-credibility of young black men operates as a fantasy that is desired, so is subsequently displaced, in order to reassert whiteness. The passage alludes to body boundaries where choreographed actions are seen to attribute directly from the 'race' of individuals. The desirable black identity that the group validate is a white machination grounded in the stereotype of the macho, urban, American male.

To interpret the differing representations of South Asians, we need to recognise the nuances in the sexual dynamics of racism. Against the hyper-masculine identity of the African/Caribbean is placed the highly *feminised* image of the South Asian secured through the discursive language of the young men. Here, the subordinate masculinities of South Asians are produced through the tropes of 'towels' and 'pyjamas'. The items connote softness and domesticity, when juxtaposed to the outdoor clothing of denim worn by whites, and the subversive street-wear of 'niggers'. Here, the turban is identified as a cultural signifier of difference and relegated to an object to wipe yourself with, transforming the Asian into an 'ass wipe'. Moreover, Mac an Ghaill (1994) has indicated that the phrase 'paki', when deployed by masculine peer-group cultures, can simultaneously articulate terms such as 'poofter'. Thus, a particular moment from the *Buddha of Suburbia* was recalled, and used to position my own black masculinity within the group.

> *Darren*:   He looks like the one off . . . *Buddha of Suburbia*.
> *Robbie*:   Oh aah — That dirty paki. He gives that bloke a blow job at the end.
> *Darren*:   I think it's him.

Thus, highly stylised images cultivate black masculinities as either violent/hypersexual in the case of African/Caribbean men; or passive/homosexual in the case of South Asians. The attractions of certain forms of black masculinity that connect up with white, working-class culture suggest that articulations of racism are interwoven with issues of gender and sexuality. The consolidation of 'racial' identities through the interplay of these complex dynamics is alluded to by Phil Cohen.

> Some ethnic attributes may be idealised because of their positive class and gender associations, whilst others are denigrated. Most typically, of course, many white working-class boys discriminate positively in favour of Afro-Caribbean subcultures as exhibiting a macho, proletarian style, and against Asian cultures as being 'effeminate' and 'middle-class'. Such boys experience no sense of contradiction in wearing dreadlocks, smoking ganja and going to reggae concerts whilst continuing to assert that 'Pakis stink'. Split perceptions, linking double standards of gender, ethnicity and class are increasingly the rule.
>
> (Cohen, 1988: 83)

The 'split perceptions' and 'double standards', that Cohen identifies, go some way to accounting for the contradictory structure of whiteness exhibited. The racially charged images of blackness allow whiteness to operate as the undisclosed equilibrium of experience. Hence, the comments 'We act like we act' and 'We wear jeans' denies the choreographic performance of skinhead style and compares white masculinities favourably against the constrained, though sometimes secretly desired, images of exotic 'Others'. It appears, then, that white masculinities are not only defined against femininity, but also against the bodies of black men. More specifically, there remains a need to move beyond a black/white dualism, towards recognising the varied expressions of racism.

In the complex formulations of racism, white masculinity, clothes and activities are seen as 'natural'. African/Caribbean identities are represented as savage and dangerous through actions and styles that convey a primitive hypersexual masculinity. Finally, South Asian identities are depicted as passive and weak, condensed into an effeminate masculinity that flirts with the homoerotic. The embodiment of whiteness is a process that relies upon recognition with racialised 'Others' to define itself. In doing so, the choreographic action situates the sociosexual position of *all* 'racial' identities, including white. Despite the attempts to convey white identities as 'natural' the descriptions suggest an embodiment of whiteness requires a highly cultivated choreographic performance, the mode of acting white. The discussions invoke a freezing of cultural identities to accentuate difference. The ambivalence is further revealed when the responses concerning 'pakis' in 'pyjamas' were made to me, an Asian researcher who dressed in jeans throughout the interviews.

'Blacks Ain't As Bad As Pakis'

The loose and fragile identifications made by the 'skins' towards African/Caribbean culture provided for a partial and contingent acceptance of certain forms of blackness. As we have seen, this did not curtail their rampant celebration of whiteness but encouraged a particular form of racism that was especially hostile to South Asians. Thus, white male heterosexual hierarchies were further exposed when I asked why the 'skins' responded differently to each of these ethnic groupings.

Robbie: Blacks ain't as bad as pakis.
Mark: We smoke their draw.
Robbie: I'd rather hang around with a black than a paki.
Leonard: Pakis smell.
Robbie: Pakis smell. It's their duty.

The white youth were capable of identifying with aspects of African/Caribbean music, style and culture, 'We smoke their draw'. However, this did not erase animosity towards African/Caribbean people *per se*, as we have seen. Further, cultural affiliations were not extended to South Asians who were placed at the base of the masculine hierarchy. Rather, cultural difference could be used to align white working-class experience with that of African/Caribbeans, and distinguish each of these ethnic groups from Asians.

*What's the difference [between African/Caribbeans and Asians], I still
   can't see it?*
Daniel: [*angrily*] 'Cos pakis stink! That's why. Don't they
   Calvin? 'Cos they wear fucking tea towels . . . .
Robbie: Hankies on their 'ead.
Mark: It's the way they dress. You get black people that dress like
   we do. Like they're dressed like we're dressed but pakis, they wear
   fucking tea cosies don' they?

The shifting discourses of racism in this extract are a clear indication
of how African/Caribbeans can be included or excluded on the basis
of style. Again, white experience is the 'norm' against which 'Others'
are judged. Conversations with the 'skins' disclosed an extensive
vocabulary which associated South Asians with being 'soft': 'pyjamas',
'towels', 'sandals', 'tea cosies'. The masculine hierarchies are diagram-
matically mapped below in Table 4.1.

When the group were asked why they permitted the involvement of
two mixed-heritage males in their peer setting they became highly
ambivalent. Daniel remarked, 'I'm not against like coons – against
pakis yeah, 'cos they smell'. However, the dynamic performance of
whiteness, could claim some blacks as 'one of us' one moment and not
so the next. When the white youth were questioned about their mixed-
heritage friends Calvin and Leonard, an attempt was made to 'claim'
whiteness on their behalf.

Table 4.1   Register of ethnic hierarchies

Social group	Masculine status	Cultural style	Perceived 'roots'
White working-class	Normal (yet ruff 'n' tuff)	Jeans (plain, neutral, regular)	White suburbia
African–Caribbean	Hyper-masculine (yet subhuman, ape-like)	Ripped jeans (street-wise, urban, threatening)	Black inner-city
South Asian	Effeminate, soft (passive, potentially homosexual)	Pyjamas, towels, hankies, sandals, tea cosies (domestic)	South Asian subcontinent

Daniel: They're alright, his mum's white so . . .

[...]

Darren: They're half-castes so they're alright, they've got a bit of white in 'em.

Robbie: Like I say, it's not so much the blacks. It's the pakis. No matter what anyone says I dislike 'em.

Darren: Pakis are like the main ones. All the people round here don't like pakis.

Robbie: It's not so much black. Mostly they don't like pakis.

The paradoxes embedded in assertions of white working-class masculinity disclose the contingency of whiteness. The interconnections between class, gender and sexuality, and how these dynamics are played out across black bodies, is vital to understanding the complex formation of white ethnicities in urban and suburban contexts. The 'skins' use a biological discourse to rationalise their affiliations with Calvin and Leonard by noting, 'They've got a bit of white in 'em'. However, in other instances this could be inverted to note how anyone of a 'mixed-heritage' background had 'a bit of paki in them'.

CONCLUDING REMARKS

I have not intended to suggest that . . . political practice necessitates the abandonment of any idea of Englishness or Britishness. We are all, no doubt fond of things which appear unique to our national culture – queuing perhaps, or the sound of leather on willow. What must be sacrificed is the language of British nationalism which is stained with the memory of greatness. What must be challenged is the way that these apparently unique customs and practices are understood as expressions of a pure and homogenous nationality.

(Gilroy, 1987: 69)

As Gilroy suggests, there are ways of engaging with Englishness that need not regurgitate the narrative of nationalism. However, the empirical evidence in this research suggests that a particular section of working-class young men are retreating into white ethnicity as a highly defensive and retentive posture. The young men in this study appeared to be consolidating their masculinities through racist practices, in a way that mutually reinforced what Back (1996: 137) refers to as 'the ideological triangle that places whiteness, Englishness and racism in an interdependent relationship'. Integrating whiteness, Englishness and racism was a means by which the young men could simulate a coherent white working-class masculinity. Here, whiteness is an embodied style, which is performatively evoked in order to purvey an inner 'truth' beyond the bodily practice of language, gesture and display. The unachievable task of conveying an imagined white coherence produces an ongoing amount of 'body work'. It appeared that the desperate status of the 'skins' encouraged them to utilise an exaggerated, 'hyper-whiteness' through bodily practice and public exhibition.

However, the project of whiteness is a masquerade that simultaneously exposes the labour required to sustain this fabrication. This incompleteness, and sense of 'lack', calls for the exhibition of a white, working-class masculinity through repetitive, strategic deployments of racism. The parodic display not only has collective significance, but is a self-confirming reiteration of whiteness for the individuals concerned. The choreography of whiteness within working-class skinhead culture thus fails to assemble an identity that is solid, sure and steadfast. Rather, the act of performance reverberates an uncertainty, an inability to truly embody white masculinity. As Hebdige goes on to explain, retreat into white ethnicity can become a 'romantic gesture' (1982: 35), a posture that offers working-class males escapism and the illusion of security in masculine performance. The nostalgic performance is seen in the skinheads' attempt to authenticate concepts of territory, 'style' and ethnic behaviour. At these moments the young men appeared as 'pale warriors' – romantic defenders of an ever-retreating, imaginary English working-class culture. The retreat into white ethnicity exposed the techniques by which whiteness was 'naturalised' in these peer-group settings and, as such, also disclosed the process whereby working-class males 'do whiteness'.

Even so, 'doing whiteness' was frequently found to be a laborious activity. For the respondents in this study, desire and fantasies of the 'Other' had to be carefully regulated through rigid routines of whiteness. The sexual desire for black icons like Tina, Janet, Whitney – and the covert admiration for the 'hard' street styles of macho black males – bears testimony to the underlying ambivalence of whiteness. Such slippages were continually defended, repaired or denied by the 'skins' disclosing the eternal struggle involved to substantiate whiteness. The morbid fascination with the screen production of the *Buddha of Suburbia*, and the verbal and physical retributions delivered to white youth who dated outside their ethnic grouping, indicated that it was at the crossroads of 'race' and sexuality that whiteness was most severely scrutinised. 'Doing whiteness' meant acting white by way of dress code, body language and a range of cultural practices. It was at these moments, when white identity was being so stringently stabilised, that the contours of whiteness became starkly visible. Nevertheless, the highly sculpted white ethnicities, so intensely refined by the young men in this study, were founded on pale imitations of black culture. The markings of this were detectable in a spectrum of bodily consumption: hairstyles, dress codes, language, cannabis use, musical preferences. The 'authentic' whiteness that the 'skins' hoped to achieve meant bleaching these 'anomalies' from existence. However, the indelible stain of blackness on skinhead style, and the lived cultures of Birmingham youth generally, make total erasure a distinct impossibility.

The continual struggle to effect a white coherence, where daily actions carry the shadow of a haunting ambiguity, throws up glimmers of hope for political action.[16] According to Jeater (1992) the moment of reinventing whiteness outside nationalist discourses may have passed, though 'new' ethnicities which critically appraise whiteness are undoubtedly in occurrence (Back, 1996; Jones, 1988). This suggests reconfigurations at a grass-roots level are a cultural possibility, where 'Brit-pop' youngsters may already be looking for variations on or within the identity 'white'. What needs to be challenged is the racist formation of white ethnicities, and the material deprivation which makes a pale warrior stance so attractive for working-class males. Anti-racism must now pay heed to the oppressive choreography of whiteness, to recognise how this combines with working-class frustration and the dynamic culture that resides in masculine peer-groups. The present task for anti-racism, as we enter the millennium, is to provide alternative performative rhythms, in tune with the lived experience of these young people.

ACKNOWLEDGEMENTS

I primarily thank the participants interviewed in this research, who willingly gave up their time. I also thank the youth workers and teachers who permitted me access into their working environments and helped organise interview spaces. A special mention goes out to Les Back and Ian Barker for their support throughout the fieldwork period. Thanks finally to Alastair Bonnett, Joyce Canaan, Máirtín Mac an Ghaill and Mary Jane Kehily.

NOTES

1. Pseudonyms have been used throughout to protect the identities of people and places.
2. The geographical significance of researching racism in the outer city is paramount, with up to ten times the number of reported incidents occurring in the English suburbs compared with the inner city.
3. The interviews were conducted as part of an Economic and Social Science Research Council grant (ESRC 000234272) investigating the social basis of racist violence among young people in outer-city areas. I was the fieldworker researching with Les Back in outer-city Birmingham, while Roger Hewitt conducted comparative analysis in the peripheries of South London. I was further supported by Ian Barker, a sociology undergraduate on work experience, who aided me throughout much of the research process.
4. I am grateful to Richard Johnson for the use of this term.
5. Although several interviews were conducted with the victims of racist violence, here I will focus on the thoughts and actions of the perpetrators.
6. Undoubtedly, conducting interviews with skinhead groups is a complex procedure. Moore (1994) relied primarily on memory work, field notes and observation during his time spent with young 'skins'. Our study employed these techniques but also included taped interview responses, photographic evidence and the use of video to capture animated performances.
7. The Richard Allen series were among the most popular pulp-fiction novels for male working-class adolescents in the 1970s. More recently, they have become precious collectors' items.
8. The term 'EastEnder' refers to people from the eastern part of London, frequently mythologised in soap opera and popular fiction as the essence of working-class Englishness. The name Joe Hawkins is itself a caricature that resonates East End working-class culture. Also see Clarke (1976: 101) for an understanding of skinhead associations with the East End.
9. See Jim Ferguson's Fashion Notebook (pp. 36–47) for nuances within skinhead style and the varied fashions that were worn in different contexts and moments in time.
10. The sporting of skinhead haircuts within contemporary gay subcultures provides a sharp parody of the masculinism associated with the crop.
11. Bomber jackets and flight jackets were part of skinhead uniform in the 1970s, with the most popular styles being olive green and black (see Marshall, 1994).
12. Despite the graffiti practices of the Kempton Dene males they were not in the National Front Party.
13. This may have been because explicit racism was not tolerated in the youth club. Furthermore, it is likely that these motifs of whiteness were specifically deployed near the local school, where harassing black pupils outside the school gates became a regular practice of intimidation.
14. An annual 'night ops' expedition which involved basic orienteering skills was to be conducted in a park. This competition involved other youth

clubs and was felt to be an opportunity for young people to stay out all night without feeling threatened. The skinhead youth took advantage of this situation and proceeded to attack South Asian youth from other clubs.

15. As Walters notes in a review of Murray Healy's (1996) book *Gay Skins*, the skinhead look 'is not entirely fixed; it clearly means different things to different people in different contexts. Yet it is not entirely free-floating: the one thing skinhead style does signify to everybody is "butch"' (1996: 8).

16. Phil Cohen has pinpointed the lack of fixity between organised racism and popular youth racism 'to be a real cause for celebration' for anti-racist practitioners.

REFERENCES

Allen, R. (1992) *Skinhead*, in *The Complete Richard Allen*, vol. 1 (Dunoon: Skinhead Times Publishing).

Allen, T. (1994) *The Invention of the White Race* (London: Verso).

Back, L. (1993) 'Race, Identity and Nation within an Adolescent Community in South London', *New Community*, 19(2), pp. 217–33.

Back, L. (1996) *New Ethnicities and Urban Culture* (London: University of Central London Press).

Bendersky, J. W. (1995) 'The Disappearance of Blonds: Immigration, Race and the Re-emergence of "Thinking White"', *Telos*, 104, pp. 135–57.

Bonnett, A. (1993) 'Forever "White"? Challenges and Alternatives to a "Racial" Monolith', *New Community*, 20(1), pp. 173–80.

Bonnett, A. (1996a) 'Anti-Racism and the Critique of "White" Identities', *New Community*, 22(1), pp. 97–110.

Bonnett, A. (1996b) '"White Studies": The Problems and Projects of a New Research Agenda', *Theory, Culture and Society*, vol. 13(2), pp. 145–55.

Brah, A. (1993) 'Difference, Diversity and Differentiation', in J. Donald and A. Rattansi (eds), *'Race', Culture and Difference* (London: Open University Press).

Brake, M. (1987) *Comparative Youth Culture* (London: Routledge & Kegan Paul).

Butler, J. (1990) *Gender Trouble: Feminism and the Subversion of Identity* (New York: Routledge).

Carby, H. (1982) 'White Woman Listen! Black Feminism and the Boundaries of Sisterhood', in *The Empire Strikes Back* (London: Hutchinson, in association with the Centre for Contemporary Cultural Studies, University of Birmingham).

Clarke, J. (1974) 'Subcultural Symbolism: Reconceptualising "Youth Culture"', unpublished MA thesis, Centre for Contemporary Cultural Studies.

Clarke, J. (1976) 'The Skinheads and the Magical Recovery of Community', in S. Hall and T. Jefferson (eds), *Resistance through Rituals* (London: Hutchinson, in association with the Centre for Contemporary Cultural Studies, University of Birmingham).

Cohen, P. (1972) 'Subcultural Conflict and the Working-class Community', *Working Papers in Cultural Studies*, no. 2, Centre for Contemporary Cultural Studies, University of Birmingham.

Cohen, P. (1988) 'The Perversions of Inheritance: Studies in the Making of Multi-racist Britain', in P. Cohen and H. Bains (eds), *Multi-Racist Britain* (Basingstoke: Macmillan).

Cohen, P. (1993) '"It's Racism What Dunnit": Hidden Narratives in the Theories of Racism', in J. Donald and A. Rattansi (eds), *'Race', Culture & Difference* (London: Open University Press).

Dyer, R. (1993) 'White', in *The Matter of Images: Essays on Representation* (London: Routledge).

Fanon, F. (1968) *Black Skin, White Masks* (London: Paladin).

Ferguson, J. (1982) 'Jim Ferguson's Fashion Notebook', in N. Knight (ed.), *Skinhead* (London: Omnibus Press).

Frankenberg, R. (1994) *The Social Construction of Whiteness: White Women, Race Matters* (Minneapolis: University of Minnesota Press).

Gallagher, C. (1995) 'White Reconstruction in the University', *Socialist Review*, 24(1/2), pp. 165–87.

Gillborn, D. (1996) 'Student Roles and Perspectives in Antiracist Education: a Crisis of White Ethnicity', *British Educational Research Journal*, 22(2), pp. 165–79.

Gilroy, P. (1987) *There Ain't No Black in the Union Jack* (London: Hutchinson).

Gramsci, A. (1971) *Selections from the Prison Notebooks* (London: Lawrence & Wishart).

Hall, S. (1993) 'New Ethnicities', in J. Donald and A. Rattansi (eds), *'Race', Culture and Difference* (London: Open University Press).

Healy, M. (1997) *Gay Skins: Class, Masculinity and Queer Appropriation* (London: Cassell).

Hebdige, D. (1982) 'This is England! And They Don't Live Here', in N. Knight (ed.), *Skinhead* (London: Omnibus Press).

Hebdige, D. (1987) *Subculture: The Meaning of Style* (London: Methuen).

Hewitt, R. (1986) *Black Talk, White Talk* (London: Cambridge University Press).

Jeater, D. (1992) 'Beef and Reggae Music: the Passing of Whiteness', *New Formations*, no. 18, pp. 107–21.

Jones, S. (1988) *Black Culture, White Youth: The Reggae Tradition from JA to UK* (Basingstoke: Macmillan Education).

Knight, N. (1982) *Skinhead* (London: Omnibus Press).

Mac an Ghaill, M. (1994) *The Making of Men: Masculinities, Sexualities and Schooling* (Buckinghan: Open University Press).

Marshall, G. (1994) *Spirit of '69: A Skinhead Bible* (Dunoon: Skinhead Times Publishing).

Mercer, K. (1994) 'Black Hair/Style Politics', in *Welcome to the Jungle: New Positions in Black Cultural Studies* (London: Routledge).

Moore, D. (1994) *The Lads in Action: Social Processes in an Urban Youth Subculture* (Aldershot: Arena).

Nayak, A. (1993) 'Racism in Birmingham: Some Underground Oversights', in L. Back and A. Nayak (eds), *Invisible Europeans? Black People in the 'New Europe'* (Birmingham: AFFOR).

Pajaczowska C. and Young, L. (1993) 'Racism, Representation, Psychoanalysis', in A. Rattansi (ed.), *'Race', Culture & Difference* (London: Open University Press).

Pearson, G. (1976a) '"Paki-bashing" in a North East Lancashire Cotton Town: A Case Study and its History', in G. Mungham and G. Pearson (eds), *Working-class Youth Culture* (London: Routledge & Kegan Paul).

Pearson, G. (1976b) 'In Defence of Hooliganism', in N. Tutt (ed.), *Violence* (London: Development Group).

Phizacklea, A. and Miles, R. (1979) 'Working-class Racist Beliefs in the Inner City', in R. Miles and A. Phizacklea (eds), *Racism and Political Action in Britain* (London: Routledge & Kegan Paul).

Regan, L. (1993) *Public Enemies* (London: André Deutsch).

Robins, D. and Cohen, P. (1978) *Knuckle Sandwich: Growing Up in the Working-Class City* (Middlesex: Harmondsworth).

Roediger, D. (1992) *The Wages of Whiteness: Race and the Making of the American Working-Class* (London: Verso).

Roediger, D. (1994) *Towards the Abolition of Whiteness* (London: Verso).

Walters, J. (1996) 'Give Me Some Skin', *New Times*, 12 October, p. 8.

Warren, D. (1995) 'White Americans as a Minority', *Telos*, 104, pp. 127–34.

Ware, V. (1993) *Beyond the Pale: White Women, Racism and History* (London: Verso).

Willis, P. (1977) *Learning to Labour* (London: Saxon House).

5 Populist Configurations of Race and Gender: the Case of Hugh Grant, Liz Hurley and Divine Brown

SARAH NEAL

INTRODUCTION

While I was as intrigued as the next person by the events surrounding Hugh Grant, Divine Brown and Liz Hurley in June 1995, what I became increasingly fascinated by were the ways in which these events were interpreted and (re)presented within the public and media landscape. At the heart of these interpretations/(re)presentations were the racialised notions and constructions of femininity, gender and sexuality. Significantly, this racialisation process occurred not only in terms of Divine Brown's blackness but equally in terms of Hugh Grant and Liz Hurley's whiteness. This chapter seeks to explore the social constructions of white and black[1] femininities and the relation of these to ideologies of race, national identity and belonging in populist discourse.[2]

Hugh Grant's payment for sex with an African–American woman pushed to the fore the antithetical constructions of white and black femininity. The events of June 1995, very much played out in the public gaze, successfully counterposed Liz Hurley, a white (upper middle-class) model and actress with Divine Brown, a black (working-class) prostitute.[3] While Liz Hurley was (re)presented as a wronged and tragic woman, more significantly she came to symbolise purity and a specific *Englishness*. The notion of Englishness was central to the media representations of both Hurley and Grant – they can be understood as caricatures of a particular (upper-class) Englishness.[4] Hugh Grant, whose public persona and whose screen character both rely on a certain sense and image of Englishness mutated into a neo-colonial figure 'lost', not in the nineteenth-century colonial terrain of 'darkest

Africa', but in its late twentieth-century equivalent – the 'urban inner city'. More specifically Grant was 'lost' in the inner area of a city particularly identified with racial tension (Rodney King, the 1992 Riots and the O. J. Simpson trial).

Divine Brown, whose very name evoked an almost comical eroticism, entered, from the outset, a particular, if ambiguous place alongside Hurley and Grant in the discursive terrains in which the event was popularly narrated and interpreted. While Divine Brown was commonly offered to the public gaze via the historical but familiar stereotype of 'black prostitute' this chapter attempts to argue that the more complex themes of miscegenation and white obsession with the black body expressed through the attraction/repulsion, adulation/hatred binaries underpinned (or were concealed) within the media (re)presentations of Divine Brown. A number of commentators (Gilman, 1985; Solomos and Back, 1996; Young, 1995) have noted that sexuality and fantasy have always played and continue to play, central roles in the shifting worlds of racism and within these fantasy/fantasised worlds the racially othered body becomes the simultaneous object of both sexual attraction and sexual disgust. As Young (1995: 149) argues: 'we find an ambivalent driving desire at the heart of racialism: a compulsive libidinal attraction disavowed by an equal insistence on repulsion'.

The chapter argues that the Grant, Brown, Hurley incident first demonstrates, the currency of gendered and racialised stereotypes within contemporary populist discourse; second, it demonstrates racialised and sexualised ambiguity around the black body; and third, it provides a context in which it is possible to identify the ways in which whiteness and white femininity are central to broader notions of race, nation and the construction of black Otherness.

RECOGNISING CONFIGURATIONS OF RACE AND GENDER ... SOME FOREGROUNDING

Whiteness, Women and Race

Until relatively recently it has been left to feminists of colour to theorise the relationship between gender and race in a variety of ways: visibilising the specific experiences of women of colour (Dadzie *et al.*, 1986; Mama, 1994); de-pathologising white feminists portrayals of women of colour (Carby, 1982; Parmar, 1981); emphasising the

importance of diversity and difference and the complexity of identity
(Brah, 1993, 1996) and emphasising the significance of race privilege
on the structural and cultural place and everyday lives of women of
colour in historical and contemporary social relations (Hill-Collins,
1990; hooks, 1982, 1989, 1994; Mirza, 1997; Williams, 1992). While
there have been moves by some white feminist scholars to connect
race and gender (see Anthias and Yuval-Davis, 1992: 98–100 for an
account of these) analysis of the relationships between white women
and race and the place of white femininity within racialised discourse
has remained an area of limited exploration in white feminist theory.
Two obvious exceptions in this particular desert of white feminist
inquiry have been the work of Vron Ware (1992) and Ruth
Frankenberg (1993). While the work of these two women is very different it shares a common thematic concern with the relationship of
white women to race. For Frankenberg this concern is explored by
arguing via qualitative data and discourse analysis that 'race shapes
white women's lives' (1993: 1) and she proceeds to note:

> any system of differentiation shapes those on whom it bestows privi-
> lege as well as those it oppresses. White people are 'raced' just as
> men are 'gendered'. And in a social context where white people
> have too often viewed themselves as non-racial or racially neutral, it
> is crucial to look at the 'racialness' of white experience.
>
> (*Ibid.*)

Echoing this Ware states that her book is:

> predicated on a recognition that to be white and female is too
> occupy a social category that is inescapably racialised as well as gen-
> dered. It is not about *being* a white woman, it is about *being thought
> of* as a white woman.
>
> (1992: xii; original emphasis)

Using this distinction Ware is able to explore how constructions of
white womanhood and white femininity have lain, and continue to lie, at
the heart of the racialised project. In relation to black men white
women have been most obviously (re)presented as victims or uniquely
vulnerable objects of black male sexuality and aggression; for example
both lynching in the United States and, more contemporarily,
'mugging', have centrally relied on particular constructions of white
femininity and white female frailty. In relation to women of colour,

white women have been most obviously (re)presented as the measure against which women of colour can be devalued and/or exoticised/eroticised. The process of de-valuation and exoticisation/eroticisation has occurred through essentialist dichotomies which vary according to particular groups of women of colour. In relation to black women the essentialist dichotomy operates along the axis of black women as sexually available/white women as sexually unavailable; black woman as sexually abandoned/white woman as sexually restrained; black woman as servant, employee/white woman as mistress or employer; black woman as dangerous, permissive, an aggressive matriarch/white woman as good, virginal, a passive compliant. While it is possible to see this dichotomy operating in its crudest or 'rawest' terms in the context of slavery it has been in no way confined to this context. Similarly it is important to note that the systematic devaluation–exoticisation of women of colour provides a means for the social (and sexual) control of *all* women, but that it operated through a process of differentiation between women, by affording race privilege to white women.

Given this, while there is a need to analyse the racialised (re)presentation of Divine Brown as 'black prostitute', it is important to note that the power of this (re)presentation relied on the ability of the media to (re)present Elizabeth Hurley as the very opposite. One of the key concerns of this chapter is then to explore the racialised (re)presentation and construction of Hurley as a white woman with all the associated meanings of white womanhood. Examining 'whiteness' is in many ways a very different, although intrinsically linked, project from examining 'blackness' because 'whiteness refers to a set of cultural practises that are usually unmarked and un-named' (Frankenberg, 1993: 1). To be white is to occupy a non-racial category and in this way whiteness becomes normative, invisible and, perhaps most significantly, thereby dominant. The task then becomes one in which whiteness is deconstructed in order to expose it as being both racially loaded and dominating. Frankenberg powerfully makes this same point when she argues:

> To look at the social construction of whiteness ... is to look head-on at a site of dominance. (And it may be more difficult for white people to say 'Whiteness has nothing to do with me – I'm not white' than to say 'Race has nothing to do with me – I'm not a racist'.) To speak of whiteness is, I think, to assign *everyone* a place in the relations of racism.
>
> (1993: 6; original emphasis)

However, some caution is needed when relocating the gaze onto whiteness. Most obviously there is a need to avoid collapsing under- standing of racism(s) into notions of skin 'colour'. While racism does have a fetishtic focus on skin 'colours' this is by no means the only terrain in which racism operates or the only signifier which racist ideologies use. As Solomos and Back warn:

> there is a danger of reifying whiteness and reinforcing a unitary idea of 'race'. In order to avoid doing this it crucial to locate any discus- sion of 'whiteness' in a particular empirical and historical context. ... Additionally, any discussion of whiteness must incorporate an appre- ciation of how gendered processes are inextricably articulated with the semantics of race.
>
> (1996: 24)

In exploring the configurations of race and gender in populist dis- course via the reporting of the Hurley, Brown, Grant event what becomes of central concern is the identification of the race-neutral indicators that the media used in its (re)presentation and construction of Hurley and Grant. Part of my project was then to tease out the indi- cators that marked Hurley and Grant as distinctively white and thereby distinctively *different* from Divine Brown. I emphasise differ- ent because difference has become the marker for race and difference has been raced/racialised. For, as Gilroy has argued, 'contemporary British racism deals in cultural difference rather than crude biological hierarchy. It asserts not that we are inferior but that we are different, so different that our distinctive modes of being are at odds with resi- dence in this country' (1993: 91–2). The notion of difference and the notion of 'distinctive modes of being' were central to the coverage of the Hurley, Brown, Grant incident, i.e. the difference between Divine Brown and Elizabeth Hurley, two women who were assigned two racially and polemically 'distinctive modes of being'. Their assignment to these locations served to obscure their points of connection, the most significant of which is that 'both make their living submitting to the dictates of male desire' (Richard Goldstein, quoted in Eisenstein, 1996: 115).

Writing in the White Feminist Self

For those white feminists who engage in the relocation of whiteness, white womanhood and white femininity, positioning these to the fore in the analysis of racialised relations, this process can involve placing/writing in the white self. Both Ware (1992) and Frankenberg (1993) incorporate autobiography into their text, although Ware more extensively than Frankenberg. The willingness to involve or incorporate the white self in this way can be understood on a number of inter-related axes: recognising the key feminist notion of the personal being political, of recognising that the everyday personalised world can or has to be politicised and/or theorised; linking this process to how issues of race shape or emerge in the personalised white world; recognising race as subjective and impacting at individual levels. As bell hooks (1994) and Nkweto Simmonds (1997) have noted, while white women have been keen in more recent years to hear black women's voices in terms of their autobiographies, there have been only limited contributions from white feminists presenting their own autobiographies within the same parameters. As hooks argues, this can lead to a situation in which women of colour are understood to present analyses of race through the lens of the personal and subjective, while white women present an analysis on more abstracted or theorised levels. Although there are exceptions (see Adrienne Rich, 1979, 1986, for example) both Ware's and Frankenberg's inclusion of autobiography can be seen as a more recent response to this situation and as a recognition of the importance of writing in the white self in the analyses of race and racialised relations. Acknowledging the importance of this, and thinking about the Grant, Hurley, Brown incident, made me remember (although I had not forgotten) an event in my own life. When I was in my early twenties, before I came out as a lesbian, I was involved in a sexual relationship with a black man. He identified himself as a militant black activist and I identified myself as a militant anti-racist. Race was very much a part of that relationship both in terms of our 'internal' negotiations around issues of race but also in our 'external' experiences as a mixed couple as viewed by the outside world. One incident among many, but which I recall with particular emotional vividness, occurred when I was walking with my former lover, arms around each other, down a road in London. A car with three young white men slowed down by the side of us and one of these men shouted out to me 'how many times do you get down and suck his black dick then?' I remember screaming back at them, the words lost in traffic and then wanting to lie on the pavement with the pain of it and my former lover holding me and silent. The incident was significant in a number of ways. First brevity, both in terms of the time it took to identify and name our transgression across race–sex boundaries – the incident must have lasted less than a minute – and in terms of the abuse itself. In this one sentence race, gender and sexuality were complexly intertwined. While both I (white woman) and my lover (black man) can be understood as being simultaneously abused by this sentence it is my role/position as a white woman that is perhaps more significant. I was reduced to and became the sexualised vehicle through which to racially abuse my lover. In this way my lover was both marginalised as a black man and reduced to 'black dick'. Thinking about this incident years later I can see that our immediate reactions to the incident were also significant – my vocality and his silence. That I could/did speak, and that my lover couldn't/didn't, can be understood as reflecting the different configurations and impact of racialised pain experienced by each of us given that I essentially only provided the means by which racism could be articulated. As Frankenberg argues in her explorations of white women in mixed relationships:

> while it is hard to measure pain, it is safe to say both that the racism that rebounds on white women has spent some of its force on the original impact it made on their non-white partners *and* that white women nonetheless feel its impact.

> (1993: 112; original emphasis)

While I draw on this autobiographical experience because it provides a particularly relevant illustration of the ways in which race, gender and sexuality are connected in both crude and complex ways (as they were in the media coverage of the Hurley, Grant, Brown affair) I also re-tell this event in order to 'locate myself in my analysis' (Ahmed, 1997: 154).

MAPPING (POPULIST) CONFIGURATIONS OF RACE AND GENDER

Methodology

Central to my approach to analysing the ways in which race and gender shaped and underpinned the Grant, Hurley, Brown incident was my interest in how the event was interpreted and carried out very much in the public gaze. It was this dimension which transported the incident from the micro, private world of the three main actors to the macro gendered and racialised world of the public. The public (populist) gaze was both built on and fed by media reporting of the event and the 'cultural meaning making' (Campbell, 1995) that the media reporting gave the incident. The relationships between the media and race and the cultural myths and common-sense stereotypes that lie at the core of this relationship have been commented on elsewhere (Campbell, 1995; Cohen and Gardner, 1982; Hartmann and Husbands, 1974; van Dijk, 1991). In order to 'unpack' the nature of the populist discourse surrounding the Grant, Hurley, Brown event my task was to interpret the (media) interpretations of the incident. I placed parameters around my methodological approach by limiting my data collection to an analysis of media text and (re)presentations by exploring the commonalty of the central themes that the media chose to highlight, both in the written and visual text, in its coverage of the story. I looked at five newspapers – the *Sun*, the *Daily Mirror*, the *Daily Express*, the *Daily Mail*, *The Times* – over a three-day period from when the story first broke (28, 29, 30 June 1995).

Hugh Grant: Colonial Figure of the 1990s – 'I Did Something Insane' (*The Times*, 28 June 1995)

Despite this paper's concern with racialised femininities these cannot be fully explored without reference to Hugh Grant. This is significant in that it demonstrates how femininities are constructed and defined in relation to masculinity and male behaviour. More specifically, however, it was via media coverage of Hugh Grant's actions and media interpretations as to the reasons for this behaviour that became the site in which antithetical images of black femininity and white femininity were constructed and (re)presented to the public gaze.

One of the dominating themes that emerged in the three-day period of press coverage which I researched was the *why* of Hugh Grant's actions. Crucially there was a distinction in this speculation which occurred in terms of not questioning Grant paying a woman for sex but questioning *which* woman he paid to have sex with him. This shared theme can be understood as containing a subtext in which there is the seemingly non-articulated articulation of racist myths and stereotypes of black women and black femininity in which black female (permissive) sexuality is a key element. For example, under the headline 'Sex Shame *Four Weddings and a Funeral* Star Lies Low as His *Stunning Model* Girlfriend Vows to Stand by Him' (my emphasis), the *Sun* stated that 'Grant's choice of street tart astonished US reporters, he could have sat at a bar and had action in three minutes' (29 June 1995). Similarly (if more extensively) the *Mirror* reported how:

> Grant, the image of the courteous English gentleman, had just finished filming his new movie when he visited a seedy LA red-light area ... the millionaire star ... didn't choose the bright lights of West Hollywood where sex can cost more than a £1000. Instead he drove along Sunset Boulevard into 'Bargain Basement City' where the goods for sale are rough trade.
>
> (28 June 1995)

What is significant here is the identification of the environment in which Brown worked. The emphasis that the media placed on geographical location can be understood as part of a process which moves focus away from Divine Brown herself, as an individual, and instead transforms her into a collective representation of the US inner city and all its attendant (racialised) social problems. In an article head-lined 'Life on Sleazy Street' the *Sun* tells of how 'hundreds of hookers in tight shorts and see-through tops line the street and regularly flash their breasts at motorists. Many became prostitutes to feed an addiction to crack. Most are under 25 and are black or Central American' (29 June 1995). The *Mirror* similarly stated that:

> In West Hollywood the hookers wear Hermes and look like extras from a Playboy video. But three miles downtown is the seedy sex shopping district ... most of the hookers working this area come from the barrio or the ghetto – Latinos or blacks looking for a fistful of dollars to support children, pimps, crack-addicted husbands, mothers, cousins or merely themselves.
>
> (28 June 1995)

The visuals that accompanied these articles play an important role in this process of presenting Divine Brown as a symbolic figure of urban malaise. For example the *Mirror* article was accompanied by two photographs. The first and larger picture showed Liz Hurley close up and beautiful. She is wearing a black suit and sunglasses; in the background the viewer is able to discern an obviously expensive environment epitomised by the hanging shop sign of 'Draycotts Wine Bar'. The smaller picture next to this is not of Divine Brown but instead shows three women in the far distance; two are women of colour, the third is white. All three are standing on the curbside and appear to be working the street amidst busy traffic. The area is obviously poor summed up by the (equivalent) background shop sign which states it is a 'Coin Laundry'.

The linked theme of amazement at who Grant paid for sex, and the environment which Brown inhabited, was not confined to the tabloid papers. For example, *The Times* also reported the story within the same framework:

> What Hugh Grant sought in the early hours of Tuesday morning was a kind of *quick, dark, utterly anonymous gratification* that makes the fictional antics of 'Pretty Woman' and even the real ones arranged by Heidi Fleiss, the convicted Hollywood madam, seem almost *civilised*.
>
> (29 June 1995; my emphasis)

The use of the word 'civilised' to describe white women who work (either fictionally or actually) in the sex industry is significant because of its racial and colonial connotations, especially when placed beside the description of the kind of sex that Grant did choose to buy (from a black woman), i.e. 'quick, dark, utterly anonymous gratification'. The racial subtext can be seen to continue in the same article:

> It was not a notable club that he [Grant] joined, and for Britain's most debonair and dashing export since David Niven it could hardly have been more horrendously unsuitable. This is why the reaction was first incredulous. Friends called the police version of Grant's darkest hour improbable, pointing out the only witness was a prostitute who stands to make a fortune from her story.
>
> (*ibid.*)

The extract is interesting because of the ways in which it seamlessly merges a number of themes, most obviously Britishness and the incompatibility of this Britishness with paid sex with an African–American woman in an inner-city environment. This incompatibility can be seen by the use of the terms 'horrendously unsuitable', 'incredulous' reactions, responses that the whole episode was 'improbable', this latter notion itself buttressed by the (old) sexist notion of who can believe a story told by a woman (particularly a 'deviant' woman). The incredulous–improbable theme was extended further by the early media rumours that Divine Brown was actually a transsexual:

'Actor Hugh Grant has been caught with a prostitute who could be a man' (*Express*, 28 June 1995); 'Sources in LAPD said Ms Brown was a known prostitute. The sources denied rumours that she was a transsexual' (*The Times*, 28 June 1995).

The theme of nation threads through the media accounts of Hugh Grant. His embodiment of a particular and traditional form of (upper-class) Englishness is continually played upon as a means of emphasising the bizarreness of the incident. Grant, whose fame as an actor rests very much on his portrayal of a caricature of Englishness, appears to inhabit this role in 'real life'. In media terms he is 'Britain's most dashing and debonair export'; he is 'the image of the courteous English gentleman'; he is the 'upper-crust actor'; he 'oozes English charm'; he is 'the actor who has epitomised 1990s style upper-class English glamour'. In this way a quintessential, neo-colonial Englishness is contrasted with the economically desperate and socially dangerous other(ed) world embodied by Divine Brown. It is the process that creates a context in which the media, and Hugh Grant himself, explain the entire incident in terms of temporary madness, an 'act of insanity' (*The Times*, 28 June 1995). In other words it is beyond a rational understanding. It is certainly not seen as relating, albeit as a footnote, to the (historical) systematic sexual exploitation of (poor) women of colour by (wealthy) white men (hooks, 1982; Davis, 1981). The 'act of insanity' interpretation of Grant's behaviour also acts to partially conceal the historical desire/disgust fantasy for the black female body in the white imagination (Young, 1995). I argue partially because the now-famous head-and-shoulders LAPD pictures of Grant and Brown, criminalised and numbered, can be read as public evidence of the perils of miscegenation. While the LAPD photograph of Brown evokes cultural and common-sense notions of black criminality, the LAPD photograph of Grant works as a visual 'penalty' of the (potential) cost incurred for white men who sexually transgress racial barriers.

Divine Brown: Desire and Repulsion – 'Red-light girlie' (*Express*, 28 June 1995); 'Hugh and the Hooker' (*Mail*, 28 June 1995); '£15 Hooker' (*Mirror*, 28 June 1995)

As I argued above, the media focus on Divine Brown moved between her as an individual and her as a collective representation of African–Americans. This section of the chapter concentrates on media (re)presentations of Divine Brown as an individual. Media constructions as to what Divine Brown was relied heavily on emphasising her difference from both Grant and Hurley. The measurement of Divine Brown against Elizabeth Hurley can be understood as being part of the dichotomous devaluation–exoticisation process that I outlined earlier. So while populist constructions of Divine Brown in the media drew heavily on racist myths and stereotypes of black womanhood, femininity and sexuality, these were intrinsically, and often crudely, tied into the notion of Liz Hurley as being the opposite.

The themes which dominated the (re)presentation of Brown rested primarily on Brown being a prostitute, on Brown's physical body and dress, on the price she charged for having sex with Grant and on the kind of sex she performed with Grant. Succinctly combining all these elements, the *Mirror* noted how:

> Ten-stone hooker Divine Brown, 23, dressed in short skirt, stockings, suspenders and high heels emerged from the shadows and negotiated a price, probably about £15. Vice squad officers watched as 5ft 4inches Brown, a convicted black prostitute ... performed oral sex on 34-year-old Grant.
>
> (28 June 1995)

This extract is interesting as it is able to fluently connect a number of racialised themes: preoccupation with the black physique and black body has long been a central tenet of racist discourse (see Butler, 1993 for a powerful exploration of this); the reference to 'emerging from the shadows' implies the 'dark', 'twilight' Other terrain to which Brown belongs, and in which she operates; her identity as a prostitute is reaffirmed in that she has been 'convicted' for selling sex prior to the Grant episode, the cheapness of the price Grant paid significantly locates her at the bottom of the constructed hierarchy of prostitution, and the emphasis on the type of sex act itself is important. Within (hetero)sexual imaginations oral sex can be understood as being perceived as one of the 'harder' or more 'deviant' sex acts. It is no coincidence that, in the abuse myself and my former lover received, it was the image of my performing oral sex that was used to attack us – my 'deviancy' in having sexual relations with a black man was extended into my performing 'deviant' sexual practices. The wide reporting of Brown performing oral sex on Grant can be interpreted in two ways which both demonstrate a duality in terms of what Divine Brown represents in populist discourse. First, the oral sex emphasis can be seen as having been racially eroticised, i.e. linked with notions of black women being sexually abandoned and permissive. The second, more complex, interpretation can be linked with miscegenation fears of the black body and the notion that a woman's mouth represents a (symbolic) castration danger to a man in that the mouth has the teeth which the vagina lacks. The white penis in a black woman's mouth can represent the white man in the ultimately powerful position *and* represent the white man in an ultimately vulnerable position. It is within the latter reading that Hugh Grant's experiences were predominantly located.

Visual depictions of both Divine Brown and Liz Hurley in the media coverage were central to the dichotomous constructions of womanhood and femininity. The amount of pictures of both women compared to those of Hugh Grant is significant in itself, reflecting the (sexist) emphasis on women's physical appearances. Again studying the types of pictures of both women can be seen as a revealing process in which Hurley is systematically associated with a particular feminine sexuality and Brown with a unambiguous physical sexuality. While *The Times*, *Mail* and *Express* all tended to rely on the LAPD head-and-shoulders photograph of Divine Brown, the *Mirror* and the *Sun* used a more diverse selection of photographs of Brown. Specific construction themes can also be discerned in these pictures. In both these papers Brown was visually directly placed next to pictures of Liz Hurley. For example the *Mirror* (30 June 1995) carried a full-length close-up shot of Liz Hurley, beautiful in a obviously expensive (Versace) green suit and high heels. Her gaze is away from the camera, which serves to emphasise her sadness and dignity. In an equivalent full-length picture of Divine Brown, Brown is wearing knee-length black leather boots, black lace knickers and a small bra-top, with a leather overcoat pulled seductively to one side. In other words she is dressed in clothing appropriate to being a 'prostitute'. As opposed to Hurley's sad, away-from-the-camera gaze, Brown smiles alluringly and directly at the camera. In a more direct counterpoising of the two women the *Sun* (29 June 1995) also uses two full-length pictures of both women side by side under the headline 'How Could Hugh?'. Hurley is shown looking directly at the camera, her expression serious. She is wearing a shoulder-strap, glitter evening dress. Divine Brown is photographed at a slight angle. She (cheekily) looks, from the corner of her eyes at the camera. She is wearing a white mini-skirt suit with a shirt knotted over her stomach and a white bowler hat. Accompanying each photograph is separate text which in bullet points works through a series of equivalent variables for each woman: age, height, body, home, love life, money, dress, tattoo, favourite spots, work, prospects. It is a crude exercise in the constructions of difference that works on the axis of both class and race. For example under the heading 'favourite spots' the reader is told of how Hurley 'enjoys dining at Princess Diana's best-loved restaurant San Lorenzo in Knightsbridge and loves attending film premieres, fashion lunches and exclusive celebrity parties'. Under the same heading we are told that Divine Brown's favourite place is 'the junction of Sunset Boulevard and Gardener, the heart of LA's red-light district'.

In the following day's issue the *Sun* carried a two-page spread. Beside an article headed 'Liz's Love For Hugh Is on Hold – Models's Bid To Blot Out Shame' there is a '*Sun* picture exclusive' titled 'Grant's Hooker on the Job'. The two features have to be analysed in relation to each other. While Hurley is associated with the key words of 'love' and 'shame', four photographs supposedly show Divine Brown's life; visual representations in which such 'pure' emotions as 'love' and 'shame' do not remotely feature; nor could they be associated with her life. The first photograph is a full-length picture of Brown titled 'Streetwise ... touting for trade on Sunset Boulevard'. The second shows Brown in the near distance, arms spread wide, entitled 'Bikini girl ... scanty outfit under leather jacket in Los Angeles'. The third picture shows Divine Brown with two other African–American women and carries the title 'Vice sisters'. The final picture has Brown lying on a table, her legs apart, with the caption 'Leg show ... she sprawls on hotel table at a wild Las Vegas Party'. The accompanying text provides more detail of this particular picture:

she sprawls on a table clad in white hot pants and black stockings with her legs spread wide apart and holding an ankle in each hand ... the picture was taken at a raunchy party where vice girls went wild after a busy night on the streets. A friend joked 'this view of Divine is one which her punters will remember well'.

(*Sun*, 30 June 1995)

The visual images operate within a highly racialised context, evoking the combined stereotypes of black women as sexually available and as having an uncontrolled sexuality. These images also serve to infantalise the women pictured, representing them very much within a primitavist (uncivilised) framework.

The media coverage of Divine Brown is dominated by the all-embracing identity it affords her, i.e. of black hooker. However, this identity contains a multiplicity of inter-related themes and is rendered more complex by white fascination which dialectically (desire/disgust) fantasises about the black female body and inter-racial sexual contact. In contrast Hurley is afforded a range of sanitised identities – actress, model, loyal girlfriend, innocent woman, wronged woman, and beautiful tragic heroine. As Brown's 'hooker' identity is fundamentally race-d, Hurley's multiple identities can be understood as centring on her whiteness. In other words, Hurley's 'innocence', beauty and 'pure' femininity are just as race-d.

Elizabeth Hurley: Tragedy and Femininity – 'I'm So Sad, So Alone' (*Sun*, 30 June 1995); 'Bewildered and Alone' (*The Times*, 30 June 1995); 'I Will Stand By My Man' (*Express*, 29 June 1995)

The media (re)presentations of Elizabeth Hurley were played out very much in the ideological framework of white womanhood and white femininity. Just as Brown came to be a collective symbol of black femininity so Hurley acted and powerfully worked as a symbol of white femininity. Similarly as Brown was measured against Hurley so Hurley was measured against Brown on a racialised axis of polemic difference. The central themes that the media mined in its ideological construction of Hurley were her idealised beauty, her tragedy and her loyalty in the face of betrayal. Ultimately Hurley became collapsed into the concepts of civilisation, refinement, goodness and purity; concepts that cannot be associated with Brown and concepts which themselves can be collapsed into a racialised notion of Englishness. It is important to note that the media's deployment of these themes operated as much on a visual level as well as within the written text. In all five newspapers studied, in the numerous and varied pictures of Hurley the reader/audience is presented with her idealised beauty and glamour in a way that serves to emphasise her tragedy and isolation. The text which accompanies these pictures also incorporates this duality. The reader/audience is informed with the details of her physical appearance and mental health. For example, the *Mirror* (29 June 1995) shows Hurley surrounded by men walking towards an expensive car. The caption with this story reads 'Silent Liz Near To Tears' and goes on to state that:

> The 29-year-old actress looked pale and gaunt behind sunglasses and heavy make-up as minders led her to a waiting Mercedes. Liz in a £2000 lilac pink two-piece Versace suit kept her head down and

refused to answer questions and looked bewildered as she was driven away.

In these pictures Hurley never looks directly at the camera, her gaze is always into the distance and grave. Both her initial silence after the story broke and the content of her ensuing statement reinforce her dignity. This statement is itself highly significant:

> I am bewildered and saddened by recent events ... I am very much alone. ... This is all very painful for me and if members of the press could find it in their hearts to give me some time to think, I would be very grateful.
>
> (*The Times*, 30 June 1995)

Hurley's words, made more appealing by their incorporation of sadness and isolation, perfectly evoke a (white) woman at a loss, unable to comprehend the circumstances that have overtaken her life.[5] Not surprisingly the statement offered the press rich pickings for headlines: 'I'm All Alone and So Sad – Liz Tells of Heartache' (*Mirror*, 30 June 1995); 'I'm So Alone, Bewildered and Sad – Anguished Liz Hints it May Be Over with Hugh' (*Express*, 30 June 1995); 'I'm Bewildered and Alone: I Have Not Been in a Fit State to Make Decisions' (*The Times*, 30 June 1995); 'I'm So Sad, So Alone – My Pain over Hugh by Heartbroken Liz' (*Sun*, 30 June 1995). The accompanying pictures of the serious, sad and 'perfect' face of Hurley are visual metaphors for what in this context become essentially *noble* emotions (loneliness, sadness, heartbreak). Yet it is Hurley's professed state of 'bewilderment' that is the emotion that is most successfully transferred into the public arena – the subtext of this bewilderment for both Hurley and the media rests on the question – How could Grant, when he had (possessed) Hurley, 'choose' Brown? The *Sun* relocates this question from its subtextual level when it asks: 'How could he choose tough old mutton when he had a tender frisky lamb at home?' (29 June 1995). Yet it is in the very nature of this 'questioning' of Grant's behaviour that it is again possible to read the dialectic of desire and repulsion in terms of the disdain shown towards Brown and the exoneration of Hurley – as Young (1995: 149) notes, 'disgust always bears the imprint of desire'.

Class, money and geography, all intertwined, also pervaded the media configurations of Hurley. Many of the papers referenced in detail Hurley's friends who were supporting her through her crisis:

The son of Tory rebel MP Bill Cash is among Liz's small group of close friends ... they include aristocrat Henry Brocklehurst, heir to Smedley Castle. Liz fled to Henry's home in London's Kensington when the scandal broke. Henry, son of Lord and Lady Ashcombe, said yesterday 'there's no question of them splitting up'.

(*Mirror*, 29 June 1995)

Hurley is thus located within the higher echelons of the English class system. Hurley's secure (public) place in 'high society' not only emphasised her Englishness but also her distance from Brown's unambiguous underclass location. Hurley's position in 'high society' is also underlined by her model identity and her employment contract as the 'face' of the huge cosmetics company Estee Lauder. In the same way geographical distance between Hurley (alone) in (rich) areas of London and Brown and Grant in the (troubled) city of Los Angeles works on a metaphoric level that symbolises the gulf (as large and deep as the Atlantic Ocean) between the two women and their antithetical forms of femininity. The humanity that is afforded Hurley which is so devoid in the (re)presentations of Brown is epitomised in the picture carried on the front page of *The Times* (30 June 1995). This shows a full-length shot of Hurley, not significantly in Versace suit or sunglasses, but in jeans and a checked shirt walking a dog in woods, captioned 'Bewildered and alone, Liz Hurley walking her dog, Nico, near her Avon home after issuing a statement after the arrest of her boyfriend Hugh Grant'. Again the Englishness of Hurley and geographical place (woods in the English countryside) are ideologically evoked to signify her actual and symbolic distance from both Divine Brown and a 'dangerous' urban landscape.

CONCLUSIONS

Purity, innocence, loyalty, sadness were the key themes in the populist construction of Hurley as a *civilised* white woman. These themes were heavily racialised in that they were systematically associated with Hurley in a way that they were systematically disassociated with Divine Brown. This was illustrated in media speculation as to the money that Brown stood to make by exploiting Hurley's 'heartache'. For example, the *Sun* declared that Brown 'stands to earn thousands from the two-minute liaison with Hugh Grant. American tabloid magazines and TV shows are offering upwards of £75,000 for her account of events in Hugh's car' (29 June 1995).

Although the polemic constructions of Hurley and Brown operated along a binary line or through an essentially simplistic dichotomous process, the means by which indicators were employed as symbols of goodness and badness were often complex and subtextual. In other words the whole event was racialised in an often race-'silent' way. The media coverage invites its audience to empathise with Hurley's 'pain', 'anguish', 'heartbreak'; identify Brown as black Other, an object of deviance and danger (but also of fascination) and explain Grant's actions in relation to Divine Brown in terms of 'insanity'.

Whiteness, white womanhood and white femininity have long played a consistent, if shifting, central role in racialised discourse. The Hurley/ Grant/Brown incident demonstrated that they continue to have currency in contemporary configurations of race and gender and that they can successfully operate in a populist arena. Hurley and Grant as white people occupied a racialised place as much as did Brown. However, while Brown's racialised identity drew on racist myths and stereotypes embodied in the identity afforded her as a 'hooker' she is also sur- rounded by a subtext which revolves around (racialised) attraction/desire and repulsion/fear of the black body. Hurley and Grant were racialised in less obvious ways, through notions of Englishness and geographical place and through concepts of innocence and through acts of 'insanity'. In other words it is harder to read the racialisation of whiteness because whiteness is the normless norm against which blackness is easily meas- ured and defined as Other, thereby occupying 'a racial category with all its attendant meanings' (Ware, 1992: 18).

NOTES

1. Given the specific focus on Divine Brown in this chapter I use the term 'black' to refer to people of African–American and African–Caribbean descent. I use the term 'people or women of colour' to refer to broader groups of people who are also racialised with social relations.
2. For the purposes of this chapter I have used the newspaper media as a key arena in which populist discourse is generated.
3. Significantly, a year after the event these antithetical constructions con tinued. Liz Hurley filled the public landscape advertising the ('noble') Red Cross organisation while Divine Brown remained locked in her sexually deviant location as she appeared on British television chat shows to promote the (pornographic) movie (in which she stars) of the event (*Richard Littlejohn Show*, June 1996).

4. Their Englishness and the related notion of nation was made all the more acute by the broader context in which the story broke. It was reported alongside coverage of the Tory Party leadership campaign and one of the hottest Junes on record.
5. It is significant that this statement echoes that made by Princess Diana after her separation from Prince Charles. Both women embody a specifically English white femininity (Ware, 1992).

REFERENCES

Ahmed, S. (1997) '"It's a sun-tan isn't it?": Auto-biography as Identificatory Practice', in H. Mirza (ed.), *British Black Feminism* (London: Routledge).
Anthias, F. and Yuval-Davis, N. (1992) *Racialised Boundaries: Race, Nation, Colour, Class and the Anti-racist Struggle* (London: Routledge).
Brah, A. (1993) '"Race" and "Culture" in the Gendering of Labour Markets: South Asian Young Muslim Women and the Labour Market', *New Community*, 19(3), pp. 441–58
Brah, A. (1996) *Cartographies of Diaspora: Contesting Identities* (London: Routledge).
Butler, J. (1993) 'Endangered/Endangering: Schematic Racism and White Paranoia', in R. Gooding-Williams (ed.), *Reading Rodney King: Reading Urban Uprising* (London: Routledge).
Campbell, C. (1995) *Race, Myth and the News* (London: Sage).
Carby, H. (1982) 'White Woman Listen! Black Feminism and the Boundaries of Sisterhood', in CCCS, *The Empire Strikes Back* (London: Hutchinson).
Cohen, P. and Gardner, C. (eds) (1982) *It Ain't Half Racist Mum* (London: Comedia).
Dadzie, S., Bryan, B. and Scafe, S. (1986) *Heart of the Race: Black Women's Lives in Britain* (London: Virago).
Davis, A. (1981) *Women, Race and Class* (London: Women's Press).
Eisenstein, Z. (1996) *Hatreds: Racialised and Sexualised Conflicts in the 21st Century* (London: Routledge).
Frankenberg, R. (1993) *The Social Construction of Whiteness: White Women, Race Matters* (London: Routledge).
Gilroy, P. (1993) *Small Acts: Thoughts on the Politics of Black Cultures* (London: Serpents Tail).
Hartmann, P. and Husbands, C. (1974) *Racism and the Mass Media* (London: Davis-Poytner).
Hill-Collins, P. (1990) *Black Feminist Thought* (London: Hyman).
hooks, b. (1982) *Ain't I a Black Woman* (London: Pluto).
hooks, b. (1989) *Talking Back: Thinking Feminist, Thinking Black* (London: South End Press).
hooks, b. (1994) *Outlaw Culture: Resisting Representations* (London: Routledge).
Mama, A. (1992) 'Black Women and the British State: Race, Class and Gender Analysis for the 1990s', in P. Braham, A. Rattansi and R. Skellington (eds), *Racism and Antiracism: Inequalities, Opportunities and Policies* (London: Sage).

Mama, A. (1993) 'Black Women and the Police: a Place Where the Law is Not Upheld', in W. James and C. Harris (eds), *Inside Babylon: The Caribbean Diaspora in Britain* (London: Verso).

Mirza, H. (ed.) (1997) *British Black Feminism* (London: Routledge).

Nkweto Simmonds, F. (1997) 'My Body, Myself: How does a Black Woman Do Sociology?', in H. Mirza (ed.), *British Black Feminism* (London: Routledge).

Parmar, P. (1981) 'Young Asian Women: a Critique of the Pathological Approach', *Multiracial Education*, 9(3), pp. 19–29.

Rich, A. (1979) *On Lies, Secrets and Silence: Selected Prose 1966–1978* (New York: Norton).

Rich, A. (1986) *Blood, Bread and Poetry: Selected Prose, 1979–1985* (New York: Norton).

Solomos, J. and Back, L. (1996) *Racism and Society* (London: Macmillan).

van Dijk, T. D. (1991) *Racism and the Press* (London: Routledge).

Ware, V. (1992) *Beyond the Pale: White Women, Racism and History* (London: Verso).

Williams, P. (1992) *The Alchemy of Race and Rights* (London: Virago).

Young, R. (1995) *Colonial Desire: Hybridity in Theory, Culture and Race* (London: Routledge).

6 Whiter Shades of Pale: Media-Hybridities of Rodney King

JOOST VAN LOON

INTRODUCTION

> The visual representation of the black male body being beaten on the street by the policemen and their batons was taken up by the racist interpretative framework to construe King as the *agent* of violence, one whose agency is phantasmatically implied as the narrative precedent and antecedent to the frames that are shown. Watching King, the white paranoiac forms a sequence of narrative intelligibility that consolidates the racist figure of the black man.
>
> (Butler, 1993: 16)

This chapter addresses the problematic of racial identification in relation to violence. More specifically, it focuses on the role of television as a technology of 'racialisation'. The objective is to provide a re-conceptualisation of violence, identity and race by problematising prevailing symbolic associations which organise most discourses on racial violence, but in particular those mobilised in news coverage of urban disorders. The argument I pursue is that *mediation* is the primary practice/process of violent identifications which constitutes rather than uncovers the logic of racialised violence. It is through mediation that racial matrices are imposed on the *sensibility* of such events as urban uprisings. The analysis evolves around the case of a videotaped beating of a Black motorist, Rodney King, by four White police officers in Los Angeles on the 3 March 1991 and the subsequent acquittal of these officers in court, by a nearly all-White jury on 29 April 1992.

The argument is based on a semiotic analysis of the formations of 'race' in the television news coverage of the 1992 Los Angeles 'riots' that immediately followed the acquittal (Van Loon, 1995). Focusing on denotation/connotation, intertextuality, chronotopicity, narrativity and discursivity, the objective of this study was to trace the racialised identity formations that emerged as the giving of an account of 'what happened' in the form of television images, sounds and texts. What appears to be the central focus of most news coverage is the function of '*race*' as a device that has been mobilised to account for the phenomena associated with rioting (for example as Black-on-White violence) and to organise explanations of the causes of such rioting.

The relationship between the acquittal and the Los Angeles riots has generally been perceived within news broadcasts as a shift from the world of opinions and ideas to that of brutal physical force (Fiske, 1994; Swenson, 1995; Van Loon, 1995). The symbolic associations in which this shift has been embedded, however, are deeply racialised. The racial element involved in the transformation of outrage (symbolic violence) to (physical) 'violence' becomes more clear perhaps when taking into account the reversed process: the transformation of the physical violence of the beating of Rodney King into the symbolic violence of the acquittal of those responsible for the assault. This justification of violence is part of the same aforementioned race struggle because it was performed by a nearly all-*White* jury, to *clear* four *White* policemen. Both police and jury are 'authorities' that function in an imagined community of which 'whiteness' is the norm. In the force exercised by these authorities resides a reconstitution of this whiteness by asserting that such violence is legitimate when it is used to *reinforce* law and order, i.e. the norms.

RACIALISATION THROUGH MYTHIFICATION

Elsewhere (Van Loon, 1995) I have argued that the televisual mediation of riots often involves a *mythification* of rioters which evacuates the *sense* from rioting and replaces it with meaning-formations that are discursively pre-constituted and therefore taken for granted.[1] This corresponds with findings of other studies (Fiske, 1994; Gooding-Williams, 1993; Keith, 1991, 1993; Lewis, 1982; Solomos, 1988; Swenson, 1995; Trew, 1979; Van Dijk, 1991). Mythification turns race into an essence and negates the very construction this entails. One particular element of mythification that I will consider more closely here is the symbolic association between violence and race: violence is identified within a racial matrix. As Houston Baker (1993: 40) has argued, violence is always–already racialised, for example in the silence of the slave before 'his' master. In the television news coverage of the 1992 Los Angeles uprisings it returned in two forms: as a lack of law and order and as a lack of (economic, political, social, cultural, racial) integration.

The association between race and violence as a *lack of law and order* appears, for example, in accounts of rioting as expressions of a lack of concern for property and people, opportunist gang-related crimes and racial antagonisms. These associations of race and violence belong to what Justin Lewis (1982) has termed the *law and order discourse*. In this view violence is the equivalent of disorder, a lack of order, whose causal structure can be attributed to race itself or, more precisely, to racial difference – the difference of race. The pertinence of race in accounts of violence as a lack of order can even be traced in explanations of riots which have no clearly articulated racial structure. For example in the disturbances on the Marsh Farm estate in Luton (7–9 July 1995) and in the Hyde Park area of Leeds (11–12 July 1995), where 'youths' were mainly held responsible, the causal attributes were predominantly sought in the 'incompleteness' of these youths which made them susceptible to 'criminal tendencies' (Van Loon, 1995). This incompleteness was not accounted for itself, but treated as a cause that presented itself in a lack of respect for law and order. Although not racialised in terms of skin colour, the racial matrix of modernity was clearly present in the symbolic association between incompleteness, violence and a lack of respect for law and order. This association is prolific in descriptions of 'rioters' and 'criminals' as a specific *'breed'* (type, stock, *race*) of people.

Closely related to the aforementioned law and order discourse is the second prominent discursive formation to which journalists and presenters often resort, to account for racialised violence in the television news coverage of disorders. This formation pictures disorders as conditioned by socioeconomic deprivation; social, cultural and political marginality, the breakdown of families, communities, and societies; racism, and a lack of racial integration. These can roughly be grouped together in what Michael Keith (1991, 1993) has termed *Social Problems Discourse*. Here violence is the equivalent of *lack itself*, that is a lack of social, cultural, political, economic, racial *integration*. Explanations and interpretations that draw on this type of discourse always deliver their accounts as attempts to uncover deeper, often hidden, causes of rioting. In contrast to law and order discourse, advocates of social problems discourse thus reject the assumption that rioting phenomena can be understood as such, and instead offer a symptomatic reading of such events as the effects (appearances) of other forces. Instead of a lack of respect for law and order, lack is addressed in terms of socialisation, integration, or equality. However, racialisation is as prominent as in the first type, since within the historicity of modernisation there is an emphasis on an association between racial difference and differential civilisation and cultural values (Goldberg, 1993). Racial difference is thus the equivalent of a lack of culture, civility and socialisation.

Once made the equivalent of lack, violence is mobilised as a discursive object to *make sense* of these disorders as a negativity that must be countered, both in terms of the legitimate force of the authority (state) and the symbolic force of 'meaningfulness' upon which the media principally operate. When law and order discourses proliferate, the 'combat' of lack is likely to be more coercive and repressive than when social problems discourses are more prominent (Keith, 1991; Solomos, 1988). Although this difference is certainly significant in political terms, it takes place on an identical fundamental assumption: racial difference equals lack equals violence. This *logic of equivalence* engenders an identification of violence as a designated set of practices associated with race in very particular terms. However, because intricately linked to 'lack', the relationship between violence and race remains itself rather elusive. Moreover, the logic of equivalence operates on the assumption that it is possible to separate the violence that is associated with disorder from the violence that is mobilised to restore order. To be more precise, the logic of equivalence grants itself the capacity and legitimacy to distinguish illegitimate from legitimate violence. This thus assumes that violence 'is' embodied in a finite set of phenomena that can be *identified* and *judged* as (il)legitimate. However, I want to argue that this claim itself is highly problematic.

VIOLENCE AND JUDGEMENT: THE BEATING OF RODNEY KING

The best way to problematise the relationship between violence and racialisation in the context of media-discourse is to look at a series of events following the beating of a Black motorist named Rodney King, by four white Los Angeles police officers, on the evening of 3 March 1991. Rodney King was stopped by officers of Los Angeles highway patrol, after a high-speed chase. As soon as he was forced out of the car, four Los Angeles police officers took over the responsibility of the arrest by delivering 56 blows on Mr King's head, body and limbs in a beating that took 81 seconds before he was handcuffed and taken to the hospital with severe injuries to his head, body and legs. However, the officers did not know that this beating was accidentally videotaped from a balcony by an amateur cameraman, who was trying out his new camera (Baker, 1993; Fiske, 1994; Swenson, 1995). As soon as he discovered what he had recorded, he went to a local police station where he was told that the police were not interested. He then went to a local television station, which immediately broadcast the tape in full. As we now know, the rest is history.

When the prosecution brought charges against the officers, it was thought that the trial should not be held in LA itself because of possible bias against the defendants, and the venue was subsequently changed to Simi Valley, a 96 per cent White suburban city on the north of Los Angeles in Ventura County. The prosecution brought the issue of the beating towards an almost-white jury (10 out of 12; the other two were a Korean and a Latino) under the format of the question whether the beating was a case of excessive violence (as the prosecution argued) or reasonable force (as the defence argued). The result of the trial is well known. The jury unanimously decided the videotape showed that the officers were using reasonable force under the collar/colour of authority and acquitted the policemen on all but one charge.

The extraordinary aspect of the case was not the beating, but the fact that it was videotaped and that the videotape was broadcast, nationwide and indeed worldwide. The violence that was being displayed seemed real beyond any reasonable doubt. The jury in court, however, judged differently: it was not an act of violence but a display of authorised procedure. The difference is conceived as a question of legitimacy: violence that is legitimate is not identified as violence but as reasonable force. The task facing the media after the trial was to attune the intuitive truth of the videotaped images (the policemen are guilty) with those of the prevailing judgements (the policemen are innocent). Hence, the question that most pundits raised immediately after the trial was 'how' this verdict could be possible? Did we not see with our very own eyes that the beating was excessive? What we thought of as *seeing*, i.e. excessive violence, was interpreted as 'reasonable force'. How can we explain this rupture between 'our' intuition and this verdict?

THE LOGIC OF THE VERDICT

Although much has been written about the way in which the jury achieved a reading of the videotape that led to the acquittal of the four police officers (Baker, 1993; Butler, 1993; Fiske, 1994; Gilmore, 1993; Gooding Williams, 1993; Lipsitz, 1994; Williams, 1993), it is necessary to repeat some of the analyses, to understand the complex mechanism by which the jury came to interpret the videotaped beating as an enactment of reasonable force and the role that can be attributed to the racial matrix of 'identification'.

First, it must be made clear that the jury never appropriated an explicitly racist stance, for example by stating that the beating was justified because Rodney King was Black. However, this exactly provided the implicit reasoning behind the acquittal. In other words, whereas 'race' was removed from the explicit interpretation of the videotape in court, this repression returned as the essense of understanding the beating. The whitewash of the beating was thus simultaneously a whitewash of the American justice system. What effectively took place was a whitewash not only of the racism behind police brutality, but also that behind the verdict itself. This was done in three ways: (1) the negation of the videotape in exchange for the story of the police officers; (2) the argument that the videotape is as such an incomplete *piece* of evidence; (3) the affirmation that the videotape was evidence of the officers' innocence.

The first whitewash (negation) can be found in the following statement by a member of the jury:

> Everybody is saying 'this videotape, this videotape' but these officers have a job to do and in doing that job they have to be given a certain amount of reasonable and that's what this is you know, reasonable force.
>
> (ABC Evening News, 30 April 1992)

This juror thus denies the denotation of the videotaped images any jurisdiction over the decision whether the beating was an exercise of reasonable force. It is not that she does not see the violence being exercised, nor really calls into question its excessiveness. Instead, her reasonability itself is an *aesthetic of rationality* (Baker, 1993) that goes beyond the intuitive sensation of violence exercised onto a defenceless body and enters that of the Black skin itself. The disclaimer of the reality of the image is realised via 'but these officers have a job to do'.

This indeed indicates that what is displayed by the videotape is at odds with the (narrative and discursive) 'reality' of policing as *doing a job*. The job requires 'reasonable force' which does not show itself in the videotape of the beating. What is intuitively encountered with the videotaped beating as a violent enactment is thus negated by means of a symbolic reference to a different logic: that of policing 'the likes of Rodney King' (an expression used by one of the defence attorneys), i.e. Black people. Such a negation thus requires a denial of intuition in an embrace of reason, which itself is fed by the very sensationality (rather than sensibility) of Rodney King's skin colour. For example, many African–Americans on the special edition of the Oprah Winfrey Show (5 May 1992) made clear that they believed such a beating would be viewed differently if the victim had been White, or if more jurors had been Black.[2] Just as policing Black people requires a police force with 'a certain amount of reasonable force', its subsequent spectacularisation requires a certain amount of 'reasonable symbolic force' (i.e. semiotic cleansing) to justify it.

In other words, the 'racism' appropriated in the whitewash is not one of an outright assertion of White supremacy (for then no legitimation would have been needed for the violence). Instead, by asserting the whitewash in terms of reasonable force, the jury did not deny the importance of legitimacy and ideology, and indeed actively engaged with the 'ideological resonance' of the videotape. The metaphor of whitewash is indeed already ideological. By embedding the brutality of physical violence within an ideology of 'reasonability', the whitewash effectively mobilised not the barbaric irrationality of tribalism (e.g. White supremacism), but the sophisticated appeal of modernity's enlightenment project, a judgement guided by Reason. It is this Reason that requires us to look not at the images as they are but elsewhere, in the *logos* of interpretations. *Logos* here refers to 'account' in the sense of the constitution of an ensemble of symbolic associations that, by being granted a law-like and systemic logic, becomes formally institutionalised as present. What the images 'mean' therefore is constituted in the formalised accounts that have already been prepared, because they are part of the symbolic order in which we become subjects of discourse.

However, the whitewash did not stop with this blatant negation.[3] A second more subtle approach was also taken. Here the video images were not simply denied but reappropriated as presenting a partial truth. Rationalisation was needed not to replace but to *complement* the image.[4] It was noted that 'several jurors said they were persuaded by the defence argument that the videotape did not tell the whole story and that Rodney King represented a threat to the officers' (ABC Evening News, 30 April 1992). The realism of the camera is not being betrayed when it is asserted that the videotape did not tell the whole story – the icons and indices of the image are *incomplete*. This 'whole story' had to be realised via *logos* because only then was it able to attain an aura of full completion. The completion was articulated in terms of the following aspects:

(1) the 'job' that these officers have to do, as mentioned by the juror;
(2) the policies and procedures of the LAPD and its training, as mentioned by Stacey Koon during the trial (in CBS Evening News, 29 April 1992 – also see Fiske, 1994);
(3) the events taking place before the videocamera started recording (e.g. a high-speed chase of Rodney King by highway patrol officers) as mentioned by Ron Allen (CBS Evening News, 29 April 1992);
(4) the context of the situation (Mr King was alleged to be 'gyrating' or 'on PCB or something'), as mentioned by Stacey Koon during the trial (Allen, 'L.A. Cops on Trial', 1993; Baker, 1993; Fiske, 1994);
(5) the 'history' of Rodney King (he was only a few days on parole) as mentioned by Ron Allen (CBS Evening News, 29 April 1992); and
(6) the 'history' and 'context' of Rodney King's race in relation to policing (as mentioned by ABC's Tim O'Brien in his report on the American justice system; ABC Evening News, 30 April 1992).

The completion through *logos*, that is, the settling of the account, worked in two steps. First it disconnects the video images from their own connotations and retrojects them into the rationalised narrative account of the officers themselves.[5] Secondly, it reconstitutes this re-contextualisation on the always-already preconstituted 'truth' of Blackness (of 'the likes of Rodney King') which always remains in excess of every possible counter-memory. In other words, 'race' is first erased as the silence of the Black man, Rodney King and the absence of Blackness in the jury, only to return in mythical form as an explanandum of the beating itself (the *obviousness* which allowed the jury to shed all doubts even before the trial had actually started). It is the assertion of obviousness which marks the jury's verdict as an enactment of *symbolic power* by which a particular (arbitrary) association of signifier and signified is *assigned* the status of naturalness (Bourdieu, 1982). Mythification 'completes' the image by replacing the sensibility of the violence with the obviousness of racial identification in three ways:

(i)   Propositions (1) and (2) indicate that the exercise of force – reasonable or not – is *always* endemic to the logic of policing, i.e. it is not an aberration from 'normal' practices of law enforcement but a regularity of the 'job', regulated and legitimised by the policies and procedures of the LA police department and its training programmes. This shows the symbolic power of *reflexivity* wherein a lie becomes truth because this truth was already a lie.

(ii) Propositions (3) and (4) indicate that the situation in which the officers encountered Rodney King was *already* interpreted by these officers before they commenced the attack, i.e. the 'whole story' of the case and the reason for the assault was already fully disclosed because the man in question was speeding and gyrating and 'therefore' on some sort of drug. This shows the operation of the symbolic power of *indexicality* in myth as asserting a truth that does not require verification because the incompletion of evidence is already complemented with White readings of Blackness.[6] The particularity that was indexed by the images could thus be translated into the universal truth of myth.

(iii) Propositions (5) and (6) give the wider social embedding of this *'always–already'* present(ed) interpretation' as Rodney King was Black, i.e. his Blackness represents the threat and the justification for the officer's response to this threat. This illustrates the operation of the symbolic power of *historicity*: as historicity is a self-selective fabrication (autopoiesis) of traces of memories and forgettings, it always–already sustains the emergence of particular truths as authoritative as they are by definition self-valorising.

Our juror did not hesitate to call upon this triple justification:

> They didn't know what they had. A man that is over 230 pounds and you pull him on the ground and four officers go into and put handcuffs on him and he throws those officers off?
>
>   (Juror quoted in ABC Evening News, 30 April 1992)

The first complement, reflexivity, shows itself in the way in which the identification of subject shifts from 'they' to 'you' to 'four officers' to 'he'. The juror first distances herself from the officers and subsequently joins them again by locating herself in an equivalence of opposition to Rodney King. The '230 pounds' indexes the monstrosity of this Other, whose extraordinary strength cannot be accounted for by reason alone. The question mark points to the possibility of knowing this Unknown. Since this knowing is not possible on the basis of ordinary 'reasonability', it has to be complemented with the indexicality of the event – the particularity for which universal reason does not work. Finally, the third complement allows the justification of the beating to move from the particular back to the universal. Reasonability is found again in the historicity of Blackness. The juror's primordial identification with Whiteness simultaneously provides an allocation of Otherness as threat, justifying self-defensive aggression (Butler, 1993). This is because, as Judy Muller explains:

> [t]he jurors were convinced that it was King who controlled the action; that he could have stopped the beating by surrendering. The officers they felt used reasonable force with the possible exception of one. ... The jury was made up of 10 Whites, one Hispanic and one Asian. Critics of the verdict are questioning whether this 'jury' of their peers gave the white defendants an edge and whether King's race was a factor.
>
> (Judy Muller, ABC Evening News, 30 April 1992)

There was a very peculiar ironic intonation in Judy Muller's enunciation of the word jury (shown in inverted commas). It is as if she agrees that this verdict disqualifies the system.[7] The usage of the juror's voice to articulate that the Whiteness of the jury was not the factor which distorted clear perception is perhaps less sympathetic than it might seem. With reference to the question whether Rodney King's 'race' was an issue, she replied: 'It didn't make any difference to me and I don't think it really made any difference to the other members of the jury' (quoted in ABC Evening News, 30 April 1992). The apparent colour-blindness of the juror allows her to deny that the verdict was a racially motivated decision. Of course, the effect of this overt negation of race was a disclosure of nothing but its opposite, and this was made blatantly clear by ABC's news editors themselves when they juxtaposed the juror's denial that race was a factor onto an image of the battered, injured and scarred face of Rodney King after the attack.

This finally brings me to the third whitewash: affirmation. Butler (1993) persuasively demonstrates how the defence (and the jury following their lead) interpreted the images of the beating as the foundation of the acquittal. She argues that the video was recontextualised in a white-visual paradigm to show that Rodney King was resisting his arrest, that he was in control of the entire situation until he was finally forced into submission, and that he therefore represented a threat to the officers involved. As Fiske (1994: 132–3) has argued, this *logorationality* was enabled by the various technologies of visual transformation and hybridisation of the video images (see below). Following Fiske, I define logorationality as the production of particular forms of knowledge on the basis of the power of 'the' word. As *logos* refers to the 'account' in which symbolic associations are institutionalised as a self-disclosing 'ensemble', the affix 'rationality' refers to the particular setting-into-work that such an ensemble enables. This setting into work is a form of power/knowledge or technology (know-how) that structures and directs the semiotic overcodings constitutive of the 'interpretations' in court. The logorationality of the court is discursive, its main technology is speech. Truth cannot be assumed; it does not speak for itself; it has to be spoken. For example, images of a tilted foot 'showed' (in the form of spoken words) resistance; Rodney King's movements were interpreted as running *at* Koon *not away* from Powell who was beating him with his baton. This re-construction of the images indicates that the materialisation of mediation is not exclusively a 'bias' of 'repression' or 'denial' of the event, but an active operationalisation of a truth as 'the Truth' – finalised by the 'judgement'.

The inauguration of this truth is realised by drawing on the *logos* of the preconstituted (given, obviousness) of the 'fact of Blackness' (Fanon, 1952/1986: 109–40). Evidence from the trial itself shows that the jury was more than susceptible to a carefully selected set of interpretations of the videotape, in particular those put forward by the defence attorneys and sergeant Stacey Koon. In other words, the videotape was not denied input, but was operationalised to provide exactly the 'evidence' of the officers' 'innocence'. For 'the likes of Rodney King', the tape thus became itself a technology of repressive racialisation, mobilised to provide a foundation of 'reasonable force' via visual evidence. In asserting that the officers used 'reasonable force', the jury thus actively sought to rationalise force exercised in the name of (White) Americanicity to conceal its primordiality under a veil of universalistic legitimacy.

The work of symbolic ordering, a making sense that is not only accountable to intuition but also to the logic of judgement itself, always resorts to reason. And immediately we can trace the racial matrix constituting the reasonability of the beating and the subsequent acquittal. It is therefore crucial not to repeat the same mistake, that is, to reason with the verdict on the basis of another judgement and appeal to reasonability. We must shift the ground of the conceptualisation of violence to a more immanent plane in which the meaningless of violence is not conceived of as a void that is in need of saturation with meaning, but disclosed as the very *madness of reason*.

MEDIA-HYBRIDITIES

The triple mechanism of argumentation constituting the acquittal clearly shows that the videotape that was brought to trial as the main witness for the prosecution, turned out to be a major witness for the defence. Many critics have pointed out that *seeing* itself cannot constitute an account (Butler, 1993; Crenshaw and Peller, 1993; Fiske, 1994; Gilmore, 1993; Gooding-Williams, 1993; Lipsitz, 1994; Swenson, 1995). Indeed, since vision is already embedded in particular discursive locations, the empiricist notion of reality as self-evident must be refuted. Images do not speak for themselves. However, this should not lead us to dogmatically deny all 'reality' to the videotaped beating. Albeit based on an all-too-easy acceptance of the illusion of transparency with which electronic media endow an event, intuitive reflections are not therefore without value. The critique of realism does not square with the strong intuitive *sense* that many people (myself included) had and still have, namely that the videotape does show excessive violence under the collar/colour of authority. The imperative not to deny intuition any real force is perhaps best expressed by an African–American woman featuring in ABC's main evening broadcast on 30 April 1992 saying: 'They told me what I saw on television did not happen and I am infuriated that they would think I am ignorant enough not to know what I saw.'

The aim of this section is to induce from this anger an agonistic analysis, or 'angry writing' as Michael Keith (1992) once called it. I posit that the problematic rupture between intuition and judgement regarding the beating of Rodney King and the acquittal of the four police officers must be located at the level of mediation itself. It is based on the prosecution's failure to understand the medium of video recording and the way it had been appropriated in court (for a similar argument, see Fiske, 1994). At the root of that failure lies the very notion of *judgement*.

Any claim to identify violence is based on the assumption that judgement always comes before violence and the failure to conceive judgement as itself symbolic violence. In the case of the verdict, the jury, who were assigned to the special function of judging the event, exercised symbolic violence in the form of what Lyotard has called 'the terror of the sublime'. The violence of judgement, however, also emerged in the more 'intuitive' response by journalists, academics, politicians, and others who claimed the capacity to read the violence from the videotape. This symbolic violence took the form of what Lyotard termed 'democratic despotism'; the judgement of the 'majority'.[8]

In both accounts, violence is conceived as an entity and subsequently defined as that which 'illegitimately' infringes upon the *integrity* of other entities. Hence it is up to judgement, i.e. discourse, to regulate the integrity of entities; i.e. to identify identities and – by default – violence. Two problems arise. First, as Parmenides and later Epicurus and Lucretius demonstrated, it is practically impossible to name all entities since the scope and diversity of entities is infinite (Deleuze, 1969/1990: 266–79). Kant further extended this with a logical bent that the idea to name all entities would have to be named itself and hence set into work an infinite regression, an *aporia* (1781/1988: 294). The second problem is of a more fundamental nature. If violence would itself be an entity, its integrity can only be identified *by default* as an infringement upon other entities. The identification of violence would thus always be by default and 'ad hoc'. Its 'identity' could then only be understood in opposition to that of an entity as it negates its integrity (including its 'own'). In other words, if violence were an entity, it could only be identified in this infinite representation (Deleuze, 1968/1994: 261). Hence one has to look for violence where it is not, that is, in excess of itself.

This leads me to state that if it is an entity, *violence is not*; *but*, as the videotape of the beating of Rodney King shows, *there is violence*. To grant the intuitive more credit than merely that of (pre-)judgement, it is therefore better to work through an alternative which takes the *excess* of violence as its point of departure. Violence is then not conceived of as integral to itself (an entity) but as a *differential* (a release of energy, for example as the splitting of atoms). As opposed to the integral which marks the attempt to capture the whole, the differential captures 'the essence' of transformation. This essence, however, is like the essence of a tri-angle (De Lauretis, 1989): a construct. This allows us to address and account for the intuitive anger that many people expressed in reaction to the verdict without reducing it to a (pre-) judgement or mistaken identification of 'what really happened'. It also allows us to differentiate between judgement and intuition as distinct modalities of violence.

In order to rescue intuition from judgement, we must look more closely at the variety of media that are involved in the casting of the beating and its interpretations: ... + *cars* + *bodies* + *batons* + *stunguns* + *handcuffs* + *camcorder* + *judicial discourse* + *photographs* + *television* + ... (c.f. Deleuze and Guattari, 1986). The differential of violence is not allocated to any medium in particular, but to the specific conjunctions of *media-hybridities*. This resonates Marshall McLuhan's enormously insightful comment that media-hybridisation is a release of energy in new forms in which violence is not an entity but an effect, a transgression. This is *the violence of mediation*:

> The hybrid of the meeting of two media is a moment of truth and revelation from which new form is born. For the parallel between two media holds us on the frontiers between forms that snap us out of the Narcissus-narcosis. The moment of the meeting of media is a moment of freedom and release from the ordinary trance and numbness imposed by them on our senses.
>
> (McLuhan, 1964: 63)

In short, I argue that media-hybridities generate violence and that different hybrid forms engender different forms of violence. It is not the nature of the media involved, but the specific assemblage in which they are being placed that determines the specific modalities of violence that are being set into work. Violence, operating in excess of any account that is rendered of it (logorationality), comes before judgement; it engenders judgement, because there is no judgement without mediation. Media-hybridities disclose 'truth' as an event and 'the truth of' the event; this disclosure is violence. We thus have to look at the specific hybrid constellations to understand what forms of truth and modalities of violence have been engendered in the mediation of the beating of Rodney King and the verdict. The following three media-hybridities have been central to the formation of the event that we associate with the beating of Rodney King, the acquittal and the subsequent disorders:

(1)   The first hybridity is *between the camcorder–videotape and legal discourse*. This hybridity is a very twisted one (Fiske, 1994). The ambiguity of the videotape, its blurred images and lack of voice-over, does not dwell comfortably with the mode of rationality of legal discourse which is highly autopoietic, i.e. self-generating (Teubner, 1989). Legal discourse only recognises its own constitutions as valid as a result of which its notions of truth and justice tend to be perceived as completely internal to its own discursive formations. Legal discourse requires interpretations based on binary specificity: something is or is not. The lack of singularity of perspective of the videotape makes it difficult for legal procedures to pin its meaning down into such a binary logic. Three significant modifications have therefore been applied to the videotape in order to make its hybridisation with legal discourse possible:

(a)   The images were sharpened, enlarged, mapped onto a grid to specify different segments leading to a fragmentation of the process which was further intensified by various markings and highlights, such as that of Rodney King's tilted leg which – the defence attorney suggested – shows Mr King's threatening behaviour and his refusal to submit (Butler, 1993).

(b)   This fragmentation of the videotape was intensified by the use of still frames which transformed the *flow* of violence, the bodies acting upon another, the movement of the arm–baton–body vectors, into a *spectacle* of positions. The aesthetics of the spectacle are quite different from that of the flow. Whereas in the flow bodies are actively engaged in an event of which violence is the effect, in the spectacle bodies are frozen in postures which can only index 'intentions', i.e. force. Whereas the flow consists of conjugations, the spectacle consists of constellations. The flow is (be)coming. The spectacle is a *déja-fait* (Debord, 1967/1994), indeed *passé*.

(c)   Time is reversed. The time of the spectacle is a monad and embodies the smallest possible interval in which no motion is possible. By stopping the flow, the time of interpretation and reflection could subsequently be stretched infinitely. This allowed the defence to ask the officers questions such as 'what were you thinking at that very moment', whilst a still frame was being used to visually anchor that 'thinking' (granting it instantaneous (split-second) accuracy). This temporal reversal consequently enabled the officers to retrospectively introject their reflections into the event, as if they *were* thinking at the moment and thus conscious of their own actions. There is no contest. Reasonability was already inscribed into the event from the outset by the very media-hybridity through which it was formed.[9]

Out of this media-hybridity comes violence as an effect. The event of the trial was marked by a *symbolic violence*: that of acquittal.[10] This violence is marked by the imposition of a closure of meaning onto the sensibility of intuition, the meaning of which is completely arbitrary. The self-evidentness mobilised by this verdict, however, is internal to the medium-hybrid in which it was cast. Outside of that, as we will see below, *it did not make any sense*.

(2) This is because most people were cast by a second media-hybridity. Instead of the camcorder–videotape–legal discourse hybrid, they encountered the *camcorder–videotape–broadcasting hybrid*. In contrast to the first one, this hybrid was very smooth. The ambiguity of the videotape was in fact extremely appropriate for the television medium (Fiske, 1994). Its blurred images, lack of voice-over and absence of editing intensified the sense of authenticity with which it emerged. This was not a staged event. Moreover, as the effectivity of television news is not based on presenting a single perspective, but always requires a doubling to turn an event into a contest, the absence of clarity and singularity helped the television medium to take a step back. It did not have to provide a clear-cut judgement, but could instead appeal to a higher truth consisting of two opposing viewpoints – guilty versus innocent. The meta-narrative of news coverage is the story that places two perspectives in opposition to one another and allows itself to wither away from binary contestation (Allan, 1995; Cottle, 1993; Dayan and Katz, 1992). The telling of the story thus always grants itself a higher ground, a purer truth, even if this truth is only the inflated reflexivity that lies are being told.

The smooth merging of the videotape and the news broadcast realised a different form of violence than that of the acquittal. The violence it engendered was that of sensibility and mood: an *indexical violence* which does not resonate with the closure of meaning at the expense of alternatives, but with the affirmation of particular experiences and/or prejudices. For people who have (directly or indirectly) experienced the brutality of the LAPD, the beating itself came as no surprise, but there was perhaps a sense of positivity that with the videotape their experiences were being vindicated. For those who always believed that the police were there to protect and serve, the video–broadcasting hybrid might have engendered a violent disjunction of experiences, and often encountered in the form of disbelief. The 'stunning effects' of the videotape (and verdict), for example, induced liberal mediators into states of shock which could only be rendered accountable with the inoculation that the officers were 'rotten apples' (and the jury were misled). Others, less inclined to give up their own prejudices, might negate the intuitive truth of the images and resort to all sorts of denials, similar to those mobilised by the jury. In all these cases there is violence, positive or negative, that attaches itself to mood and produces sense on the basis of preconceived, hence particularly situated, sensibilities.

(3)   The third hybridity is between the first and the second, hence a second-order hybridity. The trial was being broadcast itself, and in the news coverage of the trial, images of the beating were also appropriated to situate the verdict. For many people the judgement of the verdict marked a complete denial of their intuitions and experiences; a denial of their sensibilities and sense of truth and justice. This incompatibility within the medium-hybrid produced a final and most violent clash between symbolic and indexical violence that in turn materialised into new embodied constellations that we associate with the 1992 LA riots. However, for those who already have direct or indirect experience with the colour of American justice, the verdict could have been attuned very well with their intuitions and in turn have amplified the sensibilities resonating with such intuitions. As Fiske (1994) and CBS reporter Ron Allen (CBS Evening News, 29 May 1992) both indicated, many African–Americans already anticipated the verdict and were preparing for their response. The violence of these riots could thus be understood both in terms of outrage and euphoria as intuitions were both negated and affirmed.

CONCLUSION

With this case study of 'the Rodney King beating' I hope to have illustrated the interpretative strength of conceptualising violence as the effect of hybrid media. Different media-hybridities produce different forms of violence: symbolic, indexical and corporeal. The objective was to trace violence at the very grounding of racial identification. Racial difference, rather than constituting a lack with which violence can be identified, is itself already constituted by violent practices. As the case of the beating of Rodney King shows, these violent practices are not the exclusive domain of what Althusser (1971) termed 'repressive state apparatuses' but persist in judicial and political systems, as well as ideological apparatuses such as broadcasting media.

Violence is never the property of a single medium, but is always the outcome of the meeting of two or more media. Violence is an event of media-hybridisation. If we can agree that the mediation of violence is grounded in the violence of mediation, then this does not mean that we have given up on the responsibility to give an account of violent practices. All it means is that we attempt not to forget that every account that moves from intuition to judgement already entails a symbolic violence, a closure of sense into meaning at the expense of alternatives setting into work a symbolic power by which particular symbolic associations are granted a claim to 'self-evidentness' and 'naturalness', that is, mythification (Barthes, 1957/1993). Instead of reasoning, we could perhaps better render an account of the madness of reason against the aesthetics of reasonability.

Violence is the effect of hybrid media, the connectivity of technologies. Racialisation is a particular form of violence, one that allows a closure of sense into meaning by which the *sense* of Blackness (e.g., the experience of slavery) becomes a *fact* of Blackness; that which is received in silence. The silence of Rodney King, or that of O. J. Simpson, is in turn received by an exuberance of voyeurism and hermeneutic euphoria by media apparatuses which, instead of bearing witness, never stop placing meanings which perpetuate and extend the racial matrix formative of the prevailing structures of judging violence. The acquittal of the four police officers was exactly made possible because the sensibility of intuition, which is given in silence, was reconfigured in discourses which actively sought to constitute a reason within violence, a reason for violence, reasonable violence. And reasonability, we know, is merely a whiter shade of pale.

ACKNOWLEDGEMENTS

An earlier version of this chapter was presented at a Lancaster University departmental sociology seminar (7 November 1995). I thank staff and students who attended for their valuable comments, and in particular Rob Shields for his friendship and guidance. I also thank the editors for their suggestions, and the Vanderbilt Television News Archive in Nashville, Tennessee, for their kind assistance in gathering video recordings of news broadcasts. Of course, the responsibility for any misrepresentation that might occur in this chapter is mine alone.

NOTES

1. Mythification is to turn that which is particular, historical and constructed into an appearance of universality, naturalness and given-ness. This definition is derived from Barthes' (1957/1993) famous work *Mythologies*, which elsewhere (Van Loon, 1995, 1996), I have applied to the television news coverage of urban disorders (also see Gooding-Williams (1993) with reference to the 1992 LA 'riots').
2. Jill Swenson's (1995) comparative analysis of the beating of Rodney King with that of a White truck driver, Reginald Denny, points towards a similar conclusion.
3. As it violates the very 'realism' of the camera, a verdict that was simply based on a negation of the images would not have been very tenable.
4. It could be argued that to complement an image with *logos* is impossible because the mode of signification of the figure is always in excess of that of discourse (Lyotard, 1971). In other words, the assertion that the video images are incomplete, paves the way for a discursive *supplement* (Derrida, 1967/1974) which over-writes the figure. Because discourse and figure do not add up, the remainder of the images disrupts the interpretation. A deconstruction of the jury's attempt to present its discourse as a complement will therefore ultimately expose its failure to accomplish the desire to full closure.
5. This erasure is necessary for the supplement to appear as complement. The images now take on the function of visually anchoring the discourse; their role is secondary to a discursive formation which was always-already in place. Barthes (1977: 51) has argued that the anchorage of textuality into images allows particular connotations to conjure with the otherwise infinite richness of denotation to present itself as *'obvious'* (which he further explored in *Mythologies*, 1993). Such a conception of obviousness is similar to that developed by Michel Pêcheux (1982), who has associated it with the principal function of ideology as constitutive of the 'subject-form' (Van Loon, 1996).
6. Indexicality is used here as a combination of two different traditions. On the one hand, it draws upon its use within the phenomenological

(see Husserl (1913/1970: 269–71) on indication) and ethnomethodological (Garfinkel, 1967) traditions as indicating that every meaning only makes sense within a particular context. On the other hand, I draw upon its function in tradition of pragmatics (derived from the work of C. S. Peirce, 1940) as indicating a signification (e.g., smoke as indexical of fire). As Eco (1977) has argued, it takes the form of 'pointing towards' (hence index-finger), for example as the way in which epidemiologists attempt to trace the outbreak of a disease to an index case. Combined together, indexicality is a mode of symbolic spatialisation through which particular sensibilities affect intersubjectivity. It is thus a delimitation of sociation through the coordination of perspectivity. Indexicality is thus a 'tracing' of meaning, backwards, in sensibility and intuition. (I thank Rob Shields and Deirdre Boden for pursuing me to clarify this point.)

7. For such white liberal readings, the American justice system could be rescued only if the acquittal is treated as an aberration, i.e. a miscarriage of justice.

8. Lyotard, 1988a (pp. 140–2) and 1988b (pp.48–71).

9. Because of this, the content of the officers' account of their own thinking is already secondary to the form in which it was cast. The reasonability of their violence is not a matter of their own discursive gyrations, but of temporal inversion which, in turn, is a trick displayed by the medium-hybrid.

10. In Bourdieu's terms, symbolic violence refers to the closure of meaning, by which particular interpretations prevail at the expense of others and the arbitrariness of the sign is assigned a status of naturalness (Bourdieu and Passeron, 1977; Thompson, 1984). The acquisition of such a state of naturalness, however, is itself better understood as an effect of *symbolic power* (Bourdieu, 1982), because it is integral rather than differential. For a more in-depth discussion of the differences between violence and power, see Arendt (1970). Following Arendt, I merely posit that whereas violence is an effect of differentiation, power (*pouvoir*) is exercised as integration. Both are different from force (*puissance*), which is a potential or capacity, and thus static rather than kinetic, entrapped in a constellation of embodiments, rather than an effect of hybridisation (violence) or affirmation (power). (I thank Turo-Kimmo Lehtonen for the excellent discussion we had on this matter.)

VIDEOGRAPHY

Allen, E. (1993) 'L.A. Cops on Trial: The Rodney King Trial' (Columbia Home Video),
ABC Evening News, 30 April 1992.
CBS Evening News, 29 April 1992.
CBS Evening News, 1 May 1992.
Oprah Winfrey Show, 5 May 1992; broadcast in the UK by BBC2 on 27 February 1993.

REFERENCES

Allan, S. (1995) 'News, Truth and Postmodernity: Unravelling the Will to Facticity', in B. Adam and S. Allan (eds), *Theorizing Culture: Critique after Postmodernism* (London: UCL Press).

Althusser, L. (1971) *Lenin and Philosophy and Other Essays* (New York: New Left Books).

Arendt, H. (1970) *On Violence* (San Diego, CA: HBJ).

Baker, H. (1993) 'Scene ... Not Heard', in R. Gooding-Williams (ed.), *Reading Rodney King: Reading Urban Uprising* (London: Routledge), pp. 38–48.

Barthes, R. (1957/1993) *Mythologies* (London: Vintage).

Barthes, R. (1977) *Image Music Text*, essays selected and translated by Stephen Heath (London: Fontana Press).

Bourdieu, P. (1982) *Ce que parler veut dire: L'economie des echanges linguistiques* (Paris: Fayard).

Bourdieu, P. and Passeron, J. C. (1977) *Reproduction in Education, Society and Culture* (London: Sage).

Butler, J. (1993) 'Endangered/Endangering: Schematic Racism and White Paranoia', in R. Gooding-Williams (ed.), *Reading Rodney King: Reading Urban Uprising* (London: Routledge), pp. 15–22.

Cottle, S. (1993) *TV News, Urban Conflict and the Inner City* (Leicester: Leicester University Press).

Crenshaw, K. and Peller, G. (1993) 'Reel Time/Real Justice', in R. Gooding-Williams (ed.), *Reading Rodney King: Reading Urban Uprising* (London: Routledge).

Dayan, D. and Katz, E. (1992) *Media Events: The Live Broadcasting of History* (Cambridge, MA: Harvard University Press).

Debord, G. (1967/1994) *The Society of the Spectacle* (New York: Zone Books).

De Lauretis, T. (1989) 'The Essence of the Triangle or, Taking the Risk of Essentialism Seriously: Feminist Theory in Italy, the US and Britain', *Differences* (1)3, pp. 3–37.

Deleuze, G. (1968/1994) *Difference and Repetition* (London: Athlone Press).

Deleuze, G. (1969/1990) *Logic of Sense* (London: Athlone Press).

Deleuze, G. and Guattari, F. (1986) *A Thousand Plateaux: Capitalism and Schizophrenia* (Minneapolis, MN: University of Minnesota Press).

Derrida, J. (1967/1974) *Of Grammatology* (Baltimore, MD: Johns Hopkins University Press).

Eco, U. (1977) *A Theory of Semiotics* (London: Macmillan).

Fanon, F. (1952/1986) *Black Skin, White Masks* (London: Pluto Press).

Fiske, J. (1994) *Media Matters, Everyday Culture and Political Change* (Minneapolis, MN: University of Minnesota Press).

Garfinkel, H. (1967) *Studies in Ethnomethodology* (Englewood Cliffs, NJ: Prentice-Hall).

Gilmore, R. W. (1993) 'Terror Austerity Race Gender Excess Theater', in R. Gooding-Williams (ed.), *Reading Rodney King: Reading Urban Uprising* (London: Routledge), pp. 23–37.

Goldberg, D. T. (1993) *Racist Culture: Philosophy and the Politics of Meaning* (Oxford: Basil Blackwell).

Gooding-Williams, R. (1993) '"Look, a Negro!"', in R. Gooding-Williams (ed.), *Reading Rodney King: Reading Urban Uprisings* (New York: Routledge), pp. 157–77.

Husserl, E. (1913/1970) *Logical Investigations*, vol. 1 (London: Routledge & Kegan Paul).

Kant, I. (1781/1988) *Critique of Pure Reason* (London: J. M. Dent & Sons).

Keith, M. (1991) 'Policing a Perplexed Society? No-go Areas and the Mystification of Police–Black Conflict', in E. Cashmore and E. McLaughlin (eds), *Out of Order? Policing Black People* (London: Routledge), pp. 189–214.

Keith, M. (1992) 'Angry Writing: (Re)presenting the Unethical World of the Ethnographer', *Society and Space*, 10, pp. 551–68.

Keith, M. (1993) *Race, Riots and Policing: Lore and Disorder in a Multi-racist Society* (London: UCL Press).

Lewis, J. (1982) 'The Story of a Riot: the Television Coverage of Civil Unrest in 1981', *Screen Education*, 40, pp. 15–33.

Lipsitz, G. (1994) 'We Know What Time It Is: Race, Class and Youth Culture in the Nineties', in A. Ross and T. Rose (eds), *Microphone Fiends: Youth Music and Youth Culture* (London: Routledge), pp. 17–28.

Lyotard, J. F. (1971) *Discourse/Figure* (Paris: Klincksiek).

Lyotard, J. F. (1988a) *The Differend: Phrases in Dispute* (Manchester: Manchester University Press).

Lyotard, J. F. (1988b) *Le Postmoderne expliqué aux Enfants: Correspondence, 1982–1985* (Paris: Edition Galilée).

McLuhan, M. (1964) *Understanding Media: The Extensions of Man* (Harmondsworth: Penguin Books).

Pêcheux, M. (1982) *Language, Semantics and Ideology: Stating the Obvious* (London: Macmillan).

Peirce, C. S. (1940) *The Philosophy of Peirce: Selected Writings*, ed. J. Buchler (London: Kegan Paul, French, Trubner).

Solomos, J. (1988) *Black Youth, Racism and the State: The Politics of Ideology and Policy* (Cambridge: Cambridge University Press).

Swenson, J. D. (1995) 'Rodney King, Reginald Denny, and TV News: Cultural (Re-)Constructions of Racism', *Journal of Communication Inquiry*, 19(1), pp. 75–88.

Teubner, G. (1989) *Recht als autopoietisches System* (Frankfurt am Main: Suhrkamp Verlag).

Thompson, J. (1984) *Studies in the Theory of Ideology* (Cambridge: Polity Press).

Trew, T. (1979) 'Theory and Ideology at Work', in R. Fowler, R. Hodge, G. Kress and T. Trew (eds), *Language and Control* (London: Routledge & Kegan Paul), pp. 94–116.

Van Dijk, T. A. (1991) *Racism and the Press: Critical Studies in Racism and Migration* (London: Routledge).

Van Loon, J. (1995) 'Violence and Mediation: Figuring out the Racial Matrix of the 1992 L.A. Riots', PhD thesis, Lancaster University.

Van Loon, J. (1996) 'In-Finite Re-Presentations: Michel Pêcheux's Theory of Interpellation', in I. W. Hampsher-Monk (ed.), *Proceedings of the 1996 Political Studies Association Conference, 10–12 April 1996* (Glasgow: PSA).

Williams, P. J. (1993) 'The Rules of the Game', in R. Gooding-Williams (ed.), *Reading Rodney King: Reading Urban Uprising* (London: Routledge), pp. 51–5.

Part III

Complex Social Divisions and Cultural Interactions

7 Gender, Ethnicity and Politics: the Protestants of Northern Ireland
ROSEMARY SALES

INTRODUCTION

The dominance of the sectarian divide in Northern Ireland has marginalised concern with gender inequality. Politics centres around community loyalties, giving little space for alternative agendas. Women's rights have generally been seen as a lower priority than, or even in conflict with, the major political issues. While some women have gained prominence within nationalist and republican movements, Protestant women remain much less visible. The public face of the Protestant community is overwhelmingly male, represented by male political and Church leaders, and the annual displays of triumphalism by bowler-hatted, drum-beating Orangemen.

A growing body of research and activity is now addressing women's interests in Northern Ireland. Research on women has generally avoided tackling the religious divide.[1] Those studies which have examined connections between gender and sectarian divisions have focused on nationalist women,[2] while research on the Protestant community has generally ignored gender relations and Protestant women as political actors.[3] The specific experience of Protestant women remains, therefore, largely unexplored.

The past 20 years have seen major upheavals within the Protestant community. Social and economic restructuring, and policy changes brought about by 20 years of 'the Troubles', have undermined the ascendancy and loosened the ties which have bound Protestants together. While the response has often been defensive and inward-looking, it has also opened up possibilities for women to become more involved in economic and political life. Women's groups have become active on a range of issues, often challenging traditional gender relations, and developing links across the sectarian divide.

145

Another recent development has been an exploration of Protestant identities. Some have aimed to produce a more sophisticated defence of the Union in response to perceived threats from the Anglo-Irish Agreement and the Framework Document (Cadogan Group, 1995; Foster, 1995). Others, particularly women, have attempted to explore non-Unionist agendas without denying their Protestant background. This chapter developed from a contribution to a conference on 'Protestantism and Identity in Contemporary Ireland' at Queen's University Belfast in 1995, attended by academics and community activists. The discussion draws on interviews with some participants, and other women active in community groups. Pseudonyms are used except where interviewees express views which they have already declared publicly.

THE MEANINGS OF RELIGIOUS DIVISIONS IN NORTHERN IRELAND

Divisions between Protestant and Catholic shape every area of life in Northern Ireland, but religion is not an immediately visible identity. Protestants and Catholics look more or less the same and speak the same language.[4] But segregation runs deeper than between apparently more dissimilar groups in Britain. Half the population lives in areas containing over 90 per cent of one religious group (Dunn, 1995: 5). Separation is most intense in working-class ghettos, where mass unemployment further restricts social contact. According to the 1991 Census, in 35 of Belfast's 51 wards over 90 per cent of the population was of one religious group. The school system is almost entirely segregated on religious lines (Murray, 1985, 1995). Many Protestants grow up without any social contact with Catholics and only 9 per cent of marriages are 'mixed' (O'Connor, 1993: 168). Women are affected most profoundly by residential segregation since they are generally tied more closely to the home through domestic and caring responsibilities. They are more likely to be out of the labour force and, if in paid employment, they work closer to home and more often work with people from their own community.

Religious divisions are 'invisible' in another sense, since they are rarely discussed in 'polite' society. There is 'what you say in public and in "mixed" company and there is what you say in private, among your own people' (Bruce, 1994: vii). Contact between Protestants and Catholics is characterised by 'avoidance' (McAuley, 1984: 56). When discussing sectarianism in the workplace with trade unionists, I was frequently told 'religion doesn't matter here'. One official assured me that 'we never discuss politics in the union', thus demonstrating the constraints which sectarianism places on debate. In her study of Catholics in Northern Ireland, O'Connor (1993) found people unwilling to discuss 'the Troubles' openly with Protestants. A similar point was made by Jane, a Protestant community worker:

> I don't like to criticise to Catholic friends for what the IRA are doing, even though they may be more critical than I am ... there is a subconscious censorship to respect others' feelings, and no doubt they do the same.[5]

A range of theories has been developed to explain religious divisions in Northern Ireland: some, associated mainly with Protestants, place primary responsibility on Catholics, stressing for example 'cultural differences'. Others – which include left and liberal variants – may be critical of past inequalities and recommend change through legislative reform and economic regeneration to promote reconciliation within Northern Ireland. A third strand, supported primarily but not exclusively by Catholics, argues that Northern Ireland within its present borders is inherently undemocratic and un-reformable.[6] These debates have divided the left in Ireland and in Britain, leading to fundamentally different conclusions about the political situation, the progressiveness of nationalism and the possibilities of building a united working-class action within Northern Ireland.

Catholic and Protestant feminists may appear to have more in common with each other than with many of their co-religionists, but in what is defined as politics in Northern Ireland they are likely to be divided. The identification of Protestants with unionism (support for the Union with Britain) and Catholics with nationalism (support for the aspiration of a united Ireland) is by no means complete, but nevertheless overwhelming. Political developments tend to be seen through the lens of national identity, and Protestant and Catholic women are unlikely to vote for the same political party or support a common solution to the conflict.

The religious divide is now described increasingly in terms of 'ethnic' division (Bruce, 1994; Howe, 1990; McAuley, 1994). Ethnic groups involve notions of a common origin and a common fate as the basis for community. They are not, however, static entities, but are constructed in relation to specific social processes. Protestant and

Catholic ethnic identity in Northern Ireland derives from the history of the formation of the state and relations of power and dominance within it. The Northern Protestant identity is not shared with Protestants in the South of Ireland and many Protestants experience a crisis in their 'British' identity when they travel to Britain where distinctions between Protestant and Catholic have little social significance.

A distinctive feature of ethnic conflict in Northern Ireland is that it encompasses profound divisions over the constitutional position of the state the two communities share. The notion of 'parity of esteem' for the two 'cultural traditions' promoted by the official Community Relations Council suggests that tolerance and understanding can overcome sectarian differences. These traditions, however, are not merely cultural. They represent relations of power and dominance and different, and mutually exclusive, political ambitions.

The construction of ethnic identity is always gendered (Anthias and Yuval Davis, 1992). This is most explicit in nationalist mythology which uses images of woman's eternal suffering – 'Mother Ireland', 'dark Rosaleen' – as a metaphor for Ireland's oppression. Nationalists 'fashioned the male hero as one who liberated the abducted female through repossession' (Innes, 1994: 127). Republicans have also promoted more active images of women as 'freedom fighters', drawing on ancient myths of Gaelic women warriors. There is no equivalent symbolic role for women in Protestantism. Unionism is associated with conquest and settlement, and its imagery is triumphalist and masculine. There are no heroines in this world and no symbolically female territory to be liberated.

The use of religion as a 'boundary marker' for ethnic division does not mean that differences are about religion (Shirlow and McGovern, 1995). The Churches nevertheless play a powerful role in cementing community identity. Church attendance is high, particularly among women, and even for non-Church-goers 'the language of religious identity is not very distant' (Morrow *et al.*, 1994: 6). The Churches in both communities promote and reinforce notions of deference and obedience, and conformity to a rigid code of sexual behaviour.

PROTESTANT IDENTITY

Protestants have traditionally seen themselves as descendants of settlers, with strong links to Britain, particularly to Scotland. Following the defeat of the United Irishmen and the Act of Union,

Northern Protestants increasingly saw their interests as tied to Britain rather than the rest of Ireland, but it was not until partition that unionism came to dominate to the virtual exclusion of other strands of thought. With the creation of Northern Ireland, Protestant identity was constructed on the basis of economic and political power and privilege, reproduced through Unionist rule at Stormont. Class differences and struggles were accommodated within the wider political divide centring on the national question.

Unionist ideology combines a consciousness of superiority with defensiveness. Bruce argues that the monotheistic religious tradition offers radical divisions between 'the good and the bad, the saved and the unsaved, the godly and the ungodly' (Bruce, 1994: 26). This consciousness was sustained under the Stormont regime by real differences in material conditions. Catholics were the 'despised croppies' whose impoverished conditions could be taken as evidence of their inferior status.

At the same time, Protestants are a minority in Ireland as a whole, and fear being 'overrun' by Dublin, or 'outbred' by Catholics in the North. Another source of insecurity is fear of betrayal by Britain: the suspicion that – in spite of Mrs Thatcher's assertion that Northern Ireland is as British as Finchley – to the people of England, Scotland and Wales, Northern Ireland is another country, from which they would happily separate.

The 'numbers game' dominated Unionist rule at Stormont. Politics became a zero-sum game, with compromise seen as weakness or betrayal (Nelson, 1984: 16–17). This type of politics provides little scope for radical visions of the future and makes any challenge to the *status quo* potentially dangerous.

The dominant ideologies of Protestantism make a sharp separation between male and female spheres. Protestant Churches, unlike the Catholic Church, 'elevated conjugality over virginity [and] Protestant clergy were more likely to devolve the role of moral guide to husbands and fathers within the family' (O'Dowd, 1987: 14–15). Women play a vital role within the congregation, but are 'marginalised or excluded from power' within the Church (Fraser, 1995). In evangelical Christianity and the literature of the temperance movement women are represented as both more pious than men – the 'angel in the house' – and more susceptible to temptation and damnation (Brozyna, 1994).

Although Northern Ireland women do not generally conform to a stereotype of 'traditional attitudes' (Kremer and Curry, 1986), views on the family and sexuality are significantly more conservative than in Britain, with Protestants, particularly women, less liberal than Catholics (Montgomery and Davies, 1991). A recent study of domestic violence suggested that it is a prevalent but largely hidden problem, since beliefs about the place of women and the sanctity of marriage tend to condone it (McWilliams and McKiernan, 1993: 23).

The ideology promoted by mainstream religious and political movements denies women legitimacy in the public sphere. As one prominent Protestant feminist put it: 'the bonding rituals of the ascendancy, like the Orange Order or the masons, have totally excluded and rejected women' (Gordon, 1990: 7). Women have played a vital supporting role within political parties (Urquart, 1994), but have rarely stood for election themselves, or pursued an independent agenda.

The association of Protestantism with unionism has meant that women active in progressive politics often find it difficult to identify themselves as part of the Protestant community. The demands of community loyalty operate 'as a regulator of women's lives' (Moore, 1993: 78) with feminism seen as alien to Protestantism, identified with nationalism and Republicanism, and therefore something to be rejected.[7]

Protestants who oppose unionism are often assumed to be Catholics, an assumption they sometimes find it easier to leave unchallenged. Some non-Unionist Protestant women have, however, recently started to 'come out' as Protestants[8] and to reclaim a positive identity which is not based on negating their background and experience. Hazel Gordon spoke publicly about her Protestant background for the first time in 1990.[9] She explained that when she used her married name she was often thought to be a Catholic and had taken this as a compliment. But then she started to feel she was denying her identity and that 'if everybody with my views is taken for a Catholic, the decent Protestants are not being heard'. She reverted to an unambiguously Protestant name which meant 'coming out of the closet'.[10]

THE IMPACT OF CONFLICT

The past 20 years have seen a polarisation between the two communities with a reassertion of 'traditional' community values. At the same time divisions based on class have opened up within the Protestant community which have found expression in new political parties appealing to different class interests (McAuley, 1994; Price, 1995).

For Protestants, whose identity is bound up with a struggle to defend the past, the experience has been largely of alienation and loss (Dunn and Morgan, 1994). If politics is a zero-sum game, advances made by Catholics must be at the expense of Protestants. Resentment has intensified as economic restructuring destroys the industry on which the old ascendancy was based. Many working-class Protestants have lost access to jobs they felt were theirs by right, and now find themselves without skills or qualifications. Protestants increasingly express jealousy of Catholics:

Protestants had been told 'everything is OK as they were. So Catholics had felt nobody was going to give them anything and they had gone for education and training and were moving into high positions in the banks, the executive, the hospitals, while the Protestants had done nothing and were now the labourers.'[11]

'The Troubles' have seen a hardening of sectarianism, but conflicts also produce 'some fluidity in the social order' (Ridd, 1986: 3) which allows a transformation in outlook. Some of the more hardline loyalists have been most open to new ideas and become active in community groups attempting to re-evaluate the Protestant experience, and develop new strategies.

Northern Ireland's conflict presents contradictory possibilities for women. It has brought widening economic, social and political opportunities, together with pressures to conform to traditional values (Morgan *et al.*, 1994: 3–4). Inevitably, in a divided society, the impact has been different in the two communities. Catholics have fought for change, Protestants to defend the present and the past. There has been more space for radical ideas within nationalism and women have been more visible in politics.

The two communities responded differently to the presence of the security forces on the streets. For nationalist women the army has been seen as an alien force, provoking hostility or indifference. Many were politicised through community resistance in the early days of 'the Troubles'. Protestant women did not develop this experience which has provided a powerful basis for community activism in the nationalist community. Their response has been more ambivalent since the army, and even more the overwhelming Protestant police force, are seen as theirs. When conflicts have developed between Protestant communities and the RUC, the police are seen as betraying their own people.

Those involved with paramilitary organisations are overwhelmingly male. Some women have become prominent within republican organisations, but much less is known about loyalist women paramilitaries and they appear to have had less independence within the movement (Morgan and Fraser, 1995). Loyalist women's activity has centred largely on support for male prisoners, and welfare work.

Paramilitary activity depends on at least tacit support from large sections of the community and intensifies pressures for community loyalty. The use of violence against the 'other side' has been sanctioned, or at least tolerated, by large sections of the population. While Republican violence has generally aimed at what they define (however contentiously) as 'legitimate targets', loyalists have more often engaged in purely sectarian killing. In solidly loyalist or nationalist areas there is strong social disapproval of informers, while the widespread availability of guns can make it difficult and sometimes dangerous to raise agendas which conflict with those who hold power within the community. This power has been extended into the domestic sphere, with access to weapons giving men greater control over women's behaviour (Evason, 1982). Women subjected to domestic violence have been inhibited from reporting it, since this is looked on as 'squealing' (McWilliams and McKiernan, 1993).

WOMEN AND POLITICAL REPRESENTATION

Northern Ireland's current constitutional position has created a political vacuum in which local people have little control over decision-making. Women are doubly disenfranchised, with no elected representatives to pursue their interests within the formal political sphere. Throughout Northern Ireland's history, women have played little role in policy-making, either as elected politicians or within the civil service or the institutions of the welfare state. No woman has represented Northern Ireland at Westminster since the 1970s, and only nine were elected to the Stormont parliament in its 52-year life. Women have achieved some representation at local level, although this is of limited value since the powers of local councils were drastically curtailed with Direct Rule. Women won 67 council seats in 1993, just 11.5 per cent of the total (Lucy, 1994: 171). Under-representation is greatest in unionist parties.

The official language of equal opportunities is now incorporated into the public policy statements of all mainstream parties, although they remain conservative in relation to sexual politics. Some parties have structures for involving women in policy-making, such as the Unionist Party's 'women's issues committee'. Rhonda Paisley, Ian Paisley's daughter, was appointed spokesperson for women's issues by the DUP in 1987. She later withdrew from political activity, calling for 'a radical re-think of our involvement in Unionist politics', and describing the attitudes of her male colleagues as at best dismissive and at worst 'downright chauvinistic towards women involved in politics' (Paisley, 1992: 33).

Parties are now more willing to have women on their slates for council elections, but the women are expected to toe the party line, and their acceptance by male councillors is 'provisional on their domestic responsibilities not impinging on council business and responsibilities' (Rooney and Woods, 1995: 21). According to Rhonda Paisley:

> A token woman suits most aspects of Unionism – but a woman who starts to move up the political ladder reveals the insecurity of the majority of men who are still determined to keep a woman in her place.
>
> (Paisley, 1992: 33)

Many Unionist women councillors have been relatives of male politicians, and owed their election largely to that connection. Rhonda Paisley attempted to move beyond the traditional limitations placed on Unionist women. Iris Robinson, who replaced her as spokesperson on women's issues, represents the traditional view. Speaking at a conference in the Shankill, she maintained:

> I don't pretend to be anything other than a simple housewife, one that loves her country deeply. I don't have any particular skills.
>
> (Quoted in Hall, 1994: 27)

The new fringe Unionist parties have attempted to involve more women, but have as yet no elected representatives. One of the first women on the executive of the Progressive Unionist Party (PUP), was a well-known community activist whose feminism was seen as an asset by the people who urged her to join the party. Promoting a feminist agenda, however, was not easy within the macho environment in which the party operates, 'and showing men their issues are not the only issues is quite hard'.[12]

WOMEN AND INFORMAL POLITICS

Although largely excluded from formal politics, women have become increasingly active in informal organisations. Relations between Church and state in Northern Ireland have sustained a conservative family ideology, underpinned by some of the most restrictive legislation in Europe, and the 1970s saw the development of feminist campaigns which challenged conventional views of women's role.

The women's movement, like feminist campaigns everywhere, has split on grounds of ideology and tactics, but the sectarian divide has often been at the root of these divisions. The Northern Ireland Women's Rights Movement, founded in 1975, attempted to 'unite women from all political traditions or none' (Roulston, 1989: 225) and to engage working-class women. Unity proved difficult to sustain since, by attempting to avoid taking a position on the constitution, it implicitly suggested that progress could be made within the existing political framework (*ibid.*: 227). Divisions intensified during the hunger strike, when the issue of women Republican prisoners in Armagh jail 'became a metaphor for everything that has kept Irish women divided from each other' (Ward, 1991: 156). Republican women felt that the programme was limited by failing to incorporate an anti-imperialist perspective,[13] while some Protestants felt their experience was not validated in the women's movement. Julie, who joined the PUP after many years of feminist activity, recalled:

> The feminist movement tended to have a more nationalist tinge. I was denying what I was, disallowing my background and life experience. That feeling brought me back to understanding my strong Protestant identity.[14]

The movement nevertheless achieved some notable successes. Divorce became easier in 1978, and the Equal Pay and Sex Discrimination Acts were transferred to Northern Ireland. Legislation on domestic violence was strengthened and women's refuges gained public funding and support. Abortion, however, remains an unresolved issue; Northern Ireland's other 'taboo' subject. The Northern Ireland Abortion Law Reform Association (NIALRA) has had problems even in establishing an address, since organisations associated with the campaign risk losing funding.[15]

By 1980 feminists were frustrated at their inability to develop a programme which could encompass all women's struggles without the danger of sectarian splits (Ward, 1991: 156) and many women started to devote their energies to community activity. Women's centres have been established across Northern Ireland, providing advice and support and the base for a range of activities. Only a small number of women had been active in the feminist movement, but the new centres involve a much wider spectrum. Community organisations, in which women have also been dominant, have grown alongside women's centres in response to social deprivation, particularly in the inner city. Community work has traditionally been a 'safer' area for women, not quite part of the formal, public sphere. Catholics still dominate 'community development', but a substantial network of both women and community centres has developed in Protestant areas, including the Shankill Women's Forum established in 1994.

Most women's centres are in either Protestant or Catholic territory, and tend to serve one community almost exclusively. They are dependent on their communities for support, which can make it difficult to raise controversial issues such as abortion or lesbian rights. Most centre staff and users speak of the welcome for their activity within the communities, but women's activity continues to generate hostility in some quarters. When June, a community worker, carried out a research project into women's needs in East Belfast, she was threatened by people claiming to be speaking for loyalist paramilitaries and told to 'watch your back, fenian lover'.[16]

As the centres have become more established with paid staff, they are increasingly dependent on funding, including from official sources. A study of women's voluntary organisations concluded that they provide a wide range of often highly specialised services and are increasingly called upon to replace services which should be provided by statutory agencies (Taillon, 1992: 3). Some groups raised the issue of 'political vetting' and withdrawal of grants from organisations whose activities do not please funding bodies (*ibid.*: 6). Funding is often channelled through church organisations which may attempt to limit the agenda of community groups. The Shankill Women's Centre lost its grant from Belfast City Council in 1996. The centre has organised activities not traditionally considered appropriate for Protestant women, including classes in Women Studies and the Irish language and history. No reason was given for the cut, but some women suspect that the centre appeared too 'soft on nationalism'.[17]

Many women argue that they are able to cross the sectarian divide and can put aside their own political opinions in a way that men find impossible. In a notable demonstration of co-operation the Falls and

Shankill Women's Centres made a joint approach to Belfast City Council when it cut off funding for the Falls Centre, which is based in a strongly nationalist area. The success of this campaign led to the formation of the Women's Support Network and continuing work between groups from different areas.

The recent growth of community activity has produced a solid basis for women's organisation across the sectarian divide, which many women have been keen to see reflected in the negotiations about Northern Ireland's constitutional future. The Women's Coalition was formed to promote a women's agenda in the elections for the Northern Ireland Forum in 1996, the gateway to all-Party negotiations, and won nearly 2 per cent of the vote.

Much of this cross-community work has, however, been based on the politics of avoidance. The divided nature of society, and the sensitivity of the political issues, make all areas of debate potentially problematic. As one centre administrator told me: 'We don't talk about politics here. We only talk about women's issues'.[18] The separation of 'women's issues' from the mainstream political agenda, while allowing some extremely productive work to be done, risks marginalising the issues on which women can unite. Support for the Women's Coalition has not been unanimous among feminists. Many fear that unity can be maintained only so long as the peace process remains stalled, and that if serious progress were made, differences would inevitably surface.

CONCLUSION

Women have made substantial moves into the public sphere, both in employment and in the largely informal politics of community and women's groups. The energy and activity devoted to developing women's organisations have made a real difference to women's lives. They remain, however, largely excluded from formal politics, and the issues on which women have campaigned have not become part of the mainstream political agenda.

The programme of groups such as the Women's Coalition challenges traditional values in Northern Ireland, but unless women are involved with politics as it is defined in Northern Ireland, their influence is likely to remain peripheral. Women have a real interest in the outcome of negotiations on constitutional issues and the development of democratic and inclusive political structures. If they are to reconstruct the meaning of Northern Ireland politics, they face the demanding task of engaging with the issues which divide them. For Protestant women this task is doubly difficult. The ties of unionism to the ascendancy have traditionally placed it on the side of the *status quo*, while feminism and other progressive movements have been viewed with hostility. In spite of recent attempts to find more progressive forms of Unionism, the Union remains inescapably linked to exclusion and inequality. The fate of the peace process has exposed the irreconcilability of the politics of the two communities within the confines of Northern Ireland. Women within the Protestant community have been at the forefront of developing a non-Unionist politics which can embrace Protestant identity while looking forward to a more open society.

NOTES

1. For example, Cockburn, 1991; Morrissey, 1991; and most studies for the Equal Opportunities Commission for Northern Ireland (EOCNI). The EOCNI recently commissioned a report (Davies *et al.*, 1995) which examined differences in Protestant and Catholic women's labour market experience.
2. For example Edgerton, 1986; Ward, 1983, 1991.
3. For example Bruce, 1994; McAuley, 1994; Nelson, 1984. No Protestant woman is mentioned by name in the index of any of these works.
4. Irish has largely died out as a first language. There are a small number of Irish-speaking schools and, for nationalists, Irish is an important element of national identity.
5. Interview with Jane, July 1995.
6. For more detailed discussion, see McGarry and O'Leary, 1993, and Sales, 1997.
7. This point was made by a number of interviewees from both communities.
8. This phrase was used by several women at the conference 'Protestantism and Identity in Contemporary Ireland', Belfast, February 1995.
9. 'Women in Ireland in the 1990s', conference organised by WEA Women's Studies Branch, 14 October 1990.
10. Interview with Hazel Gordon, July 1995.
11. Report of a discussion at a women's centre in a Protestant area of Belfast.
12. Interview with PUP activist, November 1995.

13. Interview with Aileen, Clar na mBan member, November 1995.
14. Interview with Julie, November 1995.
15. Interview with NIALRA member, July 1995.
16. Interview with June, February 1995.
17. Interview with Pat, March 1996.
18. Interview with administrative worker, women's centre, February 1995.

REFERENCES

Anthias, F. and Yuval Davis, N. (1992) *Racialised Boundaries* (London: Routledge).

Brozyna, A. (1994) '"The Cursed Cup Hath Cast Her Down": Constructions of Female Piety in Ulster Evangelical Temperance Literature, 1863–1914', in J. Holmes and D. Urquart (eds), *Coming into the Light* (Belfast: Institute of Irish Studies).

Bruce, S. (1994) *The Edge of the Union* (Oxford: Oxford University Press).

Cadogan Group (1995) *Lost Accord: The 1995 Frameworks and the Search for a Settlement in Northern Ireland* (Belfast: Cadogan Group).

Cockburn, C. (1991) *In the Way of Women: Men's Resistance to Sex Equality* (London: Macmillan).

Davies, C., Heaton, N., Robinson, G. and McWilliams, M. (1995) *A Matter of Small Importance? Catholic and Protestant Women in the Northern Ireland Labour Market* (Belfast: EOCNI).

Department of Health and Social Services (1993) *The Northern Ireland Census 1991 Religion Report* (Belfast).

Dunn, S. (1995) 'The Conflict as a Set of Problems' in S. Dunn (ed.), *Facets of the Conflict in Northern Ireland* (London: Macmillan).

Dunn, S. and Morgan, V. (1994) *Protestant Alienation in Northern Ireland: A Preliminary Survey* (Belfast: Centre for the Study of Conflict, University of Ulster).

Edgerton, L. (1986) 'Public Protest, Domestic Acquiescence: Women in Northern Ireland', in R. Ridd and H. Callanan (eds), *Caught up in Conflict: Women's Responses* (London: Macmillan).

Evason, E. (1982) *Hidden Violence* (Belfast: Fastnet).

Foster, J. (ed.) (1995) *The Idea of the Union: Statements and Critiques in Support of the Union of Great Britain and Northern Ireland* (Vancouver: Belcouver Press).

Fraser, G. (1995) 'The Backbone of the Church: Women and the Protestant Churches in Northern Ireland', paper presented to a conference on 'Protestantism and Identity in Contemporary Ireland', Queen's University, Belfast, February.

Gordon, H. (1990) 'Women, Protestantism and Unionism', *Women in Ireland in the 1990s*, Report of conference organised by WEA Women Studies Branch, October 1990.

Graham, B. (1995) 'Unionist Ulster: a Rhetoric Lacking Place', paper presented to a conference on 'Protestantism and Identity', Queen's University, Belfast, February.

Hall, M. (1994) *Beyond the Fife and Drum*, Report of a Conference on Belfast Shankill Road (Belfast: Island pamphlets).

Howe, L. (1990) *Being Unemployed in Northern Ireland* (London: Routledge).

Innes, C. (1994) 'Virgin Territories and Motherlands: Colonial and Nationalist Representations of Africa and Ireland', *Feminist Review*, 47, pp. 1–14.

Kremer, J. and Curry, C. (1986) *Attitudes towards Women in Northern Ireland* (Belfast: Equal Opportunities Commission for Northern Ireland).

Lucy, G. (1994) *Northern Ireland Local Government Election Results 1993* (Lurgan: Ulster Society).

McAuley, J. (1994) *The Politics of Identity* (Aldershot: Avebury).

McGarry, J. and O'Leary, B. (1995) *Explaining Northern Ireland* (London: Blackwell).

McWilliams, M. and McKiernan, J. (1993) *Bringing it Out in the Open: Domestic Violence in Northern Ireland* (Belfast: HMSO).

Montgomery, P. and Davies, C. (1991) 'A Woman's Place in Northern Ireland', in P. Stringer and G. Robinson (eds), *Social Attitudes in Northern Ireland* (Belfast: Blackstaff Press).

Moore, R. (1993) *Proper Wives: Orange Maidens or Disloyal Subjects: Situating the Equality Concerns of Protestant Women in NI* (Dublin: National University of Ireland, MA Equality Studies).

Morgan, V. and Fraser, G. (1994) *The Company We Keep* (Belfast: University of Ulster).

Morgan, V. and Fraser, G. (1995) 'Women and the Northern Ireland Conflict: Experiences and Responses', in S. Dunn (ed.), *Facets of the Conflict in Northern Ireland* (London: Macmillan).

Morrissey, H. (1991) 'Different Shares: Women, Employment and Earnings', in C. Davies and E. McLaughlin (eds), (1991) *Women, Employment and Social Policy in Northern Ireland: A Problem Postponed?* (Belfast: PRI).

Morrow, D., Birrell, D., Greer, J. and O'Keeffe, T. (1994) *The Churches and Inter Community Relations* (Belfast: Centre for Study of Conflict, University of Ulster).

Murray, D. (1985) *Worlds Apart: Segregated Schools in Northern Ireland* (Belfast: Appletree Press).

Murray, D. (1995) 'Culture, Religion and Violence in Northern Ireland', in S. Dunn (ed.), *Facets of the Conflict in Northern Ireland* (London: Macmillan).

Nelson, S. (1984) *Ulster's Uncertain Defenders* (Belfast: Appletree).

O'Connor, F. (1993) *In Search of a State: Catholics in Northern Ireland* (Belfast: Blackstaff).

O'Dowd, L. (1987) 'Church, State and Women: The Aftermath of Partition', in C. Curtin, P. Jackson and B. O'Connor (eds), *Gender in Irish Society* (Galway: Galway University Press).

Paisley, R. (1992) 'Feminism, Unionism and "the Brotherhood"', *Irish Reporter*, No. 8 (Belfast).

Price, J. (1995) 'Political Change and the Protestant Working Class', *Race and Class*, No. 37, 57–69.

Ridd, R. (1986) 'Powers of the Powerless', in R. Ridd and H. Callanan (eds), *Caught up in Conflict: Women's Responses* (London: Macmillan).

Rooney, E. and Woods, M. (1995) *Women, Community and Politics in Northern Ireland: A Belfast Study* (Belfast: University of Ulster).

Roulston, C. (1989) 'Women on the Margin: the Women's Movement in Northern Ireland, 1973–1988', *Science and Society*, 53(2), pp. 219–36.

Sales, R. (1997) *Women Divided: Gender, Religion and Politics in Northern Ireland* (London: Routledge).

Shirlow, P. and McGovern M. (1995) 'Counter-insurgency, De-industrialisation and the Political Economy of Ulster Loyalism' , paper presented to a conference on 'Protestantism and Identity', Queen's University, Belfast, February.

Taillon, R. (1992) *Grant Aided or Taken for Granted? A Study of Women's Voluntary Organisations in Northern Ireland* (Belfast: Women's Support Network).

Urquart, D. (1994) 'The Female of the Species is More Deadlier than the Male? The Ulster Women's Unionist Council, 1911–40', in J. Holmes and D. Urquart (eds), *Coming into the Light* (Belfast: Institute of Irish Studies).

Ward, M. (1983) *Unmanageable Revolutionaries* (London: Pluto).

Ward, M. (1991) 'The Women's Movement in the North of Ireland: Twenty Years on', in S. Hutton and P. Stewart (eds), *Ireland's Histories* (London: Routledge).

8 The African–Indian Antithesis? The 1949 Durban 'Riots' in South Africa

RAVI K. THIARA

INTRODUCTION

Contextualised within a broader study of the South Asian diaspora, this chapter focuses on relations between two subordinate groups in a colonial context. Within South African historiography, few attempts have been made to analyse interaction between African and Indian people. Work on race and ethnicity has largely concentrated on African–white or Indian–white relations, thus omitting a crucial dimension for the understanding of ethnic conflict in South Africa.

Through the examination of a specific incident of conflict, the Durban 'riots' of 1949, an attempt is made to assess its legacy for relations between African and Indian people. I argue that any explanation needs to take cognisance of the differential structural location of the two groups while at the same time recognising the existence of physical, cultural and ideological space which results in mutual stereotyping, mistrust and suspicion. Although the Durban 'riots' were spontaneous, they were structurally predetermined by the nature of a deeply racially defined society. In this context, historical and political factors which determined inter-racial intercourse between these two groups are highlighted. In analysing the 'riots', the different agendas of the 'players' involved, and the ways in which the story was constructed by each one in the aftermath of the event, are traced. I argue that each one was redesigning the narrative to suit its own particular purposes and gain political mileage.

Although the 'riots' lasted only three days, they left an enduring psychological legacy which is of continuing significance to Indians, informing not only the way they perceive African people but also their

161

ambivalence towards majority rule. Finally, I suggest that the 'riots' have assumed a different nature – as an 'epic'[1] – rooted in people's collective memory, which has an ongoing longevity through its reproduction over the years.

INDIAN INDENTURED MIGRATION

Indian migration to South Africa was part of the larger British colonial enterprise. This population movement began in the early nineteenth century when the indenture system was devised to provide colonial satellites with a cheap, docile and disposable labour supply in the aftermath of slavery. Under indenture, workers were contractually bound to an employer for a minimum of five years, though in practice this could mean lifelong servitude under conditions not dissimilar to slavery. Unlike slavery, which spanned many centuries, Indian indentured workers were recruited and exploited within the space of 100 years.

While indentured Indians were imported to South Africa between 1860 and 1911, the earliest Indians in South Africa were imported by the Dutch East India Company as slaves[2] (Boeskin, 1977: 30–1), and a small number later brought to Natal by individual planters from India and Mauritius (Bhana and Brain, 1990: 21). 'Passenger' Indians, traders and merchants who paid their own way, and who were free and distinct from the majority, followed 15 years later. The Indian population was thus highly diverse and differentiated along class, gender, religion, kinship and linguistic lines from the early days.[3]

Indentured Indians were incorporated into a subordinate socioeconomic position as dependent bonded labour. This differential incorporation was accompanied by an emphasis on racial, cultural and institutional differences to promote racial separation. It is important, however, not to paint a picture of Indian workers as passive objects who bowed to their adverse circumstances and oppression as resistance to this adversity manifested itself in a variety of passive and active ways (Haraksingh 1987; Thiara, 1993). It is evident, though, that indenture was not only a system for maintaining a particular type of labour system, but also a mechanism of social control designed to preserve and maintain white minority privilege and dominance.

It is indisputable that indenture was crucial in the process of capital accumulation in Natal. By the time of its abolition, Natal presented diverse economic opportunities to ex-indentured workers whose mass exodus out of indenture and diversification into the entire fabric of South African society soon aroused demands for a curtailment of their freedom and rights from influential sections of the white community. The introduction of Indian indentured labour not only strengthened the bargaining position of white planters *vis-à-vis* African labour but immediately juxtaposed the two labour providers against one another.

EARLY ENCOUNTERS

Racial antagonism in South African society has deep historical roots. In this section I argue that it is necessary to examine critically the notion that Africans and Indians were racially polarised at every level of society, and that racial antipathy between the two was inherently inevitable. The crucial role of the dominant white minority in fostering and nurturing antagonistic stereotypes and relations between the subordinate groups is importantly underlined.

White policy with regard to Africans and Indians as labour providers created the larger framework in which relations between these two groups were developed. The maintenance of divisions between Africans and Indians through the racial division of labour, as well as residential segregation, ensured the dominance of the white minority. Africans and Indians were differentially racialised, which correlated closely with the roles assigned to them, and this largely ensured geographical, ideological and economic separation. Within this process the traits of one group were compared with the other, where those less pliable were negatively labelled.[4] For instance, in South Africa the industry of Indians was initially applauded and seen as an example for Africans, to teach them the value of deference and regular work, qualities crucial for white needs. In turn, African self-sufficiency was seen as indolence and a refusal to be civilised.[5]

Clearly, the importation of Indians contributed to the preservation of white supremacy. In British Guinea, for instance, this view was openly expressed by Sir Henry Barkly (Moore, 1987: 229). It was assumed that the Indian would always side with whites against African insurrection. Indeed, in South Africa the presence of indentured Indians was regarded as a military asset against possible Zulu attacks: 'In 1865 a thousand muskets were ordered from England to be stored ready for issue to coolies in an emergency' (Thompson, 1952: 35). This assumption was slowly eroded in most colonies in the face of increased incidents of Indian resistance.

Although it is apparent that close contact between Africans and Indians was minimal, often leading to conflicts at the micro-level, there is insufficient available evidence to suggest that relations between them were irrevocably bad. Initially, contact between them on the estates was largely mediated through the dominant white minority. Where Indian and African workers were employed alongside each other they were organised into separate competitive work gangs. There is evidence to suggest that African whipping boys were used on the estates and Indians were confined to the African barracks as a punishment. Indian overseers were frequently appointed to oversee African mill workers, while African and Indian policemen were used to enforce regulations and to administer punishment (floggings) of the Indians and Africans respectively (*Indian Opinion*, 6 July 1907; 15 July 1911). Outside of estates, Indians began to encounter Africans on a larger scale when they sought employment away from places of Indian concentration. The Protector's Reports provide an indication of interaction between the two groups, highlighting little else except communication difficulties (*Report of the Protector of Immigrants*, 1878: 7).

Competition over rights to land was a primary source of tension between the two groups, a conflict that was fuelled by policies aimed at systematically undermining the rights of African people. Initially, the position of Indians was distinguished from Africans by the lack of landownership; they were only able to purchase or rent land from white or African farmers in the last decade of the nineteenth century. Natal Africans were gradually dispossessed of land but were able to occupy white land[6] (Marks, 1970: 4). During this period, only land allocated to Africans was offered to Indians, creating a competitive mode; later this was used to justify the withdrawal of land rights from Indians.

Competition in the labour market was a second major point of discord. Much of the evidence suggesting the beginning of African resentment against Indians in this area, however, is mediated through whites. Nevertheless, the existence of tension, particularly in times of scarcity, cannot be doubted. Compared with a decrease in the rights of Africans, Indian economic diversification and success increased African resentment, as reflected in the following:

There are several grave objections to the Indians and Arabs. The former become domestic servants in the principal places like hotels, refreshment places etc., thereby displacing natives. Moreover, the money earned by them is not spent in the country; it is sent out of South Africa to India. This applies especially to the Arabs.

(De B. Webb and Wright, 1976: 222)

The Indian view of Africans was informed and coincided with that of whites. Generally Indians perceived themselves as being more civilised, and complained bitterly about being supervised and beaten by African policemen, their inferiors. It is evident that prejudiced sentiments were strongest amongst trader Indians who also sought to distinguish themselves from indentured workers. Evidence indicates that some Indian traders, despite having a large African clientele, were reluctant to extend credit to Africans, customarily given to Indians, unless well known to them (Padayachee and Morrell, 1991: 89). In part, Indian attitudes towards Africans reflected the retention of the traditional caste system in which dark skin colour was associated with inferiority. Indians saw themselves as being closer to whites than Africans, and hence were seen as aloof and distant (De B. Webb and Wright, 1976: 228). The African perception of Indians, on the other hand, viewed them as untrustworthy businessmen and liars.

While communication difficulties frustrated interaction between the two groups, especially until a common *lingua franca* was developed, it is apparent that differential treatment was the root cause of much of the resentment: 'Kumalo thinks natives ought to be allowed to go into magistrates' offices as clerks, just as Indians do' (De B. Webb and Wright, 1976: 231). As a result, social interaction between the two groups remained minimal. Although the work of Bhana and Brain provides some evidence of marriages between Indian men and African women (1990: 171), inter-racial marriages were rare, though Indian men frequently had liaisons with African women, much resented by African men. It is clear that Indian traders were particularly guilty, often offering credit facilities to exploit disadvantaged African women and girls (Beall, 1982: 183).

Although social contact was minimal, and individual conflicts common, there was an absence of any serious frictional encounters. Indians were an increasingly urban group while Africans largely remained rural; it was only as competition over the urban space increased that antipathy became heightened. Political organisations representing the two groups at the time were separate and autonomous; the potent legacy of deeply entrenched inequality delayed the possibility of political alliances and a common cause was not made until the 1940s.

Despite political and economic persecution, differential treatment ensured that in time Indians were able to wield a degree of economic and political power unavailable to Africans. Indians in the 1940s enjoyed a degree of socioeconomic advantage which not only re-inforced the flimsy link, but enhanced the African perception of Indian as beneficiary. I now turn to the 1940s and the 'event' which has left a potent legacy for Indians.

1940s DURBAN

Durban in the mid-1930s and 1940s was marked by rapid industrial growth and urbanisation, demonstrated not only by the expansion of the local economy, especially the industrial sector, but also the increase in population. Although there had been a substantial settle-ment of white and Indian families since the 1890s, the pattern for Africans began to change only in the 1940s when the numbers of all three groups almost doubled[7] (Burrows, 1959: 24–5). Restrictions on the inter-provincial mobility of Indians had confined the majority to Natal, so that while 2 per cent of coloureds and Africans, and 5 per cent of whites lived in Durban, it contained roughly 40 per cent of the total Indian population (Burrows, 1959: 24–5). Within this context, according to Edwards and Nuttall (1990: 5), public debate over post-war Durban was:

> informed by the relative weakness of the state, by the desire of seg-ments of local capital to restructure the urban workforce, by the increasingly vociferous racial demands of Durban's white ratepay-ers, and by the assertiveness of ever larger numbers of proletar-ianised Africans and Indians.

During the 1940s there was a concerted attempt by the central state to restrict to defined areas, though not to prevent, Indian property own-ership. On the other hand, African residence in the city remained undesired, the municipality's housing policy being primarily geared around a migrant labour system. By 1949 Africans owned 0.1 per cent of Durban's immovable property (Kuper *et al.*, 1958: 31). Although Indians faced discrimination, compared with Africans they had greater opportunity.

Cato Manor, on the outskirts of Durban and formerly occupied by Indian farmers owning small plots of land, was transformed during the rapid industrialisation. The increased urbanisation of Africans, and inadequate housing provision, turned Cato Manor into an informal settlement (Naidoo, 1984: 86).[8] The declining profitability of agriculture and rapid population growth meant that 'shack-farming', the rental of land to African shack-dwellers, became an attractive and lucrative option for Indian landowners so that, in 1950, approximately half of Durban's African population was illegally housed in shack slums on Indian-owned property (Webster, 1987: 34–5). This geographical area became a 'contested urban space, the main focus of a specifically African struggle for land and urban rights in a city which had consistently denied these' (Edwards and Nuttall, 1990: 16).

This period also marked the beginning of the blueprint for racial zoning of Durban, inspired by white anti-Indian agitation against Indian 'penetration'. The 1946 Asiatic Land Tenure Act gave legislative force to the zoning proposals. At the same time the Indian Representation Act sought to co-opt moderate Indian leaders by giving them 'a say in the administration of the zoning proposals, and dangled the carrot of Indian communal representation in parliament' (Edwards and Nuttall, 1990: 17). Cato Manor, under this new legislation, was to be zoned for Indian residence, having obvious implications for African settlement and for the nascent African shack-lords.

Such increased segregation measures intensified oppositional struggles and led to a radicalisation of political organisations, as well as attempts to increase co-operation across racial lines at the leadership level. At the popular level daily life was marked by the struggle for survival in the face of increased prices, high unemployment, lower wages, extreme poverty, housing shortages and overcrowding. This heightened competition and tension between the 'advantaged' Indian and the impoverished and 'aspiring' African. Perceptions of Indian advantage were reinforced by daily contact between the two groups, where the Indian appeared in the role of shopkeeper, landlord, or skilled worker, who began to be perceived as a block to African aspirations. Indian religious and cultural exclusivity reinforced racial boundaries; Indians were seen as a distinct group with distinct interests.

Indian–African tensions were also fanned by intense public white anti-Indianism of the 1940s when the role of white politicians in fuelling this was crucial. Indians were prominent as an election issue in white politics and the election campaign of 1948 reflected these sentiments in the speeches and propaganda of various politicians, who made numerous calls for the compulsory repatriation of Indians, calling them 'dishonest', 'land grabbers', 'unscrupulous', 'unassimilable' and 'distasteful (Moodley, 1979: 488). Indians were labelled 'foreigners' who should be given 'boats not votes', and threatened with violence. Nationalist cabinet ministers utilised public platforms to warn Indians that as 'aliens' they had no future in the country. The white press gave sanction to such anti-Indianism, leading to the general feeling that Indians could be attacked without comeback.

Indians, who lived in relative comfort in the immediate vicinity of impoverished Africans, became the 'obvious scapegoat' of their frustrations (Webster, 1987: 35). Trade in the African market was dominated by Indians and, as prices increased, resentment was expressed through African claims of Indian overcharging (Kirkwood and Webb, 1949: 4). In addition, the subjective experiences of Africans exacerbated the tension. This resentment was played out during the 'riots' when Indian shops were attacked 'while African stores were left untouched' (Webster, 1987: 33). During this period, African wages fell considerably, while the destruction of African farming, caused by a drought between 1944 and 1946, increased their dependency on the urban wage (Gawande, 1989: 33). Further African frustration at maltreatment and overcharging on Indian-owned buses was also expressed. It is important to note that, in 1943–4, 70.6 per cent of Durban Indians lived below the poverty line (Hemson, 1977), despite the success of trade unions in securing higher wages between 1937 and 1946 (Ginwala, 1976: 303). The failure of Indian unions to incorporate African concerns[9] and employer preference for Indian workers, fanned the perception that Indians were a block to African mobility (Hemson, 1977: 102–3). While conflict between Africans and Indians was informal and low-key, white anti-Indianism, reinforced by Indian 'advantage' *vis-à-vis* labour, trade, transport and land, provided an immediate focus. Thus the structural location of the two groups and the resultant politics are a critical context for an understanding of the 1949 conflict (Edwards and Nuttall, 1990: 8).

Political attempts to harness African anger at postwar food scarcity, and the heightened power of the shopkeeper, exacerbated tensions. In 1946 the South African Communist Party's (SACP) organised food campaign became focused on the 'black marketeer' and especially on Indian traders. According to Edwards and Nuttall (1990: 37) this was due to three reasons. Firstly, the anti-Indianism of the Durban whites meant that suppression of the campaign was less likely if directed at Indian traders. Secondly, in order to be effective it had to relate directly to the experiences of Africans and Indians who frequented

Indian stores. Finally, 'radical' Indians from the SACP and the Natal Indian Congress were instrumental in selecting wealthy traders who supported 'reactionary' politics.

Such attempts by political leaders to pursue class-based action within a highly racially defined context, however, fuelled popular consciousness of the exploitative 'wealthy' Indian and had important consequences for 1949, as no distinction was drawn between the poor and wealthy Indian. It is also demonstrative of the gap that existed between political leaders and 'ordinary' people, as the following highlights:

> For Party members this was an exciting experiment in popular socialism, with all the makings of a 'people's revolt'. The crowds were non-racial in character; popular anger was being directed at the worst excesses of capitalism in carefully selected Indian stores; stockpiled goods were being redistributed at controlled prices. ... The generalised looting of Indian stores three years later, in 1949, suggests that many African participants of the 1946 food campaign were drawing different conclusions to those reached by Party activists. ... A further lesson could hardly have been missed: repressive state forces had not intervened because the campaign had targeted Indian rather than white shops. In January 1949 these 'lessons' were ... to be applied with uncanny similarity, but on a far greater scale.
>
> (Edwards and Nuttall, 1990: 11)

The success of informal market networks of production and exchange provided ammunition for African demands for land, housing and business. These demands 'introduced a new element, making existing racially defined struggles over access to and control of material resources that much more volatile. Africans were newcomers in a long-standing battle between whites and Indians' (Edwards and Nuttall, 1990: 7). The co-operative movement increased in importance and significance during the late 1940s, not only as a means of survival but also as a way for emerging shack-leaders to gain a foothold in commercial life, thereby challenging African marginalisation. Organisations such as the Zulu Hlanganani Association and the Zulu Cultural Society made calls to 'displace Indians and Europeans as exploiters of the people' (Gawande, 1989: 33). Appealing to a specific 'African' nationalism, the co-operatives were implicitly anti-Indian, arguing that Indians were 'strangers' who did not 'belong', in order to negotiate gains for African traders (Riots Commission, 1949: 663–9, 304–5).

COURSE OF THE EVENT

> Stones began to fly, glass shattered. Within minutes Victoria Street became a battleground of hostile crowds, flying missiles, damaged buses, and broken glass. ... Looting began through broken shop windows. ... Both African and Indian bystanders exploited a chance for recompense. All the signs were that state power would not intervene to protect Indian property.
>
> (Edwards and Nuttall, 1990: 23)

A scuffle between an Indian shopkeeper and an African boy, witnessed by hundreds, was the 'spark' which, fuelled by rumours of Indian attacks, led to African violence against Indian people and property in Durban on an unprecedented scale. Beginning on Thursday 13 January 1949 it lasted three days. Concentrated in Cato Manor, housing both Indians and Africans, it led to 142 deaths (50 Indians, 87 Africans, 1 white and 4 unknown); 1087 injuries (503 Indians, 541 Africans, 11 Coloureds and 32 whites); the destruction of 247 houses, 58 stores, 1 school and 1 factory, while 1285 houses, 652 stores and 2 factories were damaged. Refugee camps, set up in Indian schools, remained open for eight months[10] (Kirkwood and Webb, 1949: 3).

The unrest has been broadly divided into three phases; the first began on Thursday when an Indian shopkeeper assaulted a 14-year-old African youth, whose head was gashed as a result. This incident was soon overshadowed by collective anger and frustration which became focused on Indian shops and buses. The second phase, when the purpose was more specific, began from Friday when large numbers of African migrant workers gathered in the Indian area at lunch time. Assaults were confined to Indians, many were robbed of their Friday pay. Whites gathered, some encouraging, some passive, some joining in with the looting; their response has generally been interpreted as tacit approval.[11] Press photographs give a good indication of the participants; mainly young men with the exception of one group headed by a woman, many wore the clothes of employed workers and petty traders, the red-trimmed calico uniforms of domestic workers were also prominent along with migrant and dock workers (Riots Commission, 1949).

According to some analysts the unrest widened at this point from assaults on Indians and property into a broader challenge, especially as some 1000 hostel residents began to march towards the city centre. They were met by the police[12] (Naidoo, 1984: 92) who opened fire into the crowd, on the edge of the Indian shopping area (Nuttall, 1989: 21). This action, signifying the beginning of state violence into the unrest, confined the crowds to the shack areas, which were hard to police.

The third phase was marked by mass killings, when the 'violence went beyond looting, beating and breaking to include murder, rape and burning. ... The killings and burning in Cato Manor amounted to a pogrom: the organised extermination and expulsion of all Indians' (Edwards and Nuttall, 1990: 27). Many Indians fled into the bush; some were taken away in police vans while those Indian traders with guns attempted to put up a fight. The goodwill that existed between Indians and Africans in some areas was reflected in instances where Africans risked their lives to shelter and save Indians 'who had collapsed in the grounds'. Machine guns sometimes fired 'for five minutes at a time' into the groups looting and burning buildings (*Natal Daily News*, 15 January 1949). Indians had largely been driven out of the shanty towns and neighbouring districts. There were an estimated 25,000 Indian refugees by the third day. It was the poorest Indians living in the outlying areas, whose socioeconomic position was comparable to Africans, who were the worst hit.

A number of observations need to be made about the course of events. Firstly, an assumed Indian passivity has been contradicted by some writers pointing to Indian actions such as the throwing of bottles and other missiles from balconies. Individual accounts also contradict this assumption; an interviewee made the following comment:

> If the women were alone they had to fend for themselves. My aunty barricaded the whole house with tables and things. It was a real battle but they were prepared with bush knives. Also what they did was get a pot of water, put chillie powder in it so if anyone came nearby, they would splash it in the eyes.
>
> (Interview with community activist, November 1991)

Secondly, the police response was lethargic and largely inadequate in the early stages, reinforcing a view that Indians could be attacked without reprimand. Thirdly, while white people were alerted to the unrest through the morning papers, among Africans the subject aroused much excitement, the tale becoming embellished with each telling, drawing on racial stereotypes. One version of the story stated that Madondo had been decapitated by Indians and his head placed in a mosque. This led to other equally wild rumours: that widespread venereal disease among Africans was the result of Indian lust for African women, that the diluted liquor sold by Indians caused tuber-culosis (Riots Commission, 1949: 277–8, 305–6), and that Indian men in the city were killing African men indiscriminately and raping African women (Naidoo, 1984: 86).

NATURE OF THE EVENT

> Africans put the blame on the Indians. Indians put the blame on the Whites. Whites put the blame on the Indians. The Government put the blame on the Africans and the Indians. African and Indian leaders put the blame on Government policy and its anti-Indian statements.
>
> (Naidoo, 1984: 91)

The nature of an epic is precisely that every retelling depends on when it is being retold as much as who by. In every retelling the central story gathers extraneous material which may be used to suit a particular purpose, the event thus lending itself to epic proportions and mystification. This is done not only at the political but also the popular level, the different narratives often vying with each other to assert and establish their particular version as the 'truth', often to suit specific purposes. This section traces how the story was constructed by differ-ent players in the aftermath of the event.

State

Given that state ideology has continuously emphasised friction as an inevitable marker of inter-racial relations, the state was clearly able to manipulate 1949 to propagate its own racist ideology and give it cre-dence. This was reflected in the findings of the official Riots Commission,[13] seen as 'more ideological than judicial in tone' (*Indian Opinion*, 22 August 1949), which exonerated all but the factor of Indian–African tensions as the cause. Emphasising the inevitability of racial conflict, the state sought to send out a double-edged message. Firstly, it blamed radical groups and their attempts to promote inter-racial co-operation, arguing that the unrest was a clear sign that it was unworkable. Unsurprisingly, the Commission of Enquiry found the 'riots' to be an incident of inherent racial conflict, largely due to the 'character of the parties', which had not been 'motivated by outside influences' (Kirkwood, 1949: 99). This provided valuable leverage for apartheid zoning policies. Secondly, Indians were chastised for the intervention of India, recently liberated from British rule, in the affairs of South Africa. The Report stated that 'one of the most unsettling influences upon the Native mind is the fact that South Africa has a hostile press abroad' (Kirkwood, 1949: 102). In this sense the unrest was seen as an invaluable lesson for the Indians[14] (Naidoo, 1984: 103). Given the virulent anti-Indianism of whites, the 'riots' formed part of the 'return to India' package[15] (Naidoo, 1984: 103).

It was further emphasised that a neutral state had stepped in to restore control. In particular, the 'riots' provided the state with 'ideological ammunition' to justify the 1950 Group Areas Act as a necessary measure to prevent further conflict between racial groups. The destruction of African shanty towns and the rezoning of Indian residential and trading property for white use was justified in the name of the 'riots' by municipal officials (Edwards and Nuttall, 1990: 1). The state also used the 'riots' as a demonstration of the continued 'uncivilised' state of Africans, alluding to the fact that they were not yet ready to exercise responsibility. Moreover, the unrest was used to justify racist policies to the international community, especially through the United Nations. It was stated that 'pictures of the riots should be posted on the wall of the United Nations committee room to show the world that South Africa is struggling with problems more terrible and realistic than those which can be settled by political theorising' (*Weekly Newsletter*, 22 January 1949, p. 3).

Radicals

Immediately after the unrest, the leaders of the African National Congress (ANC), South African Indian Congress (SAIC) and the SACP met in Durban, and leaders issued a public statement condemning the violence and calling for 'greater calm and understanding' (Karis and Carter, 1973: 285–8). The 'riots' delivered a severe blow to the Three Doctors Pact of 1947 which sought to create black unity against the state.

Pursuing their own particular objectives, black political activists claimed that African–Indian tension was absent and that anti-Indian violence was dictated by the racist state. The conflict erupted in the wake of mass joint action against the state planned by the nascent multiracial political alliance between the ANC and SAIC. Recognising the potentially deep damage it could cause, the Congresses blamed the 'riots' on the depressed socioeconomic conditions and discriminatory policies of the state (Karis and Carter, 1973: 285–8). As pointed out by Edwards and Nuttall (1990: 1), apart from the trader-led Natal Indian Organisation expressing concern about the possibility of the 'riots' being organised, this delicate question remained unaddressed.

Many who were critical of black leaders of the time saw the unrest as an indictment of the leadership and the inadequacy of black political organisations (Edwards and Nuttall, 1990: 1). Common mass mobilisation of Africans[16] and Indians had not been seriously addressed in Durban during the 1940s (Nuttall, 1989: 13). Clearly, the unrest threw up issues pertaining to the distance between political organisations and the masses as alliance politics were thrown into confusion.

Generally, in response to the 'riots', the promulgations of black oppositional groups stressed a common black identity and unity of Indian and African against racial oppression, attributing any incident of conflict to state manipulation and propaganda. However, within this was a failure to address issues pertaining to inter-group ignorance, mistrust, and tension. Arguing that an Indian identity was non-existent and a fabrication of the state, radical Indian political activists instead sought to emphasise class or black identity, seeing the two as mutually exclusive. While this facilitated inter-racial solidarity among political leaders, an organisational failure to deal with this issue meant that relations at a mass level remained frustrated. Undeniably, 1949 imposed a 'harsh legacy' for black politics, making unity at the mass level difficult to achieve and the task of the Congress alliance unenviable.

African Traders

The shack-lords and traders, later to become the state-recognised African leaders of the 1960s and 1970s, were the only group to make material gains from the unrest, while the situation of the majority of Africans remained unchanged. African traders, established and marginal, local squatter leaders and shack residents all sought to exploit and protect the opportunities opened up by the 'riots'. As Indian refugees returned to their homes two weeks after the unrest, 'guards' sought to protect their new acquisitions from Indians rumoured to be seeking reprisal; others extended their shacks and new residents came from other parts of the city. Petty traders mushroomed, selling goods unavailable in Indian stores. There was a flood of applications for pedlar's licences while many others traded without applying.

The Zulu Hlanganani Co-operative and Buying Club were set up by leading African traders and were overtly anti-Indian and pro-Apartheid, their major aim being to ensure a monopoly over African trade for their members (Kuper, 1965: 301–2). The organisation became a part of the Bantu National Congress in the 1950s, set up by the Government to oppose militant African nationalism. The Zulu Hlanganani Co-operative, which commemorated the 'riots' in annual celebrations, presented a petition to the Union Government in 1955 expressing concern at Indian domination in trade, provocatively evoking 1949:

> The responsible officials have since 1949 promised to rectify these mistakes but all in vain. It shall be remembered that in January 14th 1949, the riots took place between Bantu and the Indians. Trading interests are still in the hands of the Indians. We, therefore, present these grievances to you, Sir, so that they can be immediately rectified. It is not our wish to see another bloody war ... but unless things can come our way within the short space of time it is possible that our respect and endurance shall no more prevail.
>
> (Kuper, 1965: 305)

At the end of the month, when temporary municipal bus certificates expired leaving only Indian buses, rumours of an African backlash drove 500 Indians to seek safety in refugee camps. This reflected the receptiveness of ordinary people to rumours of a repetition of the 'riots' (*Natal Mercury*, 24–6 February 1949).

'Conservatives'

While the Native Advisory Board and conservatives in the Durban ANC agreed to set up a joint council with the NIC to 'promote mutual understanding', they also used the unrest to increase their bargaining power with the municipality, 'seeking specifically to advance the interests of an aspirant commercial middle class through segregation policies which excluded Indian interests from "Native" areas' (Edwards and Nuttall, 1990: 30). With the support of white officials, Advisory Board politicians were successful in setting up a wholesale trade to supply African retailers, and in ensuring support for African trade licences. These gains 'enabled the riots to be remembered as an "act of God" which launched a more prosperous African trading class' (Edwards and Nuttall, 1990: 30).

The riots have an ongoing longevity, which is reflected in the discourse of many contemporary political players. Inkatha, and its leader Chief Buthelezi, have frequently used the 'riots' as part of its anti-Indian rhetoric. Indeed, Buthelezi, in his constant proclamations for Zulu-led black unity and chastisement of Indian meddling in African politics, has often threatened a repeat of 1949. In 1976 Chief Sithole, a member of the Kwazulu Legislative Assembly, told his audience that:

> when the Congress (ANC) was composed only of Africans, there were no problems, but that the trouble started when different nations were allowed to join. We must be wary of these Indians because they want to use us as their tools, as a ladder for them to reach their goals.
>
> (Mare and Hamilton, 1987: 152)

Seven years later, despite his denial that he had used 1949 to threaten Indians, Buthelezi warned Indians to reject the proposals for the Tri-cameral parliament, threatening that: 'We have seen racial outbursts in this country and we know what mob anger can do' (Mare and Hamilton, 1987: 152). For many Indians these threats were affirmed by the unrest in Inanda in 1985, the Natal violence of 1990 further creating fresh fears.

1949 has also been central to the discourse of conservative Indians who have sought to participate in Government-created structures. The 'riots' were evoked during the Tri-cameral elections in the 1980s by conservative Indian leaders attempting to lend credence to ambiguous state reform policies and their participation in such structures.

CONSEQUENCES OF THE EVENT

While the significance of the 'riots' has been recognised, the potency of their legacy has not been fully acknowledged. A dismissal of those explanations which draw on 'common-sense' memories, as attempts to develop conspiratorial explanations (Edwards and Nuttall, 1990: 2), has often resulted in an underestimation of the potency of the collective memory at the mass level, to which I now turn.

The significance of an event is often assessed on the basis of the 'body count' or damage to property. Undeniably 1949 was a big event. However, it can be argued that it has been of greater significance at the perceptual and psychological level, leaving an enduring legacy for future relations between Africans and Indians and constantly feeding Indian fears of possible persecution under majority rule. In assessing this, it is important to look at flashpoints in relations between Indians and Africans since the 'riots', in order to see how other incidents may further furnish earlier perceptions and the use people make of them.

Affirmation of the Epic

Inanda has created enormous problems. But, although Inanda seemed to have as dramatic an impression on the psyche of Indian people as 1949 did, even now when Indian people talk of Africans in a negative way, they talk about 1949.

(Interview, May 1989)

The Inanda conflict of 1985, though generally viewed as being different in nature to 1949, further generated fear and tension, particularly in Durban since the imagery of 1949 was quickly evoked. Like 1949, 1985 was preceded by an economic recession with obvious implications for the most impoverished in South African society. The 1980s were marked by heightened political protest and unrest. In 1985, in protest against the assassination of a prominent lawyer, Victoria Mxenge, and the state of emergency, African attacks began on 'symbols of the system', but later spread to shops. In Inanda the violence turned against Indians and their property, an estimated 2000 Indians took refuge in Phoenix, an Indian township. Although it did not lead to a major confrontation, by the end of the month 75 were dead and over 1000 injured, with many Indian shops and houses destroyed (Sitas, 1986).

Indians complained that 'the government had created a situation where Africans were beginning to believe that the land was already theirs and Indians had no business remaining' (Meer, 1985: 51). Once again, Indian wealth and property were juxtaposed against African impoverishment, and Indians viewed as part of a system which systematically denied the African. The participation of some Indians in the Tri-cameral Parliament, which gave pseudo-political rights to Indians and Coloureds only, also created antipathy towards Indians. Buthelezi criticised Indian participation, stating that Africans were angry that 'Indians have entered parliament. I had warned that the new political dispensation was a recipe for violence' (*Post Natal*, 29 August 1985).

Marked by inadequate police protection, Indians formed heavily armed vigilante squads as rumours of the violence spreading into Indian areas became rife. According to a political activist who worked to allay fears:

> In Chatsworth, Bayview there is this one long road that divides the African and Indian communities. In the evening, lots of Indians formed a vigilante squad; they were armed with bush knives and sticks. There was this overwhelming fear. We were just a small group of people trying to allay this fear, we stood no chance, we just had to get out. After doing so much work in the community about 1949, we had a situation in Inanda which caused so much damage.
>
> (Interview, November 1991)

Just as 1949 was preceded by the 1947 Doctor's Pact, 1985 was preceded by the formation of the United Democratic Front. Although, at the national level, Indians and Africans were uniting in protest, in Inanda, as in Cato Manor in 1949, Indians themselves became the focus of violence. According to a prominent activist in the locality, 'the events of August 1985 [have] shattered many people and reopened divisions between communities' (interview, September 1990).

Collective Memory

The 'riots' of 1949, along with 1985, are the single largest historical factor underlying relations between African and Indian people, especially among the generation which directly experienced the unrest. At one level it can be argued that relations between the two groups are a result of the opportunism of white politicians and the state. At the popular level, however, 1949, along with other incidents of violence, is offered as proof of the violent and barbarous African 'character' which is constantly evoked to furnish fears of majority rule.

This view of Africans was reflected in the writing of Indian journalists who used terms such as 'barbarous determination' and 'Africans swept forward in their savage march' to evoke an image of 1949 and the African in the minds of Indians (Nowbath, 1949). The negative view of Africans also forms an integral part of the Indian folklore. According to an interviewee:

> When I was growing up, we used to have these little threats. When you have to eat, they say if you don't eat bama bullooloo is going to

catch you – the bullooloo is the African. So as I grew up, it was fostered in me, I had to be afraid of the African because of 1949.

(Interview, November 1991)

It is evident that while a small number of Indians are able to recognise the wider causes of the 'riots', the majority and especially those

who have seen their homes destroyed in front of their eyes, those who have seen a life-times savings go up in smoke, those who have seen their children hacked in front of them and those who have helplessly watched their daughters raped, will not, they cannot forget.

(Nowbath, 1949)

Clearly 1949 has become an entrenched part of the Indian folklore, its embellished reconstruction, reinforced by daily newspaper reports of African violence, being used to furnish fears about African and Indian relations in the future. The terror of 1949 has been passed on to successive generations in varying forms. An interviewee asserted that 'there is nobody who does not know about 1949, whatever version they have. My aunty told me a lot of stories. Most of my age group were not there but they probably know more than the people who were there' (interview, November 1991).

The year 1949 also marked a loss of faith by Indians in the newly formed political alliance between Indians and Africans. While leaders increased co-operative efforts, for the majority of Indians the 'wounds of the African–Indian riots in 1949 had not yet healed' (Kuper, 1965: 111). Additionally, a number of events reinforced and fanned mutual suspicion and mistrust. The events in Uganda were a painful reminder of the 'riots' to Indian South Africans who nurse a fear about the possibility of a Kenyan or Ugandan situation taking place in South Africa.

The events of 1949 and 1985 are generally seen as 'unusual' and 'extreme'. However, mistrust and ignorance at the mass level, despite solidarity among political leaders, is prevalent and the interests of the two groups have failed to converge, largely due to their differential economic and political location in society. The 'cultural arrogance' and social isolation of Indians, actively encouraged by apartheid policies, is often cited as a major cause of resentment against them. This was reflected in Natal's leading African newspaper, which pointed to the inevitability of 1949 given Indian economic advantage and 'a sense of snobbishness and superiority over the Africans' (Nowbath, 1949).

Generally, racial stereotyping among Africans and Indians is prevalent and any attempts to improve Indian–African relations at the mass level will continue to be frustrated as long as structural inequalities persist.

It is important to underline that despite the existence of hostility, there exists a history of common alliances between the two groups. While such developments indicate that caution needs to be exercised in painting a totally negative picture of Indian–African relations, they have a limited impact on group perceptions at the mass level. It is clear that there is a yawning gap between attempts by political leaders to forge unity and the popular response, informed by the collective memory and folklore of traumatic events such as 1949.

CONCLUSION

The chapter illustrates the re-telling of the story, the way in which the 1949 Durban 'riots' set the text for an epic. It has been argued that, in paying attention to the way the story is reconstructed, it is possible to shift the emphasis from the causes of the riots to the motives of the story-tellers. In the main it has been articulated that for Indians the 'riots' have taken on epic proportions; the story is constantly retold to justify their view of the African and their fear of change.

The chapter also highlights the use of incident in colonial politics, the way that incidents generate their own momentum, and the way that they are used for political purposes. It provides some examples of the way that people allude to the Durban 'riots', and the purposes for which they do it. The state and oppositional political leaders are among the examples discussed to demonstrate how the story has been retold for immediate political purposes.

The chapter also looks at event as message, the way in which people see and dissect the event in order to preach a particular message. The retelling of the story is fashioned not only by the internal consequences but also by external developments. For instance, 1949 is often related by Indians in South Africa to the wider field of African–Indian relations in Africa as a whole, to draw comparisons and furnish their fears about majority rule.

The history of the dominant white minority in the nurturing of antagonistic relations between Africans and Indians is importantly underlined. The role of differential incorporation and racialisation, together with their own structures, perceptions and communal organisation in determining relations between Africans and Indians, is also assessed. It has been made apparent that the profound psychological legacy left by the open violence of 1949 has created a collective memory and become an integral part of Indian folklore as an 'epic', which has been constantly used to furnish Indian fears about majority rule. This anxiety nursed by Indians, and aided by the experience of the South Asian diaspora in Africa, is shared collectively by all Indians and is continually reconstructed and transmitted. Heightened violence in the contemporary context, accompanied by the increased assertion of ethnicity, enhances the vulnerability felt by Indians as a minority group which occupies a position of relative advantage.

NOTES

1. It is not the traditional meaning of the term 'epic' that is adopted herein, i.e. the transmission of a heroic event. Instead, the concept is used to capture the transmission of a collective memory over time.
2. Evidence suggests that over 50 per cent of the early Cape slaves in the seventeenth and early eighteenth centuries originated from Bengal and South India, who, over time, were absorbed into the Cape Malay and Muslim population.
3. During the 51 years of indenture a total of 152,184 indentured migrants arrived in Natal; of these 101,468 embarked from Madras and 50,716 from Calcutta. Of the total, 104,641 were men and boys and 48,022 women and girls, a ratio of 46:100, and of the 152,184, a total of 42,415 returned to India, though recorded figures were not always accurate.
4. In some colonies, planters not only reinforced divisions between Africans and Indians but also encouraged them between Indians, labelled as 'Calcuttans' and 'Madrasees'.
5. This initial view of Indians later changed to one that viewed them as 'filthy', 'wicked', 'cunning' and 'deceitful'.
6. Between 1846 and 1864, 2.25 million acres were set aside for African occupation, and by 1874–5 of the 6 million acres owned by colonists, 5 million were occupied by Africans.
7. Between 1936 and 1951, the number of Africans rose from 71,000 to 151,000, the Indian population increased from 89,000 to 161,000, while the number of whites rose from 97,000 to 151,000.
8. There were 69 shops; 1 bicycle, 2 box and 4 clothing factories; 10 Government and 7 vernacular schools; 5 temples, 2 mosques and 5 cemeteries in Cato Manor. All were Indian-owned.

9.   The Industrial Conciliation Act of 1924 dictated that Africans could not belong to registered trade unions.
10.   African deaths and injuries were largely due to police and military action. The official Indian death figures were claimed to be low.
11.   Numerous cases of whites, men and women, inciting Africans to attack Indians were noted.
12.   It was claimed by a prominent political activist in an interview in 1985 that 'Only when the Government of India threatened to send in her fighting fleet was state police used. However, police intervention was not efficient because it would have been counter to the state's policy of divide and rule if it acted quickly and efficiently.'
13.   The Commission, problematic from the outset, refused to allow members of the affected communities to sit on it. It also refused the cross-examination of witnesses, as a result of which 18 organisations withdrew.
14.   A visiting French writer in 1948 noted the belief that an independent India would invade Natal was widespread among white Natalians.
15.   This is demonstrated in the following extract from the writing of a Natal white: 'I detested the Indians. In January 1949 when the anti-Indian pogroms began and Africans in Durban killed many Indians, burning and looting their shops and homes and attacking them in the streets, I sat down gleefully to write a letter to the Natal Indian Congress. In it I asked if this was not surely their warning to leave South Africa and return to India.'
16.   During this period, African politics displayed two disparate strands. The first, a conservative one, was articulated by 'establishment' politicians seeking to build a 'zulu nation' and who, in order to have a greater stake in the city, sought to bargain for concessions through Advisory Board structures. They sought to use segregation to African advantage, especially against Indian traders, and in this they shared the anti-Indian sentiments of whites. The second strand, articulated by the ANC Youth League in the 1940s, emphasised confrontation through mass action instead of deputation politics. Although sceptical about unity, they viewed Indians as possible allies in mass campaigns.

REFERENCES

Beall, J. (1982) 'Class, Race and Gender: the Political Economy of Women in Colonial Natal', PhD thesis, University of Natal.

Bhana, S. and Brain, J. (1990) *Setting Down Roots: Indian Migrants in South Africa, 1860–1911* (Johannesburg: Witwatersrand University Press).

Boeskin, A. J. (1977) *Slaves and Free Blacks at the Cape, 1638–1700* (Cape Town: Tafelberg).

Burrows, J. R. (1959) *The Population and Labour Resources of Natal* (Pietermaritzburg: Natal Town and Regional Planning Commission).

De B. Webb and Wright, J. B. (eds) (1976) *The James Stuart Archive of Recorded Oral Evidence Relating to the History of Zulu and Neighbouring Peoples* (Pietermaritzburg: University of Natal).

Edwards, I. and Nuttall, T. (1990) 'Seizing the Moment: the January 1949 Riots, Proletarian Populism and the Structure of African Urban Life in Durban during the Late 1940s', *History Workshop*, 6–10 February (Johannesburg: University of Witwatersrand).

Gawande, A. (1989) 'Indian–African Relations in Natal: Racial Tension and its Socio-Economic Causes', Undergraduate dissertation, Oxford University.

Ginwala, F. (1976) 'Class Consciousness and Control: Indian South African, 1860–1946', PhD thesis, Oxford University.

Haraksingh, K. (1987) 'Control and Resistance among Indian Workers: a Case Study of Labour on the Sugar Plantations of Trinidad, 1875–1917', in D. Dabydeen and B. Samaroo (eds), *India in the Caribbean* (London: Hansib).

Hemson, D. (1977) 'Dock Workers, Labour Circulation and Class Struggles in Durban, 1940–1959', *Journal of Southern African Studies*, 4(1), pp. 88–124.

Karis, T. and Carter, G. M. (1973) *From Protest to Challenge: Documents on African Politics in South Africa, 1882–1964*, vol. 2 (Stanford, CA: Hoover Institution Press).

Kirkwood, K. (1949) 'Failure of a Report', *Race Relations*, 26(4), pp. 97–106.

Kirkwood, K. and Webb, M. (1949) *The Durban Riots and After* (Johannesburg: South African Institute of Race Relations).

Kuper, L. (1965) *An African Bourgeoisie: Race, Class and Politics in South Africa* (New Haven, CT: Yale University Press).

Kuper, L., Watts, H. and Davies, R. (1958) *Durban: A Study in Racial Ecology* (London: Jonathan Cape).

Mare, G. and Hamilton, G. (1987) *An Appetite for Power: Buthelezi's Inkatha and South Africa* (Johannesburg: Ravan Press).

Marks, S. (1970) *Reluctant Rebellion: 1906–1908 Disturbances in Natal* (Oxford: Clarendon Press).

Meer, F. (1985) *Unrest in Natal, August 1985* (Durban: Institute for Black Research).

Moodley, K. (1979) 'The Ambivalence of Survival Politics in Indian–African Relations', in B. Pachai (ed.), *South Africa's Indians: The Evolution of a Minority* (Washington, DC: University Press of America).

Moore, R. J. (1987) *Race, Power and Social Segmentation in Colonial Society: Guyana after Slavery, 1838–1891* (New York: Gordon & Breach).

Naidoo, J. (1984) 'Reflection on the Two Indians of South Africa', BA dissertation, University of Durban–Westville, Natal.

Nowbath, R. S. (1949) *The Forum*, 29 January.

Nuttall, T. (1989) 'It Seems Peace But It Can Be War: The Durban "Riots" of 1949 and the Struggle for the City', paper presented at South African Historical Society Conference, Pietermaritzburg.

Padayachee, V. and Morrell, R. (1991) 'Indian Merchants and Dukawallahs in the Natal Economy, c. 1875–1914', *Journal of Southern African Studies*, 17(1), pp. 71–103.

Sitas, A. (1986) 'Inanda 1985: Where Wealth and Power and Blood Reign Worshipped Gods', *South African Labour Bulletin*, 11(4), pp. 85–119.

Thiara, R. K. (1993) 'Migration, Organisation and Inter-Ethnic Relations: Indian South Africans 1860–1990', PhD thesis, University of Warwick.

Thompson, L. M. (1952) *Indian Immigration into Natal, 1860–1872*, Cape Town: Archives Yearbook of South African History, 2.

Webster, E. (1987) 'The 1949 Durban Riots: a Case Study in Race and Class', in P. Bonnor (ed.), *Working Papers in Southern African Studies* (Johannesburg: African Studies Institute).

Part IV
Migration and Identity

9 Migration and Dislocation: Echoes of Loss within Jewish Women's Narratives

RUTH SWIRSKY

From around 1880 to the Second World War (which transformed Jewish history and Jewish identity with an awful finality), millions of Jews left their homes in Europe and emigrated to various parts of the world in two distinct waves of migrations, the larger migration from Eastern Europe in the decades around the turn of the century, and then a second, smaller migration of refugees from Nazism in the 1930s. In most histories of Jewish immigration, women disappear from view, subsumed into the male immigrant experience (Gartner, 1960; Hirschfeld, 1984), yet their experiences of migration were undoubtedly shaped by their gender as well as their ethnic origins and their class, together with the current political, social, economic and cultural conditions in the countries to which they emigrated and the characteristics of the Jewish communities already there (Hyman, 1983: 157; Jewish Women in London Group, 1989: 8). The gendered specificity of the experience of Jewish migration is now being examined, albeit largely in relation to the significance of gender in the process of acculturation of immigrants.

This chapter seeks to explore some of the ways in which Jewish women experienced and were transformed by migration with its separations, dislocation and loss, as well as the opportunities it presented. Historical analysis of the gendered specificity of the two periods of migration provides a framework within which analysis of autobiographical narratives will be integrated. Drawing on life histories enables us to fill in some of the silences of those histories. At the same time the fragmentary nature of evidence of the scars of exile raises further questions about the ways in which those narratives are constructed, as well as the particularity of migration in relation to the wider issues of life histories.

187

In relation to the experience of migration and exile, there are elements of both commonality and difference in the narratives of women
who participated in the two waves of mass migration, from Eastern
Europe from around 1880 to 1914 and from Nazi Germany and
annexed countries in the 1930s. The former was essentially economic
(though underwritten by anti-Semitism), the latter a migration of
refugees fleeing almost certain death, a political migration. This is
perhaps a somewhat artificial distinction, but it may be useful in
reflecting upon the differential impact of migration and exile and
women's feelings about the dislocation and loss. Inevitably, the
immensity of the Holocaust shaped the experiences of the refugees
from Nazism in very particular ways, especially in their mixed perceptions of and relationships to 'home'.[1] I am aware that using categories
such as 'Jewish women', or even 'Jewish women refugees', or 'Eastern
European Jewish women', clearly does not mean they all had the same
experiences or even the same responses to similar experiences; none
the less there are elements of commonality – and at another level
those elements of commonality extend across gender and ethnic
boundaries.

The two migrations differed in a number of important respects. In
the first place they were impelled by different historical forces – the
East European Jews by the rapidly worsening economic and political
climate, the German refugees by the threat of Nazism. The two migrations were differently constituted in class terms, the former overwhelmingly working class, the latter mainly middle class (because they
were more likely to have the means to enable them to emigrate). The
communities they came to were also economically, politically, socially
and culturally different, with the communities the refugees came to
having been transformed by the impact of the earlier mass migration.
Finally, the East European immigrants tended to settle in concentrated working-class communities, while the refugees from Nazism,
initially at least, tended to be dispersed geographically, though in time
they formed numerous societies and institutions which continue to
provide cultural continuity.

THE EXODUS FROM EASTERN EUROPE

Between 1880 and 1914 some 3 million Jews left Eastern Europe, the
overwhelming majority (around 2 million) going to the United States.
Only a small proportion settled in Western Europe, mainly Britain,

although many more passed through Britain's ports, staying briefly in order to purchase a cheaper ticket to their ultimate destination. About 120,000 settled, twice as many as the existing Jewish population of Britain in 1880 (Gartner, 1960: 30). This mass migration began because of severe economic hardship, and was exacerbated by the pogroms in the early 1880s, culminating in the restrictive May Laws of 1882 in Russia which legitimated discrimination and violence against Jews.

There is a small but growing literature, both in Britain and especially in the United States, which provides some excellent histories of Jewish women immigrants from Eastern Europe (Burman, 1990; Friedman-Kasaba, 1996; Glenn, 1990; Hyman, 1995; Marks, 1991, 1994). Debates about the role of women in immigrant adaptation have focused firstly on the extent to which women contributed to or hindered the process of acculturation/assimilation, and secondly on whether migration offered at least a degree of emancipation or subjected women to new forms of control and subordination (Friedman-Kasaba, 1996; Hyman, 1995).

The nature of the Eastern European Jewish culture from which they came was critical in terms of the significance of gender for these immigrant women. Portrayals of Jewish immigrant culture have frequently been framed in terms of adherence to or movement away from the traditions of the *shtetl* (Jewish Eastern Europe village). The assumption that the patriarchal nature of Jewish culture acted as a brake on Jewish immigrant women's participation in the public sphere has been predicated on the presumption of Jewish women's confinement within the home. In fact, immigrant Jewish women had their roots in a culture which enabled women to participate actively, though not on an equal basis with men, in public secular life. East European Jewish culture offered women contradictory messages. On the one hand, positions of status and power within the public sphere, sacred and communal, were reserved for men. On the other, Jewish culture permitted women relative independence in the secular sphere. It might be argued then, that 'as a consequence of their subordinate status within Judaism, women were less regulated than men and therefore ... were able to partake in all activities that were not expressly forbidden them' (Hyman, 1983. 158–9).

Immigrant Jewish culture interacted with gender and class to determine the nature of immigrant Jewish women's participation in public life (Burman, 1990; Kuzmack, 1990; Marks, 1991; Tananbaum, 1994). Paula Hyman has argued that these immigrant women challenged elements of the prevailing domestic ideology which limited women's public role and imbued their role as mothers with a spiritual significance, and that 'Eastern European immigrants and their children contested the boundaries between domestic and public life that characterised middle class gender norms' (Hyman, 1995: 8). Although those boundaries were being challenged by women in Britain and America at that time, these immigrant Jewish women brought to that process a different set of experiences and cultural presumptions.

At the same time the dislocation of migration often strained the fabric of family life and placed upon women much of the responsibility for maintaining the integrity of the family. One of the consequences of migration, therefore, was the heightened centrality of mothers within the home. It might also be argued that they came to play a more central role in the maintenance of Jewishness. There was the possibility of greater continuity between Jewish religious practice and women's domestic routines than was the case for Jewish men, for whom religious practice was centred in public ritual which was more subject to disruption in the process of assimilation from which only a minority were immune. Thus Jewish women came to be revered as good wives and mothers in relation to cultural continuity, an idealisation which obscured the part played by single as well as married women within the family economy and the public sphere (Marks, 1991). Consequently, as Hyman has argued, 'in some ways Jewish women were agents of assimilation; in others, buffers against the disruptive influences of the new society' (Hyman, 1995: 97).

Feminist scholarship has provided a sharper focus on the contradictory features of Jewish women's experience of migration and their role within immigrant Jewish society. What still remains somewhat obscured by analysis of their role within immigrant society, or even analysis of the transformative experiences of migration, is the dislocations and losses of those experiences, particularly in the British accounts, in part because of the paucity of autobiographical narratives.

Large-scale migration from Eastern Europe was largely ended by the First World War; migration continued during the two decades between the wars, but at a much-reduced level. The majority of Jews remained in Eastern Europe, to be engulfed by the unimaginable during the Holocaust. It was the Jews who lived under Nazi rule prior to the war who ironically had the greatest chance of survival because in the years leading up to war, as life became increasingly restrictive and dangerous for Jews, there was still some possibility of escape. Of the approximately 680,000 Jews living in Germany and Austria prior to Nazi rule, about 400,000 had left by October 1939 (Berghahn, 1984: 74) – though those who moved to other continental countries did not necessarily escape the fate of those who remained.

REFUGEES FROM NAZISM: FROM VICTIMS TO HEROINES?

In the 1930s, few countries were willing to give asylum to those seeking refuge, beleaguered as those countries were by the Great Depression, quite apart from more specifically political factors which shaped their immigration policies. The United States was the destination of the largest number of refugees from Nazism, taking in around 130,000. Many more would have preferred to go there, but especially in the last desperate year before war broke out, availed themselves of any possible route of escape, from Cuba to Shanghai, Argentina to Australia. Britain's restrictive immigration policies resulted in very few refugees being admitted before 1938, though ultimately about 55,000 were granted refugee status, with about half arriving between April and August 1939 (Carsten, 1984: 15).

In recent years attention has increasingly been paid to the experiences of women refugees from Nazism, and this has led to a re-evaluation of their role within that history (Kushner, 1989; Lixl-Purcell, 1988; Morris, 1996; Quack, 1995). The recovery of that experience and re-conceptualisation of that history is undoubtedly important. A striking illustration of that re-conceptualisation comes from Peter Gay, who in 1966 had dedicated a book to 'the many thousands of pilgrims ... whom Hitler compelled to discover America', including 'the spoiled wives who supported their unemployable husbands by washing floors, making candy and selling underwear'. Thirty years later, in the epilogue to the collection *Between Sorrow and Strength: Women Refugees of the Nazi Period*, he acknowledged that comment as 'cheap and gratuitous and unfair', having come now to regard those women as heroines (Gay, 1995: 353).

A number of contributors to that collection in particular bear testament to the women refugees' greater resilience, strength and adaptability than that of the men. They argue that 'women seemed to be able to adjust to the difficulties of immigration more easily than men on both emotional and practical levels' (Morris, 1995: 150); that 'on the whole – and of course with exceptions – it was the women "who carried the family through"' (Schiff, 1995: 186); that they demon-

strated an 'astounding degree of imaginativeness and talent for improvisation [and] found themselves a variety of odd jobs' (Berghahn,
1995: 77); that 'women's greater readiness to swallow their pride and
to accept whatever opportunity offered itself probably also explains
why they seem to have coped better emotionally. It was they who
became the emotional bedrock of the family, who offered comfort to
the other members of the family whilst their husbands lapsed into
depression or even committed suicide' (ibid.: 76); that 'thirty six [of
the 18,000 refugees in Shanghai] – mainly men – committed suicide. It
was the women who withstood the traumatic events far better than the
men' (Kranzler, 1995: 133).

It would seem then that an historical consensus appears to be
emerging which casts these Jewish refugee women as heroines.
Certainly the extraordinary experiences of escape and exile did
provide German Jewish women with opportunities to demonstrate
their strength and resourcefulness, and to assume greater power than
they had previously, constructing a new subjectivity on which to build
their identities and futures.

While I would not wish to contest those accounts and interpretations, there is a tendency to gloss over the trauma and damage
wrought by their experiences. Partly the rebalancing that has been
going on is a result of history being an interpretation of the past from
a present which has been transformed by feminism and its different
ways of understanding the past. And partly it may result from the
nature of the evidence on which it draws.

LIFE HISTORIES AND MIGRATION

The experience of migration brings into focus the intersection of biography and history. The life that is lived and what becomes the biography unfolds within a particular history. The disjunction wrought by
migration brings with it a particularly sharp reminder of the potency
of chance in affecting the course of the life that has been lived and the
multiple possibilities of the different lives that might have been. The
individual life and self is refracted through the narration of an autobiography and that narration ultimately leads back to us, to our identities. We each of us have a life story, an inner narrative which *is* our
lives, is us, is our identities. The disparate events and experiences of
the past are ordered and structured through a narrative account that
suggests coherence. It is perhaps inevitable that we seek to pin down

the past, give it coherence and continuity. In the course of such sense-making, ideas of 'truth' tend to be subordinated to the development of accounts which carry greater personal validity in the present.

It is the nature of the engagement with the present which determines the manner in which the past is recollected and in which the autobiographical narrative is constructed. Individuals select and structure a store of ready-made narratives; a part of a life story is compressed into one moment of self-narration which 'can be told and retold for its illustrative qualities and its ability to re-present a period in our lives' (Kehily, 1995: 24).

In constructing our life stories we draw upon ongoing stories and narrative structures available to us within our community and culture. This is evident in the autobiographical accounts I have examined. At times they begin to take on the character of what Sommer (1988) calls a 'collective testimony'. Though the women know their experiences are unique, they simultaneously recognise they are in some sense typical. In Katherine Morris's collection of autobiographical accounts of Jewish women refugees to Brazil, she describes 'the paradox of [these women] seeing their lives as both singular and representative' (Morris, 1996: 12).

Within such culturally determined narrative structures, migrant women clearly have difficulty in articulating and revealing the trauma and loss of migration, when they were migrating *to* something – a better life for economic migrants and safety for political migrants – which almost requires the construction of a narrative of progress, of moving forward. Such narratives tend to be cast within an archetypal autobiographical form which gives them a 'heroic' quality. In any case, as Hoffman suggests, 'Memory can perform retrospective manoeuvres to compensate for fate' (1991: 115); thus what tends to be emphasised is the positive aspects of the experience, in order to give meaning to the past. The autobiographical story written in the third person by Martha Glogauer (an immigrant to Brazil from Germany in 1933), under the pen name Mirjam Logat, is one such 'heroic' memoir:

> The women always found a way to get ahead, they worked, they slaved, they sacrificed, they defended themselves and supported the family. Marion, who had observed, heard and experienced so much, knew very well that she was not an isolated case, that she was only one of the many who emigrated and now fought for a new goal. She belonged to the uncounted ones, who with sheer iron will and energy struggled, stuck it out and got ahead.
>
> (Morris, 1995: 152)

Another clear illustration of such a narrative of progress is an autobiography written in 1911 by a young immigrant from Russia to
America which embodies the classic structure of 'an exemplary life'
(Stanley, 1992: 13). Mary Antin was exceptionally successful in her
project of assimilation and achievement; hers is an archetypal autobiography, the travelling of a life from difficult beginnings, overcoming obstacles and achieving success, what Stanley describes as a
progressive, linear narrative of almost mythological qualities (Stanley,
1992: 11–13). Only in the preface to the book does Antin write:

> All the processes of uprooting, transportation, replanting, acclimatis-
> ation and development took place in my own soul... . I can never
> forget, for I bear the scars. But I want to forget – sometimes I long
> to forget .
>
> (Antin, 1912/1985)

Migration to an utterly different world seals the separation of child
and young woman, which she deals with by suggesting a complete
break with that younger self:

> I was born, I have lived and I have been made over... . I am just as
> much out of the way as if I were dead, for I am absolutely other
> than the person whose story I have to tell. Physical continuity with
> my earlier self is no disadvantage. I could speak in the third person
> and not feel that I was masquerading... . I can reveal everything; for
> *she,* and not *I,* is my real heroine. My life I have still to live; her life
> ended when mine began.
>
> (Antin, 1912/1985: x)

While there is always some slippage between the 'I' who recollects
and the self who is recalled and who appears as a character in a suc-
cession of episodes (Crites, 1986: 159), Antin has formalised that
hiatus in her prefatory remarks, rather than seeking to impose continuity.[2] This strategy is also utilised by a later writer, Hilde Domin,
exiled from Germany in the 1930s. In an autobiographical essay, she
writes:

> I, Hilde Domin, am amazingly young. I was born in 1951, crying, as
> everyone does at birth. It was not in Germany, even though German
> is my native tongue... . My parents were dead when I was born.
>
> (Domin, 1988: 209–210)

But she goes on to say,

> [I am] an individual who still uses the same recipes for cooking as before and whose soufflés have not suffered, who indeed still likes to stay in bed until nine in the morning. But absolutely everything else is different.

(Ibid.: 214)

Both these women experienced their rebirth when they became writers, but my presumption is that this provided the means rather than being the ultimate cause. Perhaps it was a fatal combination of the dislocation of migration together with becoming a writer which led to the hiatus between the *I* of now and *she* who is recalled tipping over into symbolic death.

Eva Hoffman describes migration and exile as like a death. 'You are disappearing from the world in which you existed, you are losing a whole world.... [I]t is the loss of a life you have had' (Lappin, 1995: 11). And yet migration, with its implied moving forward, accords so well with the narrative structure of archetypal autobiographies, and so the loss and dislocation are only rarely referred to.

Migration entails not just physical dislocation, a dislocation of place, but a dislocation of self. The life that is lived after migration is different not simply in terms of place, of culture, usually language, of the events that are lived out; within that different life a different identity, a different self is (re)constructed, within 'a body occupying a foreign space'.[3] As Howard Stein has suggested:

> The boundaries of the self are defined by a psycho-geography of place. Uprooted from these, one may feel as though one has gained the world but lost the soul. The land of opportunity – fulfilled and failed alike – becomes the land of unfinished mourning.

(Stein, 1984: 274)

Eva Hoffman captures that sense of an individual 'lost in translation' in the title of her autobiographical reflections. However, she also recognises that, while life is immensely hard for immigrants, for the most part it is better than what was left behind – and in many cases an absolute necessity for survival – and she asks: 'where do the pangs of a bifurcated identity figure on this scale?' (Hoffman, 1991: 261). They *do* figure because migration is experienced by the individual not only in material terms, in social experience, but in terms of emotions, identity, a sense of self. Behind the gratitude for having been given a chance to rebuild a life in better or safer circumstances, behind the sense of very real achievement (for those who 'made it'), can sometimes be discerned ambivalence, faint echoes of the loss that migration entailed.

ECHOES OF LOSS

In the 1980s I was part of the Jewish Women in London Group's oral history project focusing on Jewish women immigrants and their daughters, and will draw on that research as well as on autobiographical writing of Jewish women immigrants to other parts of the world, in particular the United States. Only years later, with the publication of a number of studies which have sought to recover the role of Jewish women in migrating and rebuilding lives in new contexts, have I returned to those interviews I did in the 1980s in an attempt to interrogate them with different questions, to seek out not only the ways in which women experienced the migration differently from men, but the ways in which it left deep scars. There are only fragments in those oral testimonies, as well as autobiographies, which allow such understanding, echoes of the losses of migration, uprooting, relocation and resettlement within narratives which provide ample evidence of the adaptability and strength of these Jewish women migrants. Narratives from both migrations will be examined for what they reveal of the impact on the self of having lost the life they might have had within the world they called 'home'.

Within the narratives of two of the daughters of immigrants whom I interviewed, narratives which largely conformed to the dominant autobiographical form, echoes of dislocatory experiences could be heard in their accounts of their mothers. Both the women referred to the pain of loss and the difficulties engendered by the displacement which their mothers experienced. Rita Altman's parents emigrated from Poland to Germany just after the First World War and were refugees to Britain again in 1939. Thus the family experienced both migrations, from Eastern Europe and then again as refugees. She has considerable insight into the impact of the scars of separation on their family life as she was growing up. The process of migration for young adults frequently entails leaving parents behind; the emotional loss can generate several responses, one of which is guilt.

My mother never saw her mother again. Imagine the guilt of it. That's why we had to be good children; because they never were.

Not because they were bad but because they couldn't. My parents left their families behind and they put their guilt onto us.

(Jewish Women in London Group, 1989: 106)[4]

Rita was particularly adept at dipping into her store of 'ready-made narratives' (Kehily, 1995), which had been polished over years of telling, in her attempt to come to terms with her past of being twice diasporised, growing up as the child of Polish immigrants, *Ostjuden,* in Germany, and then later as a refugee to Britain. Indeed she comments on her story-telling thus, 'In the early days, when I was asked to tell one of my stories, I'd find that after a while a kind of trembling started... . And I thought, "How strange. I thought all that was gone and it was just a story"' (Jewish Women in London Group, 1989: 129–130).

In talking of her childhood, Rita also spoke of the particular emotional pressures on and within the immigrant extended family, which was just a dislocated fragment of what they had left behind in Poland. In discussing relations between her mother and her uncle and his wife, who had also migrated to Germany, she highlights the particular tensions within the immigrant extended family which she attributes to the effects of dislocation:

All that period of my childhood was about their belief that families should stick together, but when they were together the reality was different, they were *broiges* (fell out), they fought... . I think that probably it comes from a real sense of displacement.

(Jewish Women in London Group, 1989: 112)

The loss entailed by migration was almost unbearable for some, particularly in light of what later happened to those left behind. Ruth Adler's mother joined her husband in England in 1912 but she soon returned to Poland with the children and was then forced to stay there for the duration of the First World War, remigrating some years later. Ruth talks of her mother's loneliness in later life, made more acute by the losses of the Holocaust, and how she later came to understand the ways in which her relationship with her mother was profoundly affected by that loss:

In Poland [my mother] had interesting friends, people who read and went to plays, but there was no such friend here... . My mother had a need for friendship and really didn't get it... . In her old age she was very lonely.... . My mother's three brothers had all perished under the Nazis.... . She missed them very much, and her close friends with whom she corresponded until the war. This all rebounded on me in a way because she wanted me to be all of them. I wouldn't have put it like that to myself then, but I understood it later.

(Jewish Women in London Group, 1989: 38–9)

The Holocaust had a devastating effect on those who had left families behind in Eastern Europe when they emigrated earlier in the century, putting a final seal on the scars of separation. The longing for 'home', for the physical place and the people who constituted home, was transformed by the destruction of the Jewish communities which constituted that home.

As with the autobiographical narratives of the earlier period of migration, within those of the refugees from Nazism, only echoes can be heard of the losses, as well as the heroic resistance, the struggles against the odds. But the migration was different in that it was forced upon them. And had they stayed, life would not have continued in much the same way, as was the case for migrants from Eastern Europe earlier in the century. Being in exile could not encompass a yearning to return – or only rarely.[5] The Germany and Austria of which they felt a part had been transformed and redefined by Nazism.

Charlotte Stein-Pick, who emigrated to the United States in 1939, wrote her memoir in 1964 in the, as it transpired, vain hope that its readers would heed the lessons of the past and somehow prevent people being forced to become refugees. That avowed intent allows her to express the pain of loss and reveal the unhealed wounds of enforced exile:

> These memories were written ... to show that even those who managed to escape and rebuild their lives suffered greatly. The country which took us in was good to us; we learned to love and respect it; we have become loyal citizens. But there is no substitute for the old homeland, and the pain of having lost it violently has left deep wounds.
>
> (Lixl-Purcell, 1988: 217–18)

The women who recounted their life stories to me did not narrate their accounts for the purposes that Stein-Pick wrote her memoir. As with the narratives of East European migrants, references to the loss and dislocation of exile are fragmentary, as indeed they are in many autobiographical accounts. The largest single group of refugees admitted to Britain came on domestic permits – as domestic servants – and of course they were mainly women. Rita Altman was 17 when she arrived on a domestics permit organised by her 11-year-old brother who had come on a Kindertransport[6] to the Midlands, an extraordinary feat for a young child. He showed her photograph to Jewish families in the area, saying, 'This is my sister. She is lovely. She can cook. She can sew. She can clean. You have to get her out.' One family did agree to sponsor her, but her career as a domestic servant in Britain was particularly short-lived. 'It was horrendous. I was the ungrateful refugee – a fortnight and I was gone' (Jewish Women in London Group, 1989: 119–20).

The theme of gratitude looms large in many life stories of refugees. They had been given asylum and did not wish to appear ungrateful. Had one or other country not allowed them entry, the refugees would have experienced almost certain death. Yet ambivalence in the face of loss and hardship is also present in some of the narratives. Memories of the past are reshaped from within the present, and for many it is only the passing of time which has allowed them to see what happened in that period in a different light. In talking of her English Jewish husband whom she married during the war, Rita says:

He did me a favour too, marrying a refugee. Very cruel, you know. Never mind I was lovely and talented – it was a favour. 'It didn't matter to me', my first husband used to say, 'she was a refugee and very poor when I married her'. I had no defence against that.
(Jewish Women in London Group, 1989: 123)

The refugees had to contend not only with ambivalent gratitude for asylum and whatever acceptance and success they found. Their experiences were transformative in a different way from any other migration because of the eventual knowledge of the full enormity of the Holocaust. In talking of a cousin who lived in Luxembourg before the war Rita says:

You started relationships and it all went to naught... . And I think that is the nostalgia – if nostalgia it is – the longing to know 'What happened to him?' ... I think that's my resentment against the bloody world! ... In the end you had the internal anger, you got rid of it altogether, forgot it. Like a child who doesn't know a mother or a father and romanticises about them, and then inevitably, inevitably, makes them bigger than they are. You don't live in a reality.
(Jewish Women in London Group, 1989: 121)

Carolyn Heilbrun claims that nostalgia is 'likely to be a mask for unrecognised anger' (Heilbrun, 1988: 15); Rita clearly recognised that behind what she construed as nostalgia indeed lay anger. This occurred in a heightened form because of the Holocaust but, in any case, anger is one of a range of possible responses triggered by the emotional loss of migration. The range of responses also include guilt, evident in Rita's account of her mother's separation from her parents, as well as anxiety and denial.

Not everyone is able to articulate the pain of loss. For many the guilt of having escaped, of having survived while so many perished, led them to deny or belittle their loss and pain, which none the less affected them deeply. Esther told the following story of her mother:

> This psychiatrist was talking to my mother about the various things that had happened to her in her life. He said to her, 'You've suffered a lot of losses in your life', and went through them. And about each one she would say, 'I've come to terms with that'. One was ... about Nazism, having to leave Germany, having to part with her mother. And she just said. 'Oh, I've come to terms with all that.' And yet [after her death] I found a letter she had written to the same man, talking about the shock she'd had when the news came out about what had happened in the concentration camps, ... 'a shock I think none of us ever recovered from. I think a lot of the tension and anxiety has stemmed from then and has never gone away.' So at that point in the letter she was acknowledging the legacy of that history, but consciously to me, to him, ... when she was talking, she'd say, 'Oh no, no, no, it's in the past, it's over.'
>
> (Jewish Women in London Archive, 1985)

CONCLUSION

This exploration of the ways in which Jewish women migrating from continental Europe in the first part of this century experienced the trauma of migration is still somewhat tentative, given the fragmentary nature of the evidence. In drawing together historical and autobiographical accounts of migration, insights into the transformative effects of dislocation and exile have allowed the historical accounts to be extended to encompass something of the impact on identity of these Jewish women migrants. I have sought to examine the commonalities of migration and exile, the loss and the longing, while considering the historical (and gendered) specificities of Jewish migration which are important in terms of how that migration is experienced. The dislocation and the scars of loss manifested themselves in different emotional responses which are only occasionally revealed in autobiographical narratives.

A central difference between the two migrations was identified in terms of their being, broadly, economic and political. Economic migrants leave a home which continues to exist, with kin and community continuing to have a concrete presence which acts as reference point, a focus. Indeed in these more affluent times of accessible international travel, 'home' can be visited to provide reassurance and help dispel the longing, assuage the emotional loss, and indeed the guilt at having left. This is not to say that physical accessibility mitigates the sense of dislocation and the unhappiness of displacement. However as mobility, migration and exile have become more commonplace, they may also have become less traumatic, albeit still involving loss. In relation to the migration of Jews from Eastern Europe of a century ago, visits were rarely possible. The sense of rootedness must have been more intense in a less mobile society and so the rupture with the past and the sense of displacement, when acknowledged, was profound.

Political migrants may consist of those who are part of a political struggle and have a vision of a different society to which they might return, and those for whom exile seems irrevocable. Perhaps political migrants who cannot go back have to turn their faces more resolutely forward. In addition, there was something quite specific about the migration and exile of the refugees from Nazism, because they carried with them the sense that the departure was irrevocable, that they could not go back, ever. For the refugees from Nazism, 'home' had been tainted, destroyed. They also had to contend with the pain of the dichotomy of being German and Jewish (Morris, 1996: 24), while the migrants from Eastern Europe had no such difficulty; they were simply Jews. For the women who were refugees from Nazism, responses to the trauma included anger and denial, as well as the scars of a 'bifurcated identity' (Hoffman, 1991: 261). So while, at one level, the experience of migration and exile, of dislocation and loss, has an almost universal quality, at another it is inevitably shaped by the historical specificity of the migration.

All of us who have been migrants live our lives with a shadow of a parallel life, the life that might have been lived. Nonetheless, for all that the life of an immigrant is not the same as it would otherwise have been, and that individual's self is a different self from what it might have been, it is her life, who she has become. For some the transition, the transformation, the translation, is more successful than for others. But Hoffman argues that: 'Even in the case of people who are very positively disposed at first, some sense of loss or mourning comes upon them later, because there is no getting away from the huge fact of being severed from the past' (Lappin, 1995: 11).

NOTES

1. *We Came as Children,* the 'collective autobiography of refugees' edited by Karen Gershon, contains an extraordinary range of responses to the issues of 'home' and of being a refugee, especially in the final section of the book. However, I have not quoted from it because none of the contributions is attributed; hence the gender of the writer is unknown.

2. Kim Chernin (1994) goes further in resolving this tension, by using the clumsy 'Kim Chernin' instead of 'I', throughout her memoir of a year spent in Israel in 1973.

3. Delia Jarrett-MacCauley used this phrase in her plenary lecture at the Women's History Network Conference in 1995 (Jarrett-MacCauley, 1996).

4. The genesis of this chapter lay in that moment of Rita Altman's life story recounted to me some 10 years ago. This fragment of her narrative resonated across continents (to South Africa) and made sense of some of the stories my mother had told me of her childhood and of my grandmother's unresolved grief at being parted from her family and her home in Jerusalem.

5. The first refugee from Nazism whom I knew as a child in the 1950s was a middle-aged widow who came to the house from time to time to sew. It was somewhat confusing to me because my mother was herself a competent seamstress, and was always desperately trying to find something for Mrs Schwartz to do. It took me decades to understand why, when her pension came through, Mrs Schwartz returned to her beloved Germany, only too glad to leave South Africa, 'a country of philistines'.

6. The second largest group to enter Britain as refugees were the approximately 10,000 children who came on the Kindertransports.

REFERENCES

Antin, M. (1912/1985) *The Promised Land* (Boston, MA: Houghton Mifflin).
Berghahn, M. (1984) *German–Jewish Refugees in England: The Ambiguities of Assimilation* (London: Macmillan).

Berghahn, M. (1995) 'Women Émigrés in England', in S. Quack (ed.), *Between Sorrow and Strength: Women Refugees of the Nazi Period* (Cambridge: Cambridge University Press).

Burman, R. (1990) 'Jewish Women and the Household Economy in Manchester, *c*. 1890–1920', in D. Cesarani (ed.), *The Making of Anglo-Jewry* (Oxford: Basil Blackwell).

Carsten, F. (1984) 'German Refugees in Britain, 1933–1945', in G. Hirschfeld (ed.), *Exile in Great Britain* (Leamington Spa: Berg).

Chernin, K. (1994) *Crossing the Border: An Erotic Journey* (London: The Women's Press).

Crites, S. (1986) 'Storytime: Recollecting the Past and Projecting the Future', in T. Sarbin (ed.), *Narrative Psychology: The Storied Nature of Human Conduct* (New York: Praeger).

Domin, H. (1988) 'Among Acrobats and Birds', in A. Lixl-Purcell (ed.), *Women of Exile: German–Jewish Autobiographies since 1933* (New York: Greenwood Press).

Friedman-Kasaba, K. (1996) *Memories of Migration: Gender, Ethnicity and Work in the Lives of Jewish and Italian Women in New York, 1870–1924* (New York: State University of New York Press).

Gartner, L. (1960) *The Jewish Immigrant in England, 1870–1914* (London: Allen & Unwin).

Gay, P. (1995) 'Epilogue: The First Sex', in S. Quack (ed.), *Between Sorrow and Strength: Women Refugees of the Nazi Period* (Cambridge: Cambridge University Press).

Gershon, K. (ed.) (1989) *We Came as Children: A Collective Autobiography* (London: Papermac).

Glenn, S. (1990) *Daughters of the Shtetl: Life and Labor in the Immigrant Generation* (Ithaca, NY: Cornell University Press).

Heilbrun, C. (1988) *Writing a Woman's Life* (New York: Ballantine).

Hirschfeld, G. (ed.), (1984) *Exile in Great Britain* (Leamington Spa: Berg).

Hoffman, Eva (1991) *Lost in Translation* (London: Minerva Press).

Hyman, P. (1983) 'Culture and Gender: Women in the Immigrant Jewish Community', in D. Berger (ed.), *The Legacy of Jewish Migration* (New York: Brooklyn University Press).

Hyman, P. (1995) *Gender and Assimilation in Modern Jewish History: The Roles and Representation of Women* (Seattle: University of Washington Press).

Jarrett-MacCauley, D. (ed.), (1996) *Reconstructing Womanhood, Reconstructing Feminism* (London: Routledge).

Jewish Women in London Group (1989) *Generations of Memories: Voices of Jewish Women* (London: The Women's Press).

Kehily, M. J. (1995) 'Self-narration, Autobiography and Identity Construction', *Gender and Education*, 7(1), pp. 23–31.

Kranzler, D. (1995) 'Women in the Shanghai Jewish Community', in S. Quack (ed.), *Between Sorrow and Strength: Women Refugees of the Nazi Period* (Cambridge: Cambridge University Press).

Kushner, T. (1989) 'Politics and Race, Gender and Class: Refugees, Fascists and Domestic Service in Britain, 1933–1940', *Immigrants and Minorities*, 8 (March 1989), pp. 49–58.

Kuzmack, L. (1990) *Woman's Cause: The Jewish Women's Movement in England and the United States, 1881–1933* (Columbus, OH: Ohio State University Press).

Lappin, E. (1995) 'At Home in Exile: a Conversation between Eva Hoffman and Elena Lappin', *Jewish Quarterly*, No. 160, Winter.

Lixl-Purcell, A. (ed.), (1988) *Women of Exile: German–Jewish Autobiographies since 1933* (New York: Greenwood Press).

Marks, L. (1991) 'Carers and Servers of the Jewish Community: the Marginalized Heritage of Jewish Women in Britain', *Immigrants and Minorities* 10(1/2), pp. 106–27.

Marks, L. (1994) *Model Mothers: Jewish Mothers and Maternity Provision in East London, 1870–1939* (Oxford: Clarendon Press).

Morris, K. (1995) 'German–Jewish Women in Brazil: Autobiography as Cultural History', in Quack, S. (ed.) (1995) *Between Sorrow and Strength: Women Refugees of the Nazi Period* (Cambridge: Cambridge University Press).

Morris, K. (ed.) (1996) *Odyssey of Exile: Jewish Women Flee the Nazis for Brazil* (Detroit, MI: Wayne State University Press).

Quack, S. (ed.), (1995) *Between Sorrow and Strength: Women Refugees of the Nazi Period* (Cambridge: Cambridge University Press).

Schiff, G. (1995) ' "Listen Sensitively and Act Spontaneously – but Skilfully": Self-help – An Eyewitness Report', in S. Quack (ed.) (1995), *Between Sorrow and Strength: Women Refugees of the Nazi Period* (Cambridge: Cambridge University Press).

Sommer, D (1988) 'Not Just a Personal Story: Women's *Testimonios* and the Plural Self', in B. Brodzki and C. Schenk (eds), *Life/Lines: Theorizing Women's Autobiography* (Ithaca, NY: Cornell University Press).

Stanley, L. (1992) *The Auto/biographical I: Theory and Practice of Feminist Auto/biography* (Manchester: Manchester University Press).

Stein, H. (1984) 'Misplaced Persons: the Crisis of Emotional Separation in Geographical Mobility and Uprootedness', *Journal of Psychoanalytic Anthropology,* 7(3), pp. 269–92.

Tananbaum, S. (1994) 'Biology and Community: the Duality of Jewish Mothering in East London 1880–1939', in E. Glenn, G. Chang and L. Forcey (eds), *Mothering, Ideology, Experience and Agency* (London: Routledge).

10 Globalisation, Western Culture and *Riverdance*
JOYCE I. SHERLOCK

INTRODUCTION

Although the *Riverdance* phenomenon provides a still relatively unusual topic for social investigation, there is a growing interest in providing cultural analyses of dance. The aim of the chapter is to investigate the success of some claims for *Riverdance* by analysing aspects of the video: *Riverdance – the Show*. In the first part of the chapter some of the ways that cultural analysis has focused on physical talent and modernity, resonances and alienation, culture and commodification and art and reality in dance and music are considered. These foci are explored in relation to *Riverdance* to conclude that while the virtuosity of the dancers may account for some of its success, this aspect of the spectacle belies the institutionalisation of Irish dance in Western culture. While audiences may be responding to resonances of homeland and nostalgic memories of community, the feeling of cultural belonging can provide sinister as well as positive connotations. These can be related to both faces of nationalistic belonging. *Riverdance* may be shown to provide a sense of a new cultural identity for Ireland, but it should not be forgotten that as a cultural commodity it is serving the interests of capitalist profit-making. Representations of womanhood and social harmony in the show evoke contradictory significations which contrast with social realities of modern life in Ireland and with the lives of Irish and other dispersed peoples. Even so, it is argued that in these times of cynicism, there are those who would still maintain that cultural artefacts can represent accurately, so conveying something of the complexity of social and cultural reality towards a deeper understanding of how they might be improved for all.

RIVERDANCE

Riverdance – the Show was Britain's top-selling video during the summer of 1995 (Gold Distributors). Its success has been as a televisual and stage spectacle, since being acclaimed during the 1994 Eurovision song contest, which was followed by the video, a fund-raiser for Bosnia in Northern Ireland. The theme tune reached the top forty in the record charts, which resulted in a performance on *Top of the Pops*. There followed the stage performance of *Riverdance – the Show*, and the video. *Riverdance* featured in the Royal Variety Performance and VJ celebrations in 1995. Its popularity has led to debate on late night television shows, a feature on *How Do They Do That?* (BBC1, 13 August 1995) and advertisements in Sunday papers to sell weekend breaks to London for an extended second theatre season (for example: *Sunday Times* Supplement, 17 September 1995: *Observer*, 24 September 1995).

In late 1995 I became aware of the interest in *Riverdance* by people I encountered in the work environment. As I began to seek comments intentionally, I realised that the sorts of things which were being said echoed some of the ways of thinking about dance which I had encountered in my own dance research. At the beginning of each of the sections analysing *Riverdance,* later in the chapter, I quote a statement which exemplifies one of the ways of thinking and which relates to the structure of the theoretical discussion below. This underpins the analysis of a dance phenomenon whose popularity continues to draw media attention, but little interest from social investigators.

Physical Talent and Modernity

In spite of this, among others Novack (1990), Polhemus (1993), Sherlock (1993) and Thomas (1995) attest to a growing interest in the cultural analysis of dance. They help us to appreciate that dance forms are created by the complex interplay between individuals and institutional forces and valued by different interest groups. Novack (1990) argued for an understanding of the American 1960s 'artistic' dance form, contact improvisation, not just as artistic practice, but as a way of life. She also challenged the idea of physical movement split off from thoughts and ideas about the use of the body. This allowed her to argue that dancers are culturally reproduced yet can intentionally create new styles of dance to express different ideas of being in the world. Similarly, in Sherlock (1996) I argued that dance, just as any other cultural product in contemporary culture, may also be subject to the global dominance of modernity, that is, institutions and ideals of Western culture, configured alongside the capitalist nature of society. Thus, dance, far from being 'natural', is institutionalised not only in national contexts but at the global level. Giddens (1990) has argued for a global concept of society, given that high-speed transport and instantaneous communications have reduced space and time. Metropolitan theatres, schools of dance training and their native and colonial histories, media technology relaying images and dance music to most homes where the latest nuances of club dancing are rehearsed, take us beyond national boundaries (Sherlock, 1994).

Resonances and Alienation

Hollows and Milestone (1995) have demonstrated the significance of shifts from the local to the global through analysis of British northern or rare soul, a music and dance nightclub culture featuring 'all-nighters', mainly in deindustrialised cities situated north of Watford. The black soul resonances of living in inner-city poverty, derived more from provincial industrial northern towns of the United States, like Detroit, than the Bronx, speak to distant northern English white-working class experiences (Jones, 1988, and Gilroy, 1987, provide similar examples). The escapism of leisure from industrial labour implies pleasure and the ritual of 'going out' as well as identification with an idea of community. Bennett's (1995) study of hip-hop, in Germany, found that it was not culture which tied dispersed people of partial African origin together, but identifying with passions, recognising the expressive quality of the cultural artefact over the language.

Culture and Commodification

On a similar theme of diaspora, Horak (1995) focused on the tension between the media-conveyed market hegemony of hip-hop for young people from immigrant families in Vienna who still listen to folk music from their cultural homes. Dance and body awareness were, according to Horak (1995), important parts of forming an identity in the city as they moved between cultures.

Although these studies agree with Novack's (1990) contention that dance styles are changed by participants in relation to a search for a distinctive identity, their use of the idea of passions or resonances brings in an important somatic dimension to the analysis. This shows that music derived from one cultural location can be meaningful to another cultural group through evocations of life experiences structurally similar in capitalist relations, and can be taken on by that group to celebrate their own cultural identity. People are using dance intentionally for control over their cultural space, their presentation of self and reworking a range of styles from a rejection of institutionalised dance styles in 1960s America to dancing as a form of leisure in the 1990s. It should be remembered, though, that contemporary stylistic conventions do overlay cultures where their own dance forms have become disembedded (Sherlock, 1994) and reconstructed to look Western, while local time will have given way long ago to industrial time, planning, appointments, modern labour patterns, entertainment and cultural appreciation.

Art and Reality

Dance forms in art, social and recreational contexts are connected by global capitalist urban ways of life, displacement and a struggle for self-identity, and are constantly re-created and restated in identifying with fantasies and images of that recognition. As has been implied, the struggle for identity is situated within modern urban capitalist contexts, from which consumer culture is making vast profits. Dance and music are important means of working through self-presentation, meaningful in the particular social location of each group, but each within limits of the power relations of the market and consumer capitalism. Gilroy (1987) puts the emphasis on the power of the cultural articulation when he analyses popular black music and dance forms in the context of political organisation and action. In my examination of Ballet Rambert (Sherlock, 1988), I showed how dance style was expressive of the specific high-society culture of the 1920s and its later changes. One of its projects, to be art, was valued as part of the modern project: progress towards a better way of life for all. Reference to the critical dimension of modernism in art can remind us that dance images could represent resistance but also be appropriated as commodities misrepresenting realities which should not be forgotten.

RIVERDANCE – THE SHOW

Physical Talent and Modernity

> The vibrancy and the constancy of the footwork. You sometimes
> see that in ballet, but it left me with my mouth open.
>
> (University receptionist)

The quote suggests that it is the recognition of skill in the footwork
which thrills. Skill is often explained by notions of dance talent which
ignore the reality of years of training in unglamorous institutionalised
settings. Disciplined cooperation in this case contradicts prejudicial
stereotypes of the lazy, 'boozy', inefficient, disorganised, spontaneous, fun-loving Irishman. Because of its 'straight-laced', 'folk
authentic' image, traditional Irish folk dance with Flamenco and
Slavic influences would seem to be an unlikely basis for a hugely successful dance show. At first, a unifying theme of the show seemed to
be the dependence on variations of dance styles which rely on footwork: Irish jigs, Flamenco, tap, and a version of Russian dance along
with recognisable traditional music from these 'native' cultures. The
vivacious precision, dignity, discipline and power of the group dances
and the resonances of the music, were astonishingly moving. The
dance which first 'brought the house down', however, was about 25
minutes into the 98-minute show, called *Distant Thunder*: an 'unaccompanied hard-shoe dance routine' evoking 'the power and dramatic energy of thunder' (*Riverdance*, Video Notes (RVN)). The
virtuoso skill thrilled the audience, the controlled precision, based on
seven pairs of feet dancing as one, the power of the group, the shared
sense of identity.

In *How Do They Do That?* (BBC1, 13 September 1995), Michael
Flatley revealed that he and his co-star Jean Butler were World
Champion dancers, and that each of the group dancers had gained
recognition within the dance world. In spite of that level of talent and
ability, the show demanded long hours of rehearsal to reach the
required level of precision, just as top-level musicians would, first
coming together as an orchestra. The learned nature of dancing skills
which need constant honing to attain excellence is often forgotten.
Furthermore, amateurs, in the sense of 'lovers of the dance', are
unlikely to make a substantial living out of their teaching, yet from
their classes able pupils compete, are examined and groomed to
progress.

The compulsory establishment of Irish dancing in Northern Irish state schools, as part of National Curriculum innovation, has opened up controversy (Brennan, 1996). National dance's inclusion as an educational tool is a recognition of success for those seeking to keep the Irish cultural tradition alive, and signifies a political climate confident of the new legitimacy of Irishness. Ardagh (1995) discussed the music revival of the 1950s and 1960s which promoted the essence of the Irish cultural tradition against the threat of modern social change. One outcome was the annual *fleadh*, a huge event in Finsbury Park, London, featuring folk balladeers such as Christie Moore, and Irish rock and pop singers such as Bob Geldof and Sinead O'Connor. Traditional dance featured too, and the *fleadh* is just one of numerous summer festivals among a more informal spread of revived Irish culture such as fiddlers in village pubs, folk singers and ceili dances. Against the backcloth of the growth of television culture and pop music's dominance, Ardagh's (1995) argument celebrates the survival of traditions which seemed doomed by consumer culture. His research helps to demonstrate how able young Irish dancers are connected to a wider national cultural movement including novels, games, poetry, plays and films. The scope of the cultural movement extends to the USA, Australia and Europe, surviving through nostalgic get-togethers, away from Ireland.

In *Riverdance* the precision, power and virtuosity create a feeling of belonging, legitimating a sense of no longer needing to succumb to the subordinate social location often implied about Irishness; an establishment of control. Going to see the live show in London has taken on aspects of a pilgrimage (Hollows and Milestone, 1995). Is this a global consolidation of the revival movement, or is it a new optimism for a unified Irish identity?

Resonances and Alienation

'I get goose-bumps every time I see it', an Irish colleague said, epitomising the way some viewers experience the spectacle. The thrill of the virtuosity may well be enhanced by the resonances, not only of Irishness, but also for the imagined homeland (Anderson, 1991) romanticised and reified by emigrants. Most of the lead dancers in *Riverdance* are American Irish. There are also resonances of the experience of urban culture by different cultural groups drawn to that shared way of life. The video programme notes of *Riverdance* indicate an intention to draw out some of these features as central themes.

Filmed live from the Point Theatre, Dublin, in the afterglow of its 1991 year as European city of culture (O'Connor, 1993) the video programme notes of *Riverdance – the Show* offer us unifying themes for the programme. These are related to notions about origins and archetypal myths which are taken as common to all humanity, and explain why a name like *Distant Thunder* should provide a symbolic element to Irish dancing. Part one of the show deals with the theme that 'the root of all cultures is the quest to come to terms with spiritual and elemental forces' (RVN), a creative principle which expressed life and homeland.

The performances fit this theme through names such as *Reel Around the Sun*; songs such as *The Heart's Cry*; items drawing on the Irish nationalist movement in a jig called *The Countess Cathleen* after a play by W. B. Yeats (RVN), a cultural leader of that movement; and *Caoineadh Cu Chlainn*, a legendary warrior hero. *Distant Thunder, Firedance* and *Riverdance* signify spiritual and elemental forces. Part two, called *The Show*, is motivated by the theme of tragedy which has forced diasporas. This strategy allows 'native' dances to be exhibited, based on a conceptualisation of 'native culture, as expressed through music and dance ... a sense of identity ... brought to a new and strange place' (RVN). Here human difference and similarity are recognised.

Rural Irishness is evoked from the beginning in music, images and names, exemplified by the producer, Moya Doherty. Back-projections are based on rippling blue riverwater as of the island of lakes and grassy, rainy green fields, the emerald isle. Dances and music are performed against these projections and ones of the sun, the moon, fire, Celtic symbols of spiral design, of plates or clasps. Flatley, the glamorously 'cultureless' lead dancer, flautist and choreographer takes us through the themes and dances, tapping, flamencoing and stage dancing as in the show dance tradition. The dance *Reel Around the Sun* has the appearance of a traditional Irish dance style. This elaborates into what the video notes call an international style and Flatley leads the Irish company in a reel 'in praise of the sun's great power ... supernatural or religious significance' (RVN). They are received warmly with a celebratory cheer by the audience. The shift in dance style lies in the 'international style' including higher jumps and leaps, use of arms open in display to add drama to the spectacle, a generally more upward linear aesthetic like a balleticised show dance style. Flatley's appearance in a wide-sleeved shirt and cummerbunded trousers, his carefully arranged blond hair and intense eyes and expression engaging with the audience emphasises the individualistic cleverness of the lead dancer in his footwork and charisma as he utilises the whole stage.

For much of Part One the dress and styles draw on greens and spiritual evocations of religiosity and 'nature'. *The Hearts's Cry* is an 'ethereal vocal piece [which] forms the beginning of a celebration of womanhood, a theme which is continued in *The Countess Cathleen*' (RVN). Each item is presented in turn, *Caoineadh Cu Chulainn* being a 'lament on the uilleann pipes for Cuchulain, the great Irish hero and leader who fought the sea prior to his death' (RVN). The unaccompanied showstopper *Distant Thunder* comes next and then *Firedance,* a hot Flamenco-inspired contrast in red and gold to which Maria Pages, in duet with Flatley, draws enthusiastic audience whistles. The now much-publicised Irish-inspired *Riverdance*, a choral dance of 24 dancers, ends with the lead male and female dancers pivoting to roars from the crowd.

The standing ovation by the live audience and popularity of *Riverdance* can be explained perhaps in part by the recognition of some of the intentions to explore notions of culture, creativity and homeland being realised in the show. Apart from its and Ireland's association with water there seems to be not even a mythic foundation to Riverwoman (nor substance to any of the other myths alluded to, according to Rolleston, 1994). Perhaps the stream of people from their homeland and the dream of flowing back home is an association. It may be that those who would remember their Irishness with pride outside Ireland, scattered throughout the globe, having taken on the language and culture of the host country to become credible workers, can have no real claim to cultural homogeneity. It is the passion for an idea of homeland (Anderson, 1991), here revived in versions of songs and dances based on remembered tones and communal experiences, which makes the connection, the lyrics, the yearning, haunting melodies, the traditional dance steps. Memories of shared experience as the poor emigrant in New York are evoked in the Brooklyn Bridge in Part Two, backdrop for the black Gospel singers and Harlem Tappers. This is also a symbol of hope, disappointment, despair and struggle for New Yorkers. The bridge is deemed a place to be avoided by pedestrians in New York fearful of being mugged. The dream and the reality of the diaspora are problematic for these people where the legendary success of the Irish has become a standard to emulate.

I think there is something more which is to do with the thrill of the aesthetic, like school assemblies when still innocent, like pop concerts and being in a football crowd. It is a sense of being part of something in a connected, emotional way, nostalgic for other similar times: somatic remembering. It creates a longing for a permanent state of such pleasurable emotional intensity. But it also reminds one of the more sinister aspects of shared experience related to military precision such as political rallies. Here communal excitement can sweep one along with it. But in retrospect it is very disconcerting. It smacks of the totalitarianism of being taken over by forces beyond one's control. In the recent television series *People's Century*, an episode called *Sporting Fever* (1995) featured a British water-polo competitor at the 1936 Olympics who said that in the closing ceremony, such was the collective power of the 'Zieg Heil' mass chant for Hitler, that he had to keep his hands in his pockets to avoid joining in.

Culture and Commodification

'It's nice to see folk dance getting some recognition,' another colleague has commented. Discussing *Riverdance* is not a matter of folk authenticity for the dance form is elaborated from the folk dance schools of the city. Here a tidy, polished, tamed, formalised version of dances claimed to derive from Ireland's rural past has been institutionalised. In *Riverdance* we see it elaborated into a spectacular stage version adapted for video and television. With mass circulation, the video, as part of capitalist consumer culture, has sold well as a profit-making commodity.

Such financial success may be new for Irish dancing. Being used explicitly to promote Irish culture is not. According to Brennan (1994) the Gaelic League, formed to promote the Irish language, was inspired in 1893 by Scottish 'ceilithe' nights in London, to form a social side to the league in the form of Irish 'ceilis'. The dearth of dances inspired trips to Ireland to the 'Celtic West', to collect dances for the new canon of 'Irish' social dance. This is one example of an explicit purpose being attributed to Irish dance, and a corrective to any idea of authenticity. Such is the case in the *Riverdance* construction where many of the mythic claims in the video notes seem to be based broadly on the aftermath of the massive emigration during the famine years around 1845–7. Irish nationalist themes developed by W. B. Yeats (such as Countess Cathleen) and others around Celtic mysticism (Cuchulain) and spirituality, symbolised Dublin as culturally urban in opposition to the rural, the premodern culture of the Celtic West. The urban stands against Irish nationalism as the modern, the industrialised, both crippling the poverty-stricken old way of life and offering freedom and prosperity at the cost of alienation and displacement (O'Connor, 1993).

Riverdance is set between cultures: the culture of Irish folk traditions abstracted from nineteenth-century nationalism: Irish, Spanish, Slavic, Afro-American popular cultural manifestations reinterpreted in the logic of stage and screen. This is the culture of modernity as its effects have created diasporas and institutionalised reproductions of folk traditions. It has fostered critical attitudes related to artistic judgements, the culture of the Western bourgeoisie, still close to Matthew Arnold's nineteenth-century attempts to develop a cultural hegemony to match Britain's colonial success (Cairns and Richards, 1988). Then there is the culture of consumer capitalism linked with media technology and the logic of the market. In *Riverdance* this creative ideology is at work in the modernising of ideas of traditional styles. It is present in the artistic intentions of using themes and symbols and in the levelling international style. This is levelling up to unbelievable technical prowess, to incredible professional showmanship, to a signifying of Irishness, and perhaps other subordinate cultural groups becoming modernised, disciplined and corporate and able to partake fully in industrialised labour. Flatley bears all the signs of presenting himself as a creative genius.

Yet the show is clearly being used for other interests, such as nationalism. Referring to programme notes on the live performance of *Riverdance* there is a statement by Mary Robinson, then President of Ireland, which reads:

> The fusion of the traditional with an innovative vibrant approach has given fresh impetus to the consciousness of our Irish culture and it has brought an uplifting pride to ourselves and friends of Ireland at home and abroad.

Dawson, a dance critic writing in the same programme notes, referred to 'Confidence in heritage, confidence in progression. ... A discovery ... of self. ... "We are of Ireland".'

To possess modern technological knowledge is the primary requirement of being able to advance in the Western version of the 'good life'. Technical brilliance is no less important in dance than it is in any other branch of the market-place. Cultural critics have serious concerns about our sense of control over cultural production and representation of visions of ways of life (Baudrillard, 1985). Irishness has here achieved a recognition of skilful dignity and cultural credibility. This is no longer subordinate, the butt of jokes, terroristic. Neither is it dominant, parodic or freedom fighting. In the light of Anglo-Irish talks and the rise of nationalisms, the show may be a reminder that struggle may be a necessary condition for gaining and maintaining credible identities in modern life, in its themes of humanity overcoming tragedies such as famine and slavery. Identity may be a fantasy which has to be reconstituted in relation to what one has handed down to one as cultural roots: remnants which signify difference and personal identity in places which become home but which do not fulfil desires of belonging (Ardagh, 1993).

Art and Reality

> Its corporate image and lines of dancers is interesting. It's like the novel *The Bridges of Madison County*. Such authors, putting together bits of cultures, get taken for sensitive commentators. But it's a bad book. *Riverdance* is really kitsch – really bad – the same thing.
>
> (Lecturing colleague)

Perhaps *Riverdance* should not be discredited for its popular appeal any more than Waller's (1993) *The Bridges of Madison County* (America's best-selling novel ever). There the experience of passionate love between a middle-aged man and woman, she of Italian descent and he of Irish descent, is theorised in evolutionary terms. He presents himself as the last of a species of man to bear a magical physical and sexual spirituality, becoming extinct in the routine of modern life. Evocations of the Celtic warrior and Latin beauty are presented as fading into the emotionless rationality of contemporary life.

Those engaged in serious cultural debate might argue that explanations of the *Riverdance* phenomenon at the level of resonances, can be criticised as colluding with misinformation. *Riverdance* positively reinforces biological gender distinctions and male dominance. *The Hearts's Cry* and the *Countess Cathleen* combine a traditional, essentialist notion of spiritually pure womanhood and the controversial Irish nationalist earth mother, robust, and passionate (Cairns and Richards, 1988). Irish womanhood is epitomised as natural rather than cultivated, free in nature, spiritually archetypal, self-possessed and independent. Yet the early Christian choral resonances signify virginal purity, civilisation not nature, freedom through control in the

Heart's Cry. The words of the song are closer to nature. Likewise, the young, slim, boyish female figures of *Riverdance*, in rather short skirts, long-legged like auburn-haired Butler, gloss over the ambivalent reception of Yeats' play *Countess Cathleen* where the potential revolutionary sexuality of the idea of nationalist woman was at odds with Catholic belief (Cairns and Richards, 1988).

The contemporary boyish female physique offers other contradictions. It is closer to the 'waif' look of couturier houses or the ballet stage than the peasant woman of nationalist romance; ironically, closer possibly to the thinness of starvation. Unlike the voluptuous Irish country lass it has the adolescent look of the fashion-conscious urban consumer, dieting, flat-chested rather than maternal and nurturing, even, ironically in the wake of Irish famine and diaspora, closer to a look of malnutrition than full-blooded womanhood. This is the image of consumer culture, whether it be in the marriage market, or the world of the independent young woman. The extreme of the latter could be a belief in such control over her own choices that she should have the right to starve herself to death to achieve her self-image (Kaufman *et al.*, 1996). In *Firedance* the Spanish Pages is a complete physical contrast to the Irish females, as a fuller, maturer, female shape in Spanish dress, red, trimmed with gold, hair sleek and dark. Her intense facial expression, use of arms and trunk contrast dramatically too.

The popularity of *Riverdance* coincided with the moment when the referendum on divorce in the Republic of Ireland signalled, by the narrowest of margins, that a majority of people wish to modernise their way of life in spite of strong lobbying by the Catholic church to influence the outcome. There is a discourse which rues the loosening of the grip of the Catholic church on the Irish soul. Global capitalism is the protagonist in the drive towards modernisation. Ideas of modern manhood and womanhood are under debate, yet *Riverdance* avoids this reality. Dominant discourses of traditional heterosexuality and the family unit fit both the church and capitalist ideologies. Yet dispersion is the reality, dispersion of families and couples and young single people, in search of economically viable ways of life. Conflict also remains an ongoing feature of life in Northern Ireland, in spite of the harmonious renderings of solidarity featured in *Riverdance*.

The virtuoso dance performances evoke nostalgic memories and passions, and perhaps the hybridity which is a reality of modern life for the American–Irish or the Afro-American. A vision of a future created in opposition to the powerful aesthetic attractions of consumer culture codified in *Riverdance* and (maybe the film version of) *The Bridges of*

Madison County might have been more critically self-reflexive, but might also have been too complex for a popular cultural commodity. The show has roots in varying traditions of dance and music and cultural beliefs, and audiences have found it meaningful and moving. It is a reality of the 1990s that all forms of dance have to respond to the dictates of financial and cultural constraints. A belief in art is of cultural value to certain groups and individuals. If that belief coincides with a sense that consumer capitalism is concerned with profit only, or only art which affirms its position, then it may have something in common with cultural analyses which maintain a belief in the truth being possible, or reality being material and knowable. Such is the power of consumer culture that Mitchell (1994) voices a position which many feel is the extent of opposition possible in the contemporary climate: that there is a loss of faith that we can change the world, but it can be described critically and interpreted accurately. This means not accepting distortions and romantic opiates which dull the drive against misrepresentation and disinformation, to learn from the mistakes of history in our new constructions of cultural nationalisms as they come into the fold of a type of urban sophistication. Although *Riverdance* is uplifting, and may offer a celebration of a good way of life to some, we should also be sceptical of the extent to which popular forms are valued products of cultural groups, and how far their resonances may be nostalgic diversions from the real struggles in consumer capitalism and dance of all kinds.

REFERENCES

Anderson, B. (1991) *Imagined Communities: Reflections on the Origins and Spread of Nationalism* (London: Verso).
Ardagh, J. (1995) *Ireland and the Irish: Portrait of a Changing Society* (London: Penguin).
Baudrillard, J. (1985) 'The Ecstasy of Communication', in H. Foster (ed.), *Postmodern Culture* (Oxford: Pluto Press).
Bennett, A. (1995) 'Hip Hop am Main: The Localisation of Rap Music and Hip Hop Culture', unpublished paper presented at the British Sociological Association annual conference, 'Contested Cities', University of Leicester.
Brennan, D. (1996) 'Dance in the Northern Ireland Physical Education Curriculum: a Far-sighted Policy or an Unrealistic Innovation?', in J. Sherlock (ed.), 'Special Issue: Gender and Dance', *Women's Studies International Forum*, vol. 19, no. 5.

Brennan, H. (1994) 'Reinventing Tradition: the Boundaries of Irish Dance', *History Ireland*, vol. 2, no. 2, Summer.

Cairns, D. and Richards, S. (1988) *Writing Ireland: Colonialism, Nationalism and Culture* (Manchester: Manchester University Press).

Giddens, A. (1990) *The Consequences of Modernity* (Oxford: Polity Press).

Gilroy, P. (1987) *'There Ain't No Black in the Union Jack': The Cultural Politics of Race and Nation* (Chicago, IL: The University of Chicago Press).

Hollows, J. and Milestone, K. (1995) 'Inner City Soul: Transient Communities and Regional Identity in an Underground Urban Club Culture', unpublished paper presented at the British Sociological Association annual conference, 'Contested Cities', University of Leicester.

Horak, R. (1995) 'Diaspora Experience, Music and Hybrid Cultures of Young Migrants in Vienna', unpublished paper presented at the British Sociological Association annual conference, 'Contested Cities', University of Leicester.

Jones, S. (1988) *Black Culture, White Youth* (London: Macmillan).

Kaufman, B. A., Warren, M. P. and Hamilton, L. (1996) 'Intervention in an Elite Ballet School: an Attempt at Decreasing Eating Disorders and Injury', 'Special Issue: Gender and Dance', *Women's Studies International Forum*, vol. 19, no. 5.

Mitchell, W. J. T. (1994) *Picture Theory* (London: University of Chicago Press).

Novack, C. (1990) *Sharing the Dance: Contact Improvisation and American Culture* (Wisconsin: University of Wisconsin Press).

O'Connor, B. (1993) 'Myths and Mirrors: Tourist Images and National Identity', in B. O'Connor and M. Cronin (eds), *Tourism in Ireland: A Critical Analysis* (Cork: Cork University Press).

Polhemus, T. (1993) 'Dance, Gender and Culture', in H. Thomas (ed.), *Dance, Gender and Culture* (Basingstoke: Macmillan).

Rolleston, T. W. (1994) *Celtic Myths and Legends* (London: Senate).

Sherlock, J. (1988) 'The Cultural Production of Dance in Britain with Particular Reference to Christopher Bruce's "Ghost Dances"', unpublished PhD thesis, Laban Centre for Movement and Dance at Goldsmith's College, University of London.

Sherlock, J. (1993) 'Dance and the Culture of the Body', in S. Scott and D. Morgan (eds), *Body Matters: Essays in the Sociology of the Body* (London: Falmer Press).

Sherlock, J. (1994) 'Gidden's Modernity Thesis and Dance', *New Routes for Leisure: World Leisure Congress* (Instituto de Ciencias Socias da Universidad de Lisboa, Estudos e Investigacoes 2).

Sherlock, J. (ed.) (1996) 'Dance and the Culture of the Body: Where is the Grotesque?', 'Special Issue: Gender and Dance', *Women's Studies International Forum*, vol. 19, no. 5.

Thomas, H. (1995) *Dance, Modernity and Culture: Explorations in the Sociology of Dance* (London: Routledge).

Waller, R. J. (1993) *The Bridges of Madison County* (London: Mandarin Paperbacks).

Index

219